TAROT
Plain
and
Simple

Anthony
Louis

with illustrations
by Robin Wood

2002
Llewellyn Publications
St. Paul, Minnesota 55164-0383, U.S.A.

FIRST EDITION
Tenth printing, 2002

Cover design by Anne Marie Garrison
Editing and book design by Rebecca Zins

The Tarot cards used in this book are from *The Robin Wood Tarot*, © 1991 by Robin Wood.

Library of Congress Cataloging-in-Publication Data
Louis, Anthony, 1945–
    Tarot plain and simple / by Anthony Louis; with illustrations by Robin Wood.—1st ed.
        p.   cm.
    Includes bibliographical references and index.
    ISBN 1-56718-400-6 (trade pbk.)
    1. Tarot.   I. Title.
BF1879.T2L685   1996
133.3'2424—dc20   96–30422
                                                             CIP

Llewellyn Publications
A Division of Llewellyn Worldwide, Ltd.
P.O. Box 64383, Dept. K400-6
St. Paul, MN 55164-0383, U.S.A.
www.llewellyn.com

Printed in the United States of America

Contents

Other Books by the Author

Horary Astrology
Aprenda como leer el tarot (Spanish)

∾

Dedication

To my wife Linda and my sons David and Aaron
for their enduring love and encouragement.

Turning
Experience
into Wisdom

There are already many books on the Tarot, so why read this one? Primarily because this text presents the Tarot in language that is plain and simple, with basic, easily understandable definitions of the cards. The goal has been to remain close to the source and to let the Tarot speak for itself. The content of this book is based on existing literature about the Tarot and on many years of recording my own experiences with the cards.

I asked several friends to examine this text for user-friendliness. They found the descriptions to be clear and easy to follow, even for a complete newcomer to the Tarot. Most importantly, those who have previewed this book have found the definitions of the cards to serve as a rapid and reliable guide to Tarot interpretation, both for novices and for those with prior experience using the cards.

Why learn about the Tarot? Mainly because the Tarot is an excellent method for turning experience into wisdom. At its essence, the Tarot deals with archetypal symbols of the human situation, symbols we can relate to our own lives that help us better understand ourselves. In studying the Tarot we connect ourselves to the mythical basis of our lives, contacting the gods within us. Consulting the Tarot about a troubling situation usually gives us a fresh perspective. In every Tarot reading we ask how the cards relate to our lives and what we have learned from the consultation.

A study of the Tarot awakens our intuitive abilities. We should select a deck that appeals to our imagination and then learn to associate the various symbols on the cards with meanings that will form the basis of our understanding of the Tarot. As we learn more, our experience will add to this basic definition to further expand our grasp of what the Tarot can teach us. This process requires a certain amount of work and memorization but, with practice, the significance of the cards becomes second nature. At some point we have the experience that the symbols on the cards and their positions in a spread suggest a meaning that does not occur in the textbooks. We must pay close attention to such experiences because they indicate that our intuition has been stimulated and is offering a solution to the problem at hand.

After studying the textbooks, we come to realize that, in a particular reading for a particular person and circumstance, the cards mean what our intuition and experience tell us they mean. There are no immutable or absolute meanings for any of the cards; the basic definitions here should only serve as a general basis for your own definitions. In a good reading our inner voice suggests nuances of meaning that we may never have considered before. Such a state of intuitive awareness of the archetypal significance of the cards comes only after a period of disciplined learning and practice.

If we are reading for someone else, we must keep our explanations as clear and simple as possible. We should avoid jargon and metaphysical mumbo-jumbo. If our clients have never heard of the Golden Dawn, the Cabala, Jungian archetypes, or whatever, we do not need to confuse the issue with unnecessarily technical ideas. If we comprehend the meaning of the spread, we will be able to convey our understanding in plain English. If we don't understand what we see in the cards, we should say so. A Tarot reader has no obligation to be all-knowing, and the reader must always be respectful and honest with the client. The value of what we and the cards have to say to a particular client depends on whether the client finds our comments useful in gaining perspective on his or her situation. Some readings are extremely helpful and others are simply off-target.

Keeping these words of advice in mind, the reader is now encouraged to proceed with the text and to enjoy learning the secrets of the Tarot. Best of luck on your journey!

Chapter One

An Overview of the Tarot

For those who believe that science can explain all natural occurrences through cause and effect, the idea of a spiritual dimension to the universe may seem inconceivable. Limited to rigorous mathematical laws and a deterministic view of reality, science typically views intuitive ability, a higher self, or a spiritual world as superstition and false belief. Nonetheless, simply because spirituality is outside the scope of science does not exclude it from playing an important role in people's lives.

The Tarot is a tool for awakening our intuitive faculties, for putting us in touch with our inner world. It is a metaphorical system that leads us on the path of the mythical hero, a path of adventure and self-discovery. By tapping into the archetypal symbols on the Tarot cards as they relate to our everyday concerns, we can explore our personal mythologies and more clearly see the realities of our lives.

In essence, the Tarot is a device for meditation, reflection, contemplation, problem analysis, brainstorming, decision clarification, stimulation of intuition, self-understanding, spiritual growth, and divination. The cards of the Tarot allow us to tap

1

into a dimension of the universe that may otherwise be inaccessible. They are not necessarily predictive but often turn out to be so. They always offer an alternative view and a new perspective on the problems in our lives.

The Tarot deck consists of seventy-eight cards that are similar to modern playing cards. The Tarot contains three types of cards: the twenty-two Trumps, the forty Pips, and the sixteen Court cards. There are twenty-two Major Arcana (Greater Secrets) or Trumps and fifty-six Minor Arcana (Lesser Secrets) made up of forty Pip cards and sixteen Court or People cards.

The twenty-two Major Arcana Trumps depict in allegorical images the steps on the Fool's journey to enlightenment. The Major Arcana represents situations and inner states of profound personal, spiritual, and archetypal significance.

The forty Pip cards include four suits (Wands, Pentacles, Swords, Cups) of ten cards each. In the symbolism of the Tarot, the Pip cards represent typical situations and emotional states, all the stuff of daily life: our everyday events and struggles, our attitudes, our beliefs, and our typical behaviors.

The sixteen Court or People cards consist of Kings, Queens, Knights, and Pages of each of the four suits. The Court cards represent our web of relationships, often representing actual people in our lives. In addition, they signify aspects of ourselves, our traits, our talents, our faults, and how we relate to others. Kings and Queens suggest people of stature and authority, our elders, our parents, et cetera. Knights suggest activity, courage, energy, and the drive to take action. Pages represent children and young people, often bearing news and information.

In summary, there are a total of seventy-eight cards in the Tarot deck consisting of:

A. The twenty-two Major Arcana or Trump cards depicting the Fool's journey toward enlightenment, and

B. The fifty-six Minor Arcana cards consisting of:
   (1) The forty Pip cards (Ace through ten of each suit), and
   (2) The sixteen Court cards (Page, Knight, Queen, and King of each suit).

Early History

Historical records of Tarot decks date from the fourteenth century; according to Tarot expert Arthur E. Waite, there is no history of the Tarot prior to that date. Some Tarot enthusiasts claim that the Tarot dates back thousands of years, but there is no scholarly evidence to support this view.

People used the early Tarot decks for card games and gambling. The earliest existing mention of Tarot cards occurs in the year 1332, when King Alfonse XI of Leon and Castile issued a proclamation against their use. The Roman Catholic Church also condemned the Tarot as a device of the devil and referred to the cards as "the Devil's Bible" or "the Devil's Picture Book."

The name *Tarot* may derive from the fourteenth-century Italian decks called *tarocchi,* meaning "triumphs" or "trumps." These decks, consisting of seventy-eight cards divided into four suits plus twenty-two trump cards, were used to play a game called *tarok.* The French absorbed the Italian word *tarocchi* into their language as the French *tarot,* and the sixteenth-century Parisian card makers called themselves *tarotiers.* In Germany there also existed a card game called *tarock.*

Part of the popularity of the Tarot springs from the intriguing pictures of the twenty-two Major Arcana cards. One theory suggests that the Major Arcana were originally a form of *ars memorativa,* a Renaissance pictorial memory system used to teach initiates of occult disciplines.

Widespread written material was unavailable until Gutenberg's invention of the printing press in 1436. The masses did not learn to read or write until well after the Reformation, and literacy was not a societal norm until the twentieth century. In the absence of general literacy, the symbols and pictures of the Tarot, with their allegorical references to archetypal myths and images, captured the popular imagination. Like the apple in the Garden of Eden, the forbidden nature of the Tarot further enhanced its appeal.

At some point people began to use the cards for fortune telling. Playing cards readily lent themselves for divination in Western culture, with its long history of using anything that can be randomized and interpreted symbolically to predict the future. From the fourteenth century onward, the Gypsies used the Tarot for fortune telling and spread this practice in their nomadic wanderings throughout Europe.

With the modern shift in popular thought to a scientific worldview, divination fell into ill repute. Modern Tarot writers tend to focus on the use of the cards for self-understanding and self-actualization. Yet, most people who work with the Tarot eventually realize that the cards have an uncanny tendency to indicate future events. Whether you use the cards for divination, to awaken your imagination, or to foster spiritual growth, studying the Tarot is an exciting journey.

The Golden Dawn

The nineteenth and early twentieth centuries saw a resurgence of interest in occult disciplines, including astrology, the Tarot, ritual magic, the Hebrew Cabala, Gnosticism, geomancy, et cetera. The magical order of the Golden Dawn was the most influential group to spearhead this movement. The writings of the members of the Golden Dawn continue to influence occultism to the present day.

Arthur Edward Waite, a member of the Golden Dawn, published his famous book, *The Pictorial Key to the Tarot,* in 1910. Waite commissioned artist and dramatist Pamela Coleman Smith to create a Tarot deck under his direction. Waite used symbols from a variety of occult philosophies to design his cards. The Waite deck has become the most popular and influential Tarot deck of the twentieth century.

Jung and the Tarot

The correspondence between the random distribution of Tarot cards in a layout and the events in a human life is a matter of mystery. Modern science, lacking explanatory concepts for such phenomena, prefers to believe they are products of superstition. In contrast, psychoanalyst Carl Jung (1875–1961) offers an explanation based on the principle of synchronicity, or meaningful coincidence.

In his practice of psychoanalysis, Jung noticed that events in the outside world often corresponded symbolically with the psychological states of his patients. He noted that sometimes these meaningful coincidences gave the "impression that there is a sort of foreknowledge of the coming series of events." Jung argued that the synchronistic coincidences were improbable chance happenings whose "only recognizable and demonstrable link between them is a common meaning, or equivalence." He likened his idea of synchronicity to Leibniz's concept of pre-established harmony (the belief that the universe follows a divine plan) and to the ancient Greek idea of cosmic sympathy or correspondence (the belief that the same laws that apply to the greater universe also apply to human affairs).

A Picture of the Moment

In developing his theories, Jung researched ancient systems of divination, including the *I Ching*, the Tarot, and astrology. Writing about the Chinese divinatory system the *I Ching*, or *Book of Changes*, Jung said that modern science "is based upon the principle of causality, and causality is considered to be axiomatic truth. . . . While the Western mind carefully sifts, weighs, selects, classifies, isolates, the Chinese picture of the moment encompasses everything down to the minutest nonsensical detail, because all of the ingredients make up the observed moment." Like the *I Ching* or the astrological chart, the Tarot spread is also a "picture of the moment" encompassing a cross-section of the space-time continuum that is an integral part of the entire fabric of space-time.

The idea of a space-time continuum comes from Albert Einstein's theory of relativity. Einstein rejected the idea that space (length, width, and height) and time are unrelated and separate concepts. Instead, he reasoned that space and time are really different dimensions of the same universe. In other words, time is an essential aspect of being and we cannot describe anything that exists without referring to the time when it exists. The time that something comes into being is an essential part of its make-up and identity. If you had the same physical body but were born into a different time period, you would be a different person than you are today. Divinatory arts like the Tarot and astrology help us to gain access to the quality or nature of the time under consideration.

Jung wrote of the Tarot that "the set of pictures on the Tarot cards [are] distantly descended from the archetypes of transformation." He described the Tarot as part of a symbolic process that is "an experience in images and of images." According to Jung, the symbolic process begins when we encounter a blind alley or impossible situation. Jung regarded the goal of the study of the Tarot (or of any symbolic process) to be "illumination or higher consciousness, by means of which the initial situation is overcome on a higher level." Many modern Tarot experts regard the use of the cards as a means to get in touch with the archetypal wisdom of the collective unconscious, from which we may access fundamental images depicting the human condition.

The Need for a Mood of Faith and Optimism

Jung also took note of parapsychology researcher J. B. Rhine's finding that the mood of the subject plays a determining role in success at ESP experiments. Rhine noticed that subjects who initially did well at guessing hidden patterns did worse the longer they persisted at the task.

Based on his research, Rhine correlated the subject's worsening mood with the subject's poorer performance at the ESP experiment. As Jung put it, "an initial mood of faith and optimism makes for good results." The less interested the subject becomes, the more skeptical or resistant to the experiment, and the worse the results become. According to Jung, "the affective factor has the significance simply of a condition which makes it possible for the phenomenon to occur, though it need not." Rhine's and Jung's observation that a mood of positive expectation improves psychic awareness has important implications for the optimal use of the Tarot.

Psychological Projection and the Tarot

If Jung's concept of synchronicity helps us understand the divinatory potential of the Tarot, the theory of modern psychological projective testing helps us understand the Tarot's use for self-understanding. Most of us are familiar with the Rorschach ink blot test or the Thematic Apperception Test, where a series of ambiguous pictures are presented to the subject, who is then asked to state what he or she sees in the cards. The trained psychologist interprets the subject's responses and provides a psychological profile based on the content and pattern of those responses. The Tarot cards function like the Rorschach ink blots or the TAT pictures in providing ambiguous stimuli onto which we can project the contents of our psyches. If we contemplate our projections, we can learn much about the inner workings of our minds.

Writing in *New Realities* magazine (May/June 1990), bio-chemist L. J. Shepherd explained how the Tarot furthers her process of self-understanding:

> Readings help me confront myself in a spirit of optimism. They bring up points of view I had not considered and often surprise me with a profound response to a superficial question. They remove me from the echo chamber of my own circular thoughts and give me a way to focus on a particular issue, a way to dialogue with myself. Just as the progress and direction of science is determined by the question we ask, so is our personal growth. Our questions express our vision, lead us into the future, focus a light in the realm of the unknown. Zen masters do not teach by lecturing. They wait until the student asks a question; only then is the student ready to hear the answer and mature enough to use the knowledge.

The Barnum Effect

Not all scientists are as open-minded or spiritually attuned as biochemist L. J. Shepherd. Writing in *New Scientist* magazine (December 3, 1988), Christopher Joyce forecast dire consequences to the entire fabric of society because of interest in the New Age disciplines. Mr. Joyce warned of "harm to be done when a large portion of the public rejects rational, empirical thinking, the basis of everything from paper clips to computers." Perhaps Mr. Joyce condemns what he does not understand, and may benefit from a paraphrase the words of Jesus:

What profiteth a man if he gains all the paper clips and computers of the world and loses his soul?

Mr. Joyce cites P. T. Barnum, who said, "There's a sucker born every minute." The Barnum effect is the name given to our tendency to believe personality profiles when they are ambiguous and flattering and appear to be generated specifically for us (e.g., the horoscope in the newspaper). While I agree that vast numbers of gullible people (suckers) populate the world, I maintain that an earnest study of the Tarot will convince the open-minded reader of its value.

Some Personal Research

This book grew out of my own efforts to learn the Tarot. As I read various books on the Tarot, I noticed that different authors had contradictory opinions about the meanings of many of the cards. Could Christopher Joyce be correct? Is the Tarot simply based on the Barnum effect? After struggling to resolve such contradictory information, I decided to let the cards speak for themselves. To this end, I set up a method to discover their meaning in the circumstances of daily life.

Each morning I laid out five cards and recorded the spread in a notebook. I placed the first four cards consecutively in the four corners of a square and then placed the fifth and final card in the center of the square to represent the central theme of the day. I called this the "theme and variations" spread. Every evening I reviewed the day's happenings. I considered events in my personal life, my feelings, and happenings in the world at large to see what connections the daily events and emotional climate had with the five cards drawn in the morning. Here is a schematic diagram of how I spread the cards:

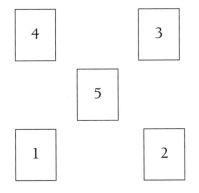

It was uncanny how each evening I could relate an event or an interaction of the day with each one of the cards. From the various books on the Tarot, I made an outline of the standard meanings of the seventy-eight Tarot cards. Each evening I added to this outline, modifying or changing what the textbooks had to say to conform with the actual daily feelings and occurrences. For example, on the day basketball star Magic Johnson announced he was HIV positive, my morning spread had produced the Tower Trump, the Three of Swords reversed, the Ten of Swords reversed, the Six of Cups reversed, and the Eight of Pentacles reversed. Because of the predominance of Swords with the Tower Trump, I had been expecting some jolting news about illness, death, or conflict. The absence of Wands, which symbolize budding life, from the spread was also significant.

After laying the five card spread daily for several weeks, I eventually consulted the spread less often. I got into a rhythm with the cards and learned to rely on my intuition to decide when to lay a new five card spread. Sometimes I would draw only one or two cards from the deck. If the time did not feel right to do another spread, I would draw some clarification cards to further expand the meaning of the original spread. The next case study illustrates this practice.

On Thursday, March 19, 1992, the following cards appeared in the five card spread:

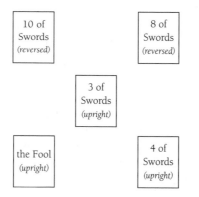

Several aspects of the spread immediately struck me. The appearance of the Fool, a Major Arcana card, in position one suggested that a matter of importance was about to unfold. The Fool is an archetype for the beginning of a significant personal journey, and the Major Arcana cards herald important events in our lives. The remaining four cards were all of the suit of Swords. As with the above Magic Johnson spread, the predominance of Swords suggests themes of hostile forces, stress, tension, conflict, illness, endings, death, or strife. The central card is the Three of Swords upright in position five. The Three of Swords is called the "stormy weather for the emotions" card. It can herald a difficult emotional period, often involving a loss. Concretely it symbolizes necessary cutting or severance. In health readings, the Three of Swords suggests a need for surgery.

The Four of Swords in position two depicts the need for rest, meditation, respite, or recuperation. It can refer to time spent in the hospital. The Eight of Swords reversed in position three suggests the removal of a blockage, limitation, or obstruction. The Ten of Swords reversed in position four is sometimes called the "disaster averted" card. Frequently the Ten of Swords reversed advises a need for prayer and warns of a message about death.

Given the serious nature of the spread, I decided not to do a new spread until this one had played itself out. On Monday morning, March 23, 1992, I learned that the wife of an esteemed colleague had died over the weekend. Then, on Monday evening, my eight-year-old son's best friend developed unexpected neurological symptoms. He needed emergency neurosurgery to relieve a sudden life-threatening buildup of cerebrospinal fluid pressure from a blockage in his brain. My wife and I are good friends with the boy's parents, and all of us were emotionally devastated (indicated by the Three of Swords).

On Tuesday, March 24, 1992, I decided to pull a clarification card from the deck. As I was shuffling, the Lovers card fell out upright. I have found that when cards seem to pop out of the deck during shuffling as if of their own accord, the message of the card is always significant. I happened to be using the Waite deck at the time, which depicts the Archangel Raphael, patron saint of healing, overlooking two lovers. I took this to be a sign of powerful healing forces being available. I set the Lovers card down and drew another card for clarification, as I had originally intended. The clarification card was the King of Cups upright. The King of Cups is a card of the compassion and advice of a kindly, dedicated physician.

On Wednesday, March 25, 1992, the MRI scan revealed that a brain tumor was causing the blockage. Because I am a physician, I became very active in helping the boy's family get the best medical care (in Tarot terminology, I tapped into the King of Cups part of my personality during the coming weeks). On Sunday, March 29, 1992, I accompanied the boy's parents to visit a neurosurgeon for a second opinion. The consulting neurosurgeon met with us at his home on a Sunday afternoon. Another King of Cups, he did not charge for the consultation, saying, "You do this work because you love children." Surgery was set for Thursday, April 2, 1992.

To allay my anxiety, I decided to draw three more clarification cards on Monday, March 30, 1992. The cards that appeared were the Magician upright, the Ace of Pentacles upright, and the Judgment card upright. Two Major Arcana cards accorded with the gravity of the situation. The Magician symbolized the neurosurgeon, who could do modern magic using his technical skill to remove the brain tumor. The Ace of Pentacles represented a hopeful new beginning in the material realm, a card of good health. The Judgment card signifies rebirth or the resurrection from the dead, the phoenix rising from its ashes. I took this to be another favorable health card. Just a few years ago, before the invention of the MRI scan, this boy's tumor would have gone undetected until it was too late for adequate treatment.

On Tuesday, March 31, 1992, I drew a final clarification card to alleviate my anxiety before the surgery. This time the Ten of Swords reversed appeared. Recall that the Ten of Swords reversed had come up in the original spread. I took this to mean an escape from death and the need to rely on a higher power. On Wednesday, April 1, 1992, the night before the surgery, the parents' church conducted a special prayer service. More than a hundred friends of the family attended to pray for the boy, reflecting the need to rely on a higher power. The surgery went well and the boy had a nice recovery. On Saturday, April 4, 1992, four days after I drew the Ten of Swords reversed, I received news of the death of a colleague. The Ten of Swords can represent an escape from death as well as the news of a death.

The boy had surgery for his brain tumor and did well for about a year when a recurrence was detected. He then had a second surgery and a course of chemotherapy. On Wednesday, January 18, 1995, the boy was due for an MRI scan to check the state of his tumor. That morning I again drew the Three of Swords and felt quite upset. The next day I learned the results of the scan: the tumor, which was now inoperable, had begun to grow again. The image of a heart being pierced by three swords clearly depicts the emotional state of all who are close to this boy. At the time of this writing, however, the tumor is in remission and the boy is doing well.

My personal research has convinced me of the truth of the cliché that a picture is worth a thousand words. No book can adequately describe the meanings of the Tarot symbols. Each student will gradually develop a set of meanings and associations for the Tarot cards that is uniquely his or her own. A book like this can only show the student some of the paths others have traveled.

ᨆ

Chapter Two

How to
Spread and
Interpret
the Cards

There is no right or wrong way to spread the cards. Many Tarot readers design their own spreads for particular situations. A handful of methods for laying the cards have become popular because of their widespread practice or their ties to other occult disciplines. Two of the most popular spreads are the Celtic Cross spread and the Horoscope spread.

Each card position in a spread carries a particular meaning that helps you interpret the significance of the card falling in that position. The meaning of an individual card in a reading will depend on many factors: its position in the spread, the surrounding cards, the nature of the question, and the reader's intuitive awareness. The art of reading a spread is that of weaving together a story that links and synthesizes the meanings of the cards with the meanings of their positions in the spread. Tarot interpretation is an imaginative, intuitive, and creative process, not unlike appreciating a work of art. In fact, Tarot experts Mueller and Echols view Tarot spreads as "the artful expression of your life, your living canvas."

The Tarot allows you to tap into your own imaginative powers. As a Tarot practitioner, you should feel free to design your own spreads as the need arises. Eventually you will settle on a few spreads that meet your needs in varying situations. The beginner would do well to start with simpler layouts before proceeding to more complex ones. I will describe several spreads in order of increasing complexity, but first let me comment on choosing a deck and preparing to lay out the cards.

Choosing Your Deck

There are dozens of Tarot decks on the market. How do you decide which to use? Choosing a deck is a personal and subjective decision. Fortunately, most New Age stores will have both picture books on the Tarot and several different Tarot decks on display. Browse through some books and look at the cards. Select a deck that appeals to you for its images, colors, textures, and whatever strikes your fancy. As you progress in your study of the Tarot, you will come to view your deck as a work of art and a valued advisor. If you become a Tarot enthusiast, you will eventually own several Tarot decks to use on different occasions.

The major producer of Tarot decks in the United States is U.S. Games Systems, Inc., 170 Ludlow Street, Stamford, CT 06902. My two favorite decks are the Universal Waite deck from U.S. Games Systems and the Robin Wood deck from Llewellyn Publications. I like these decks for their colorful images and the fact that all the cards have pictorial representations. Some decks have only markings but no pictures on the Pip cards. I recommend that beginners start with a deck that has pictures on all the cards. The drawings on the cards help stimulate the imagination and awaken the intuition.

Getting to Know Your Cards

Once you have chosen a deck, you need to get to know your cards. Take them out. Look at them. Describe them out loud. Meditate on them. Write descriptions of the cards in a notebook. Note your reactions. Which cards do you like and which do you dislike? What emotions does each card stir up in you? What is the predominant mood of the card? How do the various colors in the card affect you? Which aspects of the card jump out and grab your attention?

Make up stories about the people, animals, objects, and events on the cards. Draw two cards and make up stories combining the meaning and symbolism of both cards. Free-associate to each image on a card and keep a record of your associations. Your ability to read a Tarot spread will depend on your developing a gut feeling for each of the seventy-eight cards. Rachel Pollack refers to Tarot cards as "seventy-eight degrees of wisdom."

In getting acquainted with the cards, it helps to reflect on the meanings of the discrete elements that comprise the overall picture on each card. For example, mountains can represent major challenges, and rocks or hills, minor ones. Animals often signify our instincts and animal nature or desires. Water is a universal symbol of feelings and emotions. Birds can represent thoughts and spiritual aspirations. Several authors (e.g., Guiley, Mann, Mueller, and Echols) provide lists of symbols and their suggested meanings.

In addition to the discrete symbols, the colors used in the Tarot pictures also have significance. The following list provides some common symbolic meanings of various colors.

Color	Significance
Black	The color of night. Death, endings, darkness, mystery, the occult, destruction, resurrection, negativity, sin, materialism, ignorance.
Blue	The color of the sky and the oceans. Spirit, idealism, contemplation, reflection, emotion, the unconscious, devotion, feelings, intuition.
Gold	The color of the sun and the metal gold. Attainment, illumination, success, glory, radiance, the divine.
Gray	The color of storm clouds. Mourning, grief, sadness, penitence, depression, wisdom born of experience, reconciliation.
Green	The color of vegetation. New life, hope, serenity, fertility, growth, safety, security, abundance, health, youth, vitality.
Orange	The color of fire and the lion. Pride, ego, splendor, ambition, authority, decisiveness, vitality, force.
Purple	The traditional color of royalty. Power, pomp, pride, justice, esoteric understanding.

Continued on next page

Color	Significance
Red	The color of blood and the planet Mars. Life, force, desire, action, vitality, strength, energy, courage, aggression, sex, wounds, death, passion.
Silver	The color of the moon. Mystery, reflection, hidden knowledge, the goddess within, feminine intuition, emotions, inner life, psychic ability.
White	The universal color. Purity, illumination, daylight, joy, happiness, life, truth, openness, enlightenment.
Yellow	The color of the sun and of urine. Illumination, intellect, caution, the will, masculine power.

Caring for Your Cards

Most people take care of valued objects; tarot cards are no exception. Tarot enthusiasts traditionally wrap their cards in silk and store them in a small box, usually of pine. Such a symbolic treasuring of the cards creates an optimal atmosphere for their use.

There are, unfortunately, many superstitions about the proper care of the cards. Some authors warn of the terrible danger of cards absorbing bad vibrations if they are not carefully shielded from contamination by other people. Because I view the cards as simply a tool that enables us to tap into archetypal images, I regard such superstitions as nonsense. If bad vibrations exist, they come from deep inside our psyches and warrant self-reflection and understanding.

Hopeful Expectation

Jung noted the importance of an attitude of hopeful expectation as a necessary condition for the success of Rhine's ESP experiments. The Tarot reader should cultivate a sense of optimism and trust that the Tarot cards appearing in the spread will provide important clues to the matter at hand. As the Tarot practitioner gains experience, such an attitude will become second nature.

Meditative Shuffling and Stilling the Mind

In addition to reading the cards with hopeful expectation, the Tarot practitioner should create a quiet, almost sacred, atmosphere in which to lay out a spread. Some devise their own rituals, like the ones used by the great religions, to create such an atmosphere; for example, a common method is to pray for divine guidance before conducting a reading. Objects like candles, silk cloths, and incense can help establish a contemplative atmosphere.

A Tarot reading optimally begins with the reader and the querent (person asking the question) stilling their minds to allow the shuffling of the cards to occur in a calm, reflective, meditative state. The querent shuffles the deck while contemplating the question of the moment. At some point during the act of meditative shuffling, it will feel right to stop mixing the cards. Most Tarot readers then have the querent cut the deck (often in three piles from left to right, reassembling them in the reverse order). The reader then lays out the cards in a previously chosen symbolic pattern or spread for interpretation.

Cards That Jump Out While Shuffling

During the process of meditative shuffling, it often happens that a single card or a small group of cards seem to jump out of the deck and turn themselves upright. Cards that make themselves visible in this manner are always significant, and the reader should study them carefully before proceeding with the originally intended spread.

For example, a man requested a reading about a family matter, and while he was shuffling the deck, out popped the Nine of Pentacles followed by the Eight of Swords. The Nine of Pentacles depicts a financially secure woman sitting in solitary enjoyment of her lavish garden. The Eight of Swords portrays a solitary woman who is trapped and restricted by a ring of swords thrust into the ground around her.

The client then described how restricted his wife felt by her employment and child care arrangements. She had the chance to retire with a special bonus, but the client insisted that she keep working because he was worried about finances. Now he and his wife were financially secure, but rarely saw each other because they had to work different shifts to share in the care of their infant daughter. Both he and his wife felt solitary and hemmed in by circumstances. The client regretted placing his worries about finances ahead of his concern for family and marital happiness. The two cards that jumped out of the deck exactly portrayed the most pressing issue on the client's mind.

Keeping a Tarot Notebook

While you are learning the Tarot, it is important to review the cards and their meanings frequently. An excellent way of doing this is to keep a Tarot notebook of the images and feelings that you associate with each card. Adding to the definitions as you progress, and reviewing your early impressions along with your current ones, gives you a more comprehensive view of the nature of the cards. Another option is to write your ideas and impressions directly in this book, adding to the definitions given here.

The One Card Spread

This is probably the simplest way for beginners to start using the Tarot on a daily basis. Nothing could be easier. In a reflective state of mind, you shuffle the cards and, when it feels right, you either cut the deck, lifting off the top card, or you draw a card at random from the pack. Note the current date and the name of the card in your Tarot notebook. This step is important if you want to learn the Tarot. Review your notebook from time to time. You will be amazed how your knowledge of the symbols continues to grow.

Before looking up in a textbook anything about the meaning of the card, simply study its images on your own. What do you see when you look at the card? What thoughts and feelings does it stir up in you? How would you describe the card to another person? What action is taking place? Who are the characters on the card? What situation are they grappling with? What might they be feeling? Does the card remind you of any event, feeling, or person in your own life? Let your imagination roam. Pretend to have a discussion with the characters or images on the card. What questions do you ask? How would they respond? Even if your thoughts about the cards seem silly or embarrassing at the moment, record them anyway; later they may take on profound significance.

Note your reflections about the card in your notebook. You may wish to carry the card with you and examine it periodically during the day. What events and images occur in the course of your day that relate to the images on the card? Note them in your notebook also. Study the card again before retiring. You may have a dream or fantasy that further elaborates the meaning of the card. Record such dreams and ideas in your notebook.

After recording your own dreams, reflections, and fantasies about the card, look up the delineation of the same card in this or any other book on the Tarot. How does your personal experience of the card clarify, elaborate, or differ from the descriptions in the text? Again record your comments in your Tarot notebook. Remember that your personal experience with the cards is your primary source of learning. The words in this or any other book are secondary sources designed to stimulate your own intuitive faculties. Eventually your Tarot notebook will become your most meaningful textbook on the Tarot.

The Clarification Card

Often you will want more information than a single card provides. If a nagging question arises from your one card spread, you can meditatively draw another card to clarify the situation. This clarification card will add a further dimension of meaning to the significance of the original card. In fact, in any Tarot spread you can always draw another card or series of cards to clarify the meaning of any of the original cards in the spread.

The Three Card Spread

As the name implies, this layout consists of three cards spread side by side as follows:

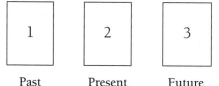

| Past | Present | Future |

The first card drawn will show some significant aspect of the events or feelings leading up to the present situation. The second card will clarify your present state, and the final card represents the future possibilities of the matter under investigation.

The Five Card Spread

After shuffling and cutting the deck, spread five cards in order as follows:

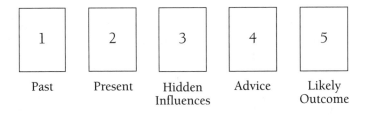

| 1 | 2 | 3 | 4 | 5 |
| Past | Present | Hidden Influences | Advice | Likely Outcome |

The first or past card represents influences leading up to the present situation. The second or present card reflects your current thoughts, feelings, and actions in the matter. The third or hidden influences card points to aspects of the question you may have overlooked or which are operating out of your awareness. The fourth or advice card often offers a practical suggestion about how to proceed. The final or likely outcome card suggests the probable outcome of following the advice of the spread.

The outcome card should not be interpreted as a deterministic or fated turn of events. In Tarot readings, an outcome is simply a likely course of events suggested by the forces in effect at the time of the spread. The querent is free to make his or her own decisions, which may alter the future course of events. If the outcome card is positive, the querent will still need to lay the requisite groundwork to bring it about. If the outcome card is negative, the reader should help the querent analyze why a negative outcome is likely from the other cards in the spread. The querent is then able to alter choices or actions to bring about a more favorable outcome.

The Horoscope Spread

The horoscope spread is a favorite among astrologers. Because the horoscope is a mandala symbolizing the entire life of the individual, the horoscope spread is excellent for a general reading. Starting with the first house of the horoscope, lay the cards in a circle, placing one card in each of the twelve houses. Many readers place a final thirteenth card in the center of the wheel as an overall indicator or summation of the entire spread. On the other hand, some readers prefer to start with a central card signifying the core question and then lay out twelve cards in the twelve houses of the horoscope surrounding the central card.

Here is a schematic diagram of the horoscope spread:

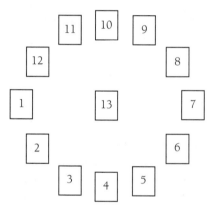

Each card symbolizes matters specific to the house in which it lies. The following list briefly describes the matters each house signifies:

House	Significance
First House	Physical body, Self, sense of identity, personal needs, appearance, health, vitality, the start of an enterprise, mother's father, father's mother.
Second House	Money, income, finances, wealth, values, possessions, movable goods, resources.

Continued on next page

House	Significance
Third House	Siblings, neighbors, close kin, local travel, short trips, conscious mind, writing, early education, communications, letters, phone calls, examinations, local environment.
Fourth House	Father, elders, home, family, real estate, land, roots, foundations, internal needs, emotional security, the grave.
Fifth House	Children, speculation, risks, hobbies, gambling, games, self-expression, romance, affections, pleasures, creative endeavors, fun, vacations, love affairs.
Sixth House	Illness, work, duty, daily routine, pets, perfection, tedium, drudgery, service, employees, father's siblings.
Seventh House	Spouse, mate, partners, marriage, committed relationships, contracts, law suits, open enemies, opponents, personal consultants, those on an equal footing with us, father's father, mother's mother.
Eighth House	Sex, death, taxes, other people's money, loans, legacies, goods of the dead, other's resources, insurance, partner's money, research, personal transformation, deep understanding, occult interests.
Ninth House	Long distance travel, religion, the law, higher education, philosophy, religion, higher mind, foreign interests, broadcasting, publication, forecasting, spouse's siblings.
Tenth House	Mother, career, profession, ambition, superiors, governors, success, public standing, reputation, status, society, discipline, structure, destiny.
Eleventh House	Friends, groups, clubs, social activities, societies, advice, detachment, hopes and wishes, humanitarian concerns.

Twelfth House   Solitude, confinement, hospitalization, retreat, sacrifice, hidden matters, secret liaisons, psychological problems, undoing, secrets, meditation, the unconscious, the subconscious mind, mother's siblings.

The Twelve Month Spread

The layout for the twelve month spread is identical to that of the horoscope spread. The difference is that the card in the first position represents the influences in effect during the current month, the card in the second position represents the influences during the next month, and so on around the wheel. The card in the thirteenth position signifies the general theme of the coming year.

The Celtic Cross Spread

The Celtic Cross is a favorite among Tarot readers and one which you ought to master. Arthur Edward Waite recommended this spread as the "most suitable for obtaining an answer to a definite question." The Celtic Cross spread carries the Christian symbolism of making the sign of the cross as you lay out the cards.

The spread often begins by consciously picking a significator card to represent the querent or the question itself. Some practitioners omit a significator card and simply lay out the other cards of the spread. I prefer to omit the significator card, thus allowing all seventy-eight cards of the deck to be able to appear in any of the ten Celtic Cross positions.

Choosing A Significator Card. If you use a significator card, it can be any of the seventy-eight cards in the deck. When the card comes from the Court cards, it generally signifies a person. Any of the Major Arcana or Pip cards might signify a situation. For example, the Justice card can represent a legal matter, and the Ten of Pentacles can symbolize a family gathering.

Kings and Knights represent men, the King being the older and more mature of the two. Queens and Pages represent women, the Queen being the older and more mature of the two. If you know the querent's astrological sign, you can use the following correspondences to select a significator.

Sign	Suit
Fire signs (Aries, Leo, Sagittarius)	Wands
Earth signs (Taurus, Virgo, Capricorn)	Pentacles
Air signs (Gemini, Libra, Aquarius)	Swords
Water signs (Cancer, Scorpio, Pisces)	Cups

An alternative is to select a significator that physically describes the querent. The following table offers some guidelines, and you should feel free to make exceptions as the situation warrants. For example, a dreamy, imaginative, dark-eyed, black-haired young man may best be signified by the Knight of Cups rather than Pentacles. Some Tarot readers simply let the querent pick a card from the deck that they feel most resembles them. The basic idea is that the significator should describe the person or matter under scrutiny.

Suit	Complexion	Hair	Eyes
Wands	Fair, freckled	Yellow, auburn, reddish	Dark or light
Cups	Fair, medium	Light brown, blonde, gray	Gray, blue, hazel
Swords	Dull, olive	Brown, black	Light
Pentacles	Dark, sallow, swarthy, ethnic	Black, very dark brown	Brown, dark

Having selected the significator, lay it facing you on the table and proceed to shuffle the rest of the cards. If there is a figure of a person on the card, note which direction that figure is facing. This will be important for laying the fourth card of the spread.

Cut the deck into three piles and reassemble the piles in reverse order so that the last pile to be cut goes on top. Here is a schematic for the Celtic Cross Spread:

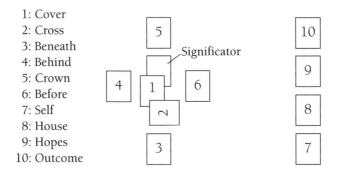

1: Cover
2: Cross
3: Beneath
4: Behind
5: Crown
6: Before
7: Self
8: House
9: Hopes
10: Outcome

(1)   Take the top card from the deck and turn it face up on the significator as you say, "This covers you." The cover card often reveals the substance of the question, the problem at hand, the present influences, the current state of the querent, and the general atmosphere now surrounding the matter. Consider this card as representing where the querent is at with regard to the question.

(2)   Take the second card and lay it face up and sideways across the first card, and say, "This crosses you for good or for ill." The crossing card shows the nature of obstacles and opposition or the lack of them, what forces may help or hinder the querent, and what problems or difficulties are in the way. This card will show conflicts, hang-ups, challenges, difficulties, and issues you need to confront, but will also show opportunities and resources.

The crossing card is traditionally read in its upright, rather than reversed, position. A positive card here means few obstacles to overcome and can point to areas of support, growth, and opportunity. A negative card will reveal factors that challenge, block, or modify the situation. To interpret this card, ask yourself what is the nature of the challenge or asset represented by the card. What is helping or hindering the querent?

Rachel Pollack regards the first two cards of the Celtic Cross spread as a "micro-cross" that captures the essence of the entire spread, and I have found this to be true. For example, a young man once asked about a relationship. His covering card was the Major Arcana Temperance card and his crossing card was the Two of Swords. The querent's dilemma was that he was involved in a steady relationship but had met someone new and was considering whether to have an affair. The first two cards of his Celtic Cross depicted his dilemma perfectly. The Temperance card reflected his ideal of a steady commitment—his current situation—and the Two of Swords reflected his conflict about cheating on his girlfriend.

(3) Take the third card and place it face up below the other cards, and say, "This is beneath you." The beneath card shows past influences affecting the matter, past experiences, repetitive behavior, motivations, where the question comes from, internal factors, and the roots or foundation of the current situation. This card shows from where the querent is coming from.

(4) Take the fourth card and place it face up to the left of the significator and say, "This is behind you." (Some readers place this card on the side of the significator that the significator is looking away from. If the significator card is not looking either right or left, they place the fourth card to the left of the significator.) The behind or recent past card shows influences that are just passing out of existence. This card can refer to events, feelings, communications, situations, or even dreams during the past few weeks. Such happenings usually have a connection with the question under consideration.

An alternative method for placing card four is to decide in advance that the position either to the right or left of the significator will represent the recent past position. Then the sixth card will be placed on the other side of the significator, representing the near future position.

(5) Take the fifth card and lay it face up above the other cards, and say, "This crowns you." The crown card is one of potentiality. It shows the querent's ideals, goals, options, intentions, avenues of development, possibilities, and

opportunities. It reveals alternative future results, potential new directions, and often the best possible outcome. Given the challenges and assets of card two, the crowning card helps us see how the querent might resolve the situation, where the question might lead, and what options are open for growth and resolution. Regard card three as advising you where you might be headed and how you might take advantage of the matter at hand.

(6)   Take the sixth card and lay it face up to the right of the significator and say, "This is before you." The before or immediate future card reveals forthcoming circumstances and influences coming into being in the near future. These may be new people, fresh ideas, or future situations. This card shows what will happen within the next few weeks in the matter. The happenings referred to by card six will require attention or action to resolve the matter inquired after. The way you attend to such near-future events will affect the potential outcome shown by the crowning card.

The cards you have laid out now form the shape of a cross. To the right of the cross you will lay four more cards, one above the other, in the shape of a pillar or staff.

(7)   At the base of the pillar place the seventh card face up and say, "This is your Self." (Waite used the term "yourself" but I prefer the Jungian connotation of calling this the "your Self" card.) The Self card symbolizes where you stand on the issue. It reveals your state of mind, your self-view, your feelings, attitudes, secret wishes, and how you see the current situation.

(8)   Above the Self card, place the eighth card face up, and say, "This is your environment and those around you." (Waite called this the "house" card.) The environment card shows how those around you view the matter as well as your interactions with these people in your life. Card eight represents the opinions of family, friends, coworkers, and others involved in the matter. It also reveals how outside influences and environmental factors, including your residence, might affect the outcome.

(9) Above the environment card, lay the ninth card face up and say, "This is your hopes, fears, and expectations." This card can help you clarify what you fear as well as what you expect or want from the current situation. Positive cards show your hopes and wishes, and negative cards show your fears and doubts. Sometimes the card in this position reveals unexpected factors that will influence the outcome.

(10) Now place the final, tenth card face up at the top of the column as you say, "This is what will come." This summation or final outcome card symbolizes the most likely future result—where the spread has been leading, the final resolution of the matter. It is the culmination of all the other cards in the spread and cannot be read in isolation. In particular, you should compare the final outcome card with both the crown card (card five) and the immediate future card (card six).

A Court card in position ten often indicates that the outcome depends on another person who will bring the matter to its conclusion. If so, you can take the Court card in the tenth position and use it as a significator for a new Celtic Cross spread. Alternatively, and more simply, if a Court card appears in the final outcome (tenth) position, you can draw a clarification card (or cards) to see what the person signified by the Court card in position ten will do. The court cards also have abstract meanings that can represent the final outcome.

In summary, the Celtic Cross spread answers a logical sequence of questions that help you to clarify your feelings and motivations about a matter. Card one shows where you are at when you ask the question, and card two reveals the obstacles you face or resources at your disposal. The third card highlights the potentials of the situation and the various options open to you. The fourth card shows where you are coming from regarding your question. Cards five and six point to recent past and near future events or feelings related to your inquiry. Card seven suggests your self-view, whereas card eight reveals how others view the matter. Card nine shows what you hope for and expect, and card ten summarizes the previous nine cards to show where matters are headed.

Reversed Cards

Reversed cards have multiple connotations and are sometimes difficult to interpret. Some authors suggest using only upright cards and will turn cards over if they appear reversed in a spread. The practice of using only upright cards limits the number of distinct delineations to seventy-eight, whereas the use of reversed cards doubles the number of possible card interpretations.

I feel that a reversed card must have some significance even though its meaning may at times be elusive. If nothing else, reversed cards call attention to themselves and require extra effort to view in a spread. The only card that is naturally reversed in the Tarot is the Hanged Man, which may provide a clue to the meaning of the other Tarot cards appearing in their reversed position. The Hanged Man advises us to view matters from a different, and often more spiritual or internal, perspective. Perhaps cards falling reversed also challenge us to change our outlook or approach to the upright meaning of the card.

Some authors believe that, like the cards of the suit of Swords, reversed cards may carry a negative association. A predominance of reversed cards in a reading can sometimes suggest problems, obstacles, delays, hindrances, difficult decisions, the need for mental effort, anxieties, worries, illnesses, stress, bad news, and broken relationships—but only if the actual content of the cards is consistent with this interpretation. Remember that each card, whether upright or reversed, must be interpreted in the context of the entire spread.

Reversed cards are not necessarily negative. The archetypal meaning of a card remains the same regardless of its orientation, but the subject's experience of the meaning of the card may change. A reversed card in a Tarot spread is similar to a retrograde planet in a natal horoscope, and the energy symbolized may be more inner than outer directed.

Sometimes a reversed card simply means that the upright meaning is difficult to grasp or express. For example, the King of Cups is a card of compassion. When reversed, the King of Cups may refer to a man who lacks compassion (the negative meaning) or to a man who has difficulty expressing his tender emotions. It can also refer to our inability to appreciate the man's affectionate nature. The upright card may express itself in an overt, conscious manner whereas the same card reversed may express itself secretly or behind the scenes.

If the upright card carries a positive connotation, the same card reversed may indicate that the usually positive qualities are being taken to excess. If the upright card carries a negative connotation, the reversed position may mean the ending of a difficult situation.

Tarot cards speak to us only in pictures. With the traditional rectangular decks, the cards in a spread may fall either upright or reversed in orientation. With some newer square or round Tarot decks, the cards in a spread may be oriented in even greater numbers of directions. Most, but not all, Tarot readers believe that the orientation of a card in a spread, whether upright or reversed or having some other bearing, signifies an aspect of the querent's situation.

To grasp the nuances of meaning in reversed cards, the reader should reflect on the possible significance of a picture turned upside down. If the upright card carries a stressful meaning, the same card reversed may either emphasize or diminish the intensity of the upright message. A reversed card may express the opposite meaning of its upright position in that a card that is overturned may reverse the meaning of the upright card. The reversed card may represent the upright situation being over and therefore done with.

Flipped cards require more effort to view and suggest that the querent is having a hard time understanding the significance of his or her situation. The difficulty the viewer experiences trying to appreciate a reversed card may reflect a prolonged or chronic condition. Often the upright card suggests an overt, objective meaning while the same card reversed signifies a hidden, more personal, subjective meaning. A reversed court card can signify a person who is not as trustworthy or reliable as the figure in the upright card would be. A reversed court card could also symbolize someone who is working behind the scenes or who is expressing the shadow side of his or her personality.

Here is a listing of some possible meanings of reversed and upright positions:

Upright Meaning	Reversed Meaning
acceptance	rejection or resistance
acute	chronic
conscious	unconscious
correct use	abuse
direct	retrograde
easy to express	hard to express
easy to understand	hard to understand
external	internal
faith	lack of faith
fast	slow
in process	over or done with
logical	intuitive
moderation	excess
mundane	spiritual
normal expression	going overboard, excess
objective	subjective
obvious	subtle
one way	the opposite way
outside	inside
overt	covert, hidden
positive	negative
presence of	absence of, need for
proceeding smoothly	problematic, stressful
public	private
quick	delayed
real	imagined
trustworthy	unreliable
uninhibited	restricted
wanting to	holding back
yang	yin

As an example of interpreting a reversed card in a spread, the Ten of Swords reversed in the spread about the boy with the brain tumor (in Chapter 1) indicated an escape from death and the need to rely on a higher power. In the same spread, the Eight of Swords reversed suggested the removal of some type of blockage or hindrance.

As another example, the Justice card reversed appeared in my morning meditation on the day of the announcement of the Rodney King police brutality verdict that led to the 1992 riots in Los Angeles. In its reversed meaning, the card indicates injustice is being done; many felt that the verdict of innocence for the policemen was unjust and that the accused police had acted unjustly toward Rodney King. The Eight of Pentacles reversed (indicating fraudulence) accompanied Justice reversed, suggesting the unemployment and lack of opportunity that helped fuel the riots in the black communities of Los Angeles.

Chapter Three

Putting
It All
Together

In Greek mythology, Ariadne, daughter of King Minos of Crete, gave Theseus a clew (ball) of thread to guide him through the Minotaur's labyrinth. Grateful for the thread that saved his life, Theseus married Ariadne when he escaped from the labyrinth.

Like Theseus, the Tarot reader must follow Ariadne's thread when interpreting any of the more complex spreads. The best way to learn is by doing. The remainder of this chapter will present three actual Celtic Cross spreads from my notebook. I hope the reader will find these useful and instructive examples of the Tarot in practice.

Sample Celtic Cross Spread 1

The querent is an assistant dean at one of the New York state universities. She is a single woman in her late thirties who values her work as an educator. Because of the state budget crisis, New York decided to lay off several assistant deans and to redistribute their duties among other employees of the university. There was to be an immediate cut in positions at the beginning of May 1992, and a second round of cuts several months to a year later. On April 21, 1992, the querent asked, "Will I lose my job this year (1992)?" She was worried that she might lose her job within a few weeks of asking the question.

We did a Celtic Cross spread. Because of the querent's position as an assistant dean, we chose the Queen of Wands (looking to the right) as her significator. The Queen of Wands represents a career woman. Her looking to the right is significant in the Celtic Cross spread because many readers place the card representing future trends to the right and past trends to the left. In other words, her future is in front of her and her past is behind her. This is how the reading went:

This covers you:	the Three of Cups upright
This crosses you:	the Two of Cups
This is beneath you:	the Seven of Wands upright
This is behind you:	the King of Pentacles upright
This crowns you:	the Three of Pentacles upright
This is before you:	the Star (Seventeen) upright
This is your Self:	the Seven of Cups reversed
This is your environment:	the Fool (Zero) reversed
This is your hopes and expectations:	the Four of Wands upright
This is the outcome:	Judgement (Twenty) upright

Before examining the individual cards, the reader should get an overall feel for the spread. One way to do so is to group together the various factors reflected in the ten cards of the spread. We made the following lists based on this spread:

3 Cups	6 Pip Cards
2 Wands	1 Court Card
2 Pentacles	3 Major Arcana
0 Swords	
3 Major Arcana	
10 Total Number of Cards	**10 Cards in Spread**
8 Upright	
2 Reversed	
10 Cards in Spread	

Given the querent's obvious state of stress and worry, the absence of Swords is a striking feature of the spread. Could this mean her worry is not supported by the cards? The theme of the absent swords is repeated in the small number of reversed cards in the spread.

The abundance of Cups suggests an emotional or relationship matter is foremost on her mind. The three Major Arcana cards reflect the significance of this issue for the querent. After all, her livelihood is at stake. The Major Arcana cards suggest issues of great importance to the querent and often imply that the forces of destiny play a role in the matter. The presence of a single court card, the King of Pentacles, suggests that a practical, money-conscious, older man is involved in the question (possibly Governor Mario Cuomo or the government official who hatched the plan to rid the assistant deans from the university).

Another useful tool is to add up the numerical values of all the numbered cards in the reading and then reduce the sum to its numerological digit (1–10) or master number (11 or 22) [see Appendix B for further numerology information]. Court cards are not numbered so we can skip them when doing the addition. In this reading, $3 + 2 + 3 + 7 + 17 + 7 + 4 + 0 + 20$ equals 63, which reduces numerologically to $6 + 3$, or 9. In numerology, nine is a number of endings and completions. Nine suggests the end of one cycle, clearing the decks, and preparation for another cycle to begin. Certainly the significance of nine is apt for this reading about ending a phase of one's career.

Now for the individual cards in the Celtic Cross. The Three of Cups covering the querent is a card of celebration and happiness, an odd card to draw when one is facing unemployment. The Three of Cups is a suggestion that she will not be in the first round of layoffs and therefore will have cause for celebration. The crossing by the Two of Cups, a card of mutual sharing, is another hopeful sign. This crossing is less an obstacle than a partnership or helping hand. Perhaps the job crisis is precipitating thoughts of marriage or settling down, or maybe a colleague will come to her assistance.

The querent is crowned by the Three of Pentacles. This is a card of skilled craftsmanship and recognition for competence at one's profession. As the crown card, the Three of Pentacles shows a possible positive outcome or the best the querent can hope for. There is a suggestion that the querent's competence at her job will be recognized and will work to her advantage. If she is laid off, she should be able to secure a new job that uses her skills and talents.

The Seven of Wands lies beneath her and shows the foundation of the situation and past influences. The Seven of Wands shows a young man taking a stand and defending his position.

The King of Pentacles behind the querent refers to a recent past event. Here the King most likely signifies a miserly older man of temporal power who set the process of layoffs in motion. Abstractly, the King of Pentacles can refer to the state budget.

The Star, a hopeful Major Arcana card, lies before the querent and denotes an event in the near future. The Star is such a positive card that the querent can soon expect good news and helpful assistance. The Star often advises the client to begin developing a special talent.

The Self card is the Seven of Cups reversed. This card reflects the querent's troubled fantasies and worries about the impending layoffs. It suggests that her worries about losing her job soon may be unfounded.

The environment card is the Fool reversed. The state of New York is acting foolishly in laying off its assistant deans. The people around her feel she is in a precarious situation.

The hopes and expectations card is the Four of Wands upright. This is a card of security, prosperity, and laying down roots. Clearly the querent has security on her mind. The Four of Wands, along with the many Cup cards in the spread, raises the possibility that marriage is on her mind.

The outcome card is Judgement (Twenty), a Major Arcana card. The outcome will be a significant event in her life. The Judgement card depicts a rebirth or a resurrection, the entering of a new phase of existence. The Judgement card in the outcome position is a positive indicator. She is unlikely to lose her job in 1992. Even if she does lose her current job as assistant dean, this will be a welcome change that will open doors and lead to an important new phase in her career. An eventual positive career change (rebirth) is the likely outcome.

The actual outcome: Although many other New York state employees were laid off, this querent did not lose her job in 1992. She was finally laid off in 1994, much to her relief as the job had become unbearable. A lifelong animal lover, at the time of this writing she is happily pursuing a new career working with pets, a special talent she had long done as a hobby.

Sample Celtic Cross Spread 2

During the 1992 United States presidential election campaign, my friend Rachel, a staunch Democrat, became worried that Ross Perot might be elected President. Based on what she had read about his background and personality, she believed that he would be unfit to run the country. On June 13, 1992, at the height of Mr. Perot's popularity, Rachel asked, "Will Ross Perot become President?"

To answer Rachel's question, we did a Celtic Cross spread. Because the question was about a non-personal issue, we decided not to use a significator card for Rachel. Here is the result of the spread:

This covers you:	the Emperor upright
This crosses you:	the Fool
This is beneath you:	the Devil upright
This is behind you:	the Page of Wands reversed
This crowns you:	the King of Cups upright
This is before you:	the Three of Pentacles upright
This is your Self:	Temperance upright
This is your environment:	the Ace of Cups upright
This is your hopes and expectations:	the Nine of Swords reversed
This is the outcome:	the Nine of Cups upright

Before examining the individual cards, the reader should get an overall feel for the spread. One way to do so is to group together the various factors reflected in the ten cards of the spread. We made the following lists based on this spread:

3 Cups	4 Pip Cards
1 Wands	2 Court Card
1 Pentacles	4 Major Arcana
1 Swords	
4 Major Arcana	

10 Total Number of Cards   **10 Cards in Spread**

8 Upright
2 Reversed

10 Cards in Spread

The presence of three Cup cards in the spread indicates that this question is of great emotional importance to Rachel. In fact, she was distraught at the thought of a Ross Perot presidency. The abundance of Major Arcana cards underscores the significance of this question for the country.

The appearance of the Emperor in position one of the Celtic Cross summarizes the matter at hand: Who will be king? The Emperor is crossed by the Fool, reflecting Rachel's fear that a man whom she considered foolish might run the country.

I was surprised by the King of Cups in the crown position. Often this card shows the best possible outcome. It seemed to me that Bill Clinton most resembled the King of Cups (emotional, compassionate, concerned with others' welfare), but at the time his popularity was quite low and it seemed that either Bush or Perot would win the election.

The Devil in the third (or "beneath") position mirrors Rachel's view that Ross Perot's motives might be based on greed or a lust for power and control. The Devil reflects unbridled passions and the dark side of human nature.

The Page of Wands reversed in the near past location reflects Rachel's discouragement at the news of Perot's strong standing in the polls. The upright Three of Pentacles in the near future position suggests some imminent, positive event affecting Rachel's material security.

Occupying the Self spot is the Temperance card, reflecting Rachel's desire for a person of moderation in the White House. She viewed Perot as occupying an extreme position. The Ace of Cups in the environment position emphasizes Rachel's emotional concern about the matter for herself and her family.

The hopes and expectations card is the Nine of Swords reversed. The Nine of Swords is called the nightmare card, and reflected Rachel's fear that a Perot presidency would be a time of despair and oppression. The reversed position of the Nine of Swords holds out the hope that Rachel's "nightmare" will not be realized, and that there is light at the end of the tunnel for her.

The actual outcome: The final outcome card is the Nine of Cups upright. This card is called the wish card, and in the summation position of the Celtic Cross indicates that Rachel will get her wish. Ross Perot will not be elected.

Sample Celtic Cross Spread 3

The following Celtic Cross spread was done on October 26, 1994. The client is a physician from the Dominican Republic who had done his medical training in Europe. His question was whether he would pass the examination that would allow him to practice medicine in the United States. Four Major Arcana (the Hanged Man, the Chariot, the Magician, and Justice) appeared in the spread, suggesting this is a very important question on the client's mind. The entire spread is as follows:

This covers you:	Eight of Cups reversed
This crosses you:	the Hanged Man
This is beneath you:	the Chariot upright
This is behind you:	the Five of Pentacles reversed
This crowns you:	the Seven of Cups reversed
This is before you:	Ace of Pentacles upright
This is your Self:	the Magician upright
This is your environment:	the Seven of Pentacles upright
This is your hopes and expectations:	the Eight of Swords upright
This is the outcome:	Justice reversed

Before examining the individual cards, the reader should get an overall feel for the spread. One way to do so is to group together the various factors reflected in the ten cards of the spread. We made the following lists based on this spread:

2 Cups	6 Pip Cards
0 Wands	0 Court Cards
3 Pentacles	4 Major Arcana
1 Swords	
4 Major Arcana	
10 Total Number of Cards	**10 Cards in Spread**

6 Upright
4 Reversed

10 Cards in Spread

The covering card, which signifies the question, is the Eight of Cups reversed. This card often represents travel or relocation related to leaving a difficult emotional situation in search of greater personal satisfaction. Because Cups symbolize one's emotional life, the reversed Eight of Cups sometimes represents depression due to problems in a relationship. In matters of timing, the Eight of Cups suggests that the client will need to give the matter a month (or one cycle of the moon) to work itself out. In relationship questions, this card often means that someone who has gone away will return within a month.

The crossing card (obstacles, opposition) is the Hanged Man, suggesting a state of sacrifice and suspension. The client may be feeling unable to move forward or backward; all he can do is wait and be patient. This card symbolizes transitions and turning points in one's life—a time to reflect and prepare for the next move. It also suggests that past sacrifices and hard work are about to pay off.

Beneath the covering card is the Chariot, a card symbolic of determined effort, of taking the reins and directing one's course in life. The Chariot's location in the spread suggests that the client is coming from a position of hard work and of sustained and concentrated energy toward a particular goal. This card also represents travel and/or the purchase of a new car in the near future.

The card in the recent past position is the Five of Pentacles reversed. This is often called the poverty card, and its reversed position suggests a recent emergence from a financially difficult situation. In fact, about a month before the reading, the client had begun a new job after a period of unemployment.

The card in the near future position is the Ace of Pentacles, a very positive card suggesting increased income and financial success. Aces symbolize new beginnings and Pentacles have to do with finances and material success. A gift or luck at lotto are possibilities.

The crowning card is the Seven of Cups reversed. This card represents conscious plans and intentions and possible future developments. The reversed Seven of Cups suggests that the client has decided to focus very realistically on his goals and to avoid excessive daydreaming about the future. This card can also signify a period of disillusionment.

The card representing the client's state of mind, his Self card, is the Magician, a card symbolic of resourcefulness, self-discipline, and the creative force of will. The Magician often represents those who manipulate nature for some definite purpose. Physicians who make use of natural forces to heal their patients are included in the symbolism. The Magician, along with the Chariot and the Seven of Cups reversed, suggests that the client is quite determined to achieve his goal.

The Seven of Pentacles occupies the position representing how other people see the client. The Seven of Pentacles symbolizes pausing midway through a project to assess where one has come from and where one is headed. Sometimes the figure on this card is viewed as worrying about his future. Together with the Hanged Man in the crossing position, the Seven of Pentacles suggests that the client is in a state of waiting or suspension before proceeding toward some goal.

The Eight of Swords lies in the position representing the client's hopes and fears in the matter. The Eight of Swords is a card of feeling all alone, trapped and frustrated by circumstances. Perhaps the client fears being restricted or blocked in reaching his goals.

The final outcome card is Justice reversed. The Justice card has to do with getting what you deserve. In its reversed position, there is a suggestion that there may be a delay in justice being done or that the client will suffer some unfair treatment in the final outcome. Perhaps his examination scores will not truly reflect what he knows, or perhaps he will be the victim of some type of discrimination or legalistic complication.

A synthesis of the overall spread is positive. Several cards suggest that the client has worked very hard toward his goal and is extremely determined to succeed. The cards representing his emotions suggest elements of worry and depression, perhaps about a personal relationship. His financial situation is definitely improving. There is a possibility of travel and the purchase of a car in the near future. In the context of the entire spread, Justice reversed in the final position suggests that he will pass his examination but there may be some delay, complication, or disappointment with the results. Perhaps he will need to take the examination a second time. He will know more within a month's time.

The actual outcome: The client learned a month after the Tarot reading that he had failed the examination and would need to take it a second time.

∽

Chapter Four

The
Major
Arcana

Below you will find a list of key words and phrases for each Tarot card, a description of typical situations that the card may represent, and an accounting of some types of people the card suggests. You will also find sayings and phrases related to the central themes of each card. As you use your cards, please add to the meanings in this book and discard those you do not find helpful in your understanding of the cards. When you use the delineations in this book, bear in mind that only one or a few of the meanings supplied for each card may fit your situation.

One difficulty beginners face in reading the Tarot is that symbols are multidimensional. Sometimes a cigar is just a cigar, but it can also be a phallic symbol, a source of pleasure, a cause of medical illness and discomfort, and so on. How do you know which nuance of symbolic meaning to use in your reading? Your choice of interpretation will depend on the context in which the symbol occurs, the nature of the question, the surrounding cards, your past experience, the feedback you receive from the querent, and, most importantly, on your intuition and inner guidance. The ancient Greek philosopher Heraclitus said that you cannot step into the same river twice. In the Tarot, you cannot read the same card twice.

Because the Tarot depicts archetypal human feelings and situations, no single textbook can exhaust all the possible meanings of each card and no author has all the answers. In the Tarot, each picture is worth far more than the proverbial thousand words. No verbal description can adequately capture the meanings of the cards. The descriptions here are suggestions and guidelines for compiling your own book on the Tarot. Don't accept anything in this book at face value unless you can prove it in your own experience.

A note of caution about reversed cards: in the following pages I have artificially divided meanings of the cards by upright and reversed positions. Remember that every card has a core archetypal meaning that is only slightly modified by the card's orientation. A reversed card simply indicates a shift in emphasis of the core meaning of the card. For example, one querent who was having problem after problem with rental property drew the Six of Swords in its reversed orientation. She clearly wanted to sell the property and leave a difficult situation behind. The reversed Six of Swords, a card indicating the inability to leave one's troubles behind, seemed to be telling her that the problems would continue for a while longer.

For some cards, I have indicated both positive and negative meanings. Which meaning you use depends on the rest of the spread. If the tone of the spread is generally negative—for example, a strong predominance of Swords and reversed cards—then the negative meaning is more likely to apply. In addition, I occasionally refer to numerology and astrology in explaining the cards. The appendices of this book go into further detail about these topics, and it would be useful to review these for more information.

In summary, I urge the reader to accept my suggestions as guidelines to possible interpretations of reversed cards. Use your intuition and judgment when doing an actual reading. You will discover meanings that I did not write about or never even thought of. Best wishes as you start this exciting journey and follow the Fool on the road to enlightenment.

∾

The Major Arcana or Major Trumps

When a Major Trump card appears in a reading, the querent can expect significant life changes and feelings of considerable importance. The Major Arcana cards often refer to the workings of fate. The querent may be swept up in a flow of events not entirely in his or her control. The Major Arcana trumps refer to matters of great significance, to personal transformation, and to life crises.

The Jungian Archetypal Journey

Many Tarot experts believe that the series of situations depicted in the Major Trumps represent an archetypal story of human development—the journey traveled by the Fool (Trump 0). According to Jung, archetypes are abstract forms, patterns, or models in humanity's collective unconscious. The characters of the great myths portray various archetypal behaviors and reactions. Archetypes appear in infinite varieties of symbols and become known personally through the powerful feelings that accompany them. The most basic Jungian archetype is that of the Self (with a capital S), an inner archetype that encompasses all, as opposed to the personal self (with a small s). The archetypes reside in our collective unconscious and appear to us in our dreams, myths, and fantasies. In addition, we project the archetypes outward and see them manifest in other people as well as in our own actions.

All of the Major Arcana cards have a specific archetype assigned them, though not all are labeled as being specifically Jungian in the following descriptions. They are approached from a Jungian standpoint by virtue of the concept of archetypes, which Jung referred to as the universal situations, feeling states, and behavior patterns of the collective unconscious. These archetypes are only potential ways of thinking, feeling, and acting. Jung compared the archetypes to a dry river bed that becomes active only when water begins to flow; for us, archetypes become active only when our behavior follows one of their universal forms.

Before proceeding with the Major Arcana in detail, let us review the stepwise journey of the Fool as he travels from card to card.

Trump 0, the Fool: The journey begins. A young man, appearing fresh and innocent and full of potential, is about to embark on a journey. Looking skyward, he stands at the edge of a precipice, apparently unaware of the abyss at his feet. His faithful dog barks to warn him of the danger of leaping into the unknown. Because of the original, adventurous, independent, and free spirit of the Fool, astrologers often associate the planet Uranus with this card. Jungians connect the Fool with the archetype of the Divine Child (the myth of the deity sending an infant to enlighten humankind).

Trump 1, the Magician: The Fool now learns to focus his creative energy and to use tools and instruments to manifest his desires. Astrologers associate the logic, conscious awareness, objectivity, adaptability, and industry of the Magician with the planet Mercury. Jungians link the Magician to the alchemic figure Mercurius (the world-creating spirit) and to the archetype of the Trickster.

Trump 2, the High Priestess: Something is missing from the Magician's logic, objectivity, and ability to manipulate the material world. In the High Priestess Trump, the Fool comes in contact with the hidden, spiritual, unconscious, and intuitive aspects of the universe. Like the sun and the moon, the Magician and the High Priestess complement one another. Astrologers associate the High Priestess with the Moon, ruler of the night.

Trump 3, the Empress: Having learned about objective and subjective reality, the Fool is now ready to meet the parental archetypes: the Empress-Mother-Womb and the Emperor-Father-Phallus. The Empress is the great earth-mother. She represents nourishment, fertility, and abundance. She feels, she heals, she nurtures, she gives birth, she is able to give and receive love. Astrologers associate the fruitful and loving aspects of the Empress with the planet Venus, although many aspects of the Moon are also present in this card. Jungians connect the Empress with the archetype of the anima (the feminine aspect of the personality).

Trump 4, the Emperor: The complement to the Empress is the Emperor. They are mother and father, wife and husband. The Emperor represents dominion, authority, order, reason, power, and control. Astrologers connect the Emperor with the forceful and pioneering first sign of the Zodiac: Aries, the Ram. Jungians see in the Emperor the archetype of the animus (the masculine aspect of the personality).

Trump 5, the Hierophant: In this trump the Fool learns about traditional values and moral requisites. The Hierophant, or Tarot Pope, is conservative, deliberate, traditional, pious, and orthodox. He is the carrier and transmitter of ancient wisdom and religious teaching. Astrologers associate the Hierophant with the fixed sign Taurus, the Bull. Jungians relate the Tarot Pope to the persona, or mask we wear in social interactions.

Trump 6, the Lovers: The Fool is now ready to learn about duality, yin and yang, temptation, decision, attraction, choice, friendship, union with a significant other, sexual adjustment, and romantic relationships. Astrologers associate the Lovers card with the dual sign Gemini, the Twins.

Trump 7, the Chariot: Having learned in the Lovers card about duality, yin and yang, and light and dark, the Fool must now learn to control and balance opposing forces to run a steady course. In this card the Fool realizes that life involves conflict and compromise, that there is no light without darkness, that we must all integrate our shadow. Astrologers associate the Chariot with the nurturing, protective sign Cancer, the Crab.

Trump 8, Strength: In this Trump, the Fool learns to trust himself, to develop self-confidence and inner strength. Astrologers associate the Strength card with the extroverted, creative, child-oriented and proud sign Leo, the Lion.

Trump 9, the Hermit: Here the Fool learns to look within, to meditate, to reflect in solitude, to trust one's inner guidance. The Hermit embodies the old adage, "Know thyself." Astrologers associate the Hermit with the prudent, service-oriented sign Virgo, the Virgin, goddess of the harvest.

Trump 10, the Wheel of Fortune: In this card the Fool learns that much of life is random and unpredictable, full of ups and downs. He understands that he cannot take any day for granted because it may be his last. He comes to appreciate the workings of fate—that there are forces beyond his control—and of karma, that what he sows he shall reap. Astrologers associate the Wheel of Fortune with the beneficent, expansive planet Jupiter.

Trump 11, Justice: Despite the randomness of the universe, there is a certain justice or fairness in its structure that reflects a need for balance and harmony in our lives. The Justice card reinforces the lessons of karma: our actions do have consequences for which we are held accountable. Society sets up a system of justice to try to ensure fair treatment of its members. Astrologers associate the Justice card with Libra, the Scales, the sign of balance and harmony.

Trump 12, the Hanged Man: In this card the Fool comes to appreciate the need to let go, to avoid living in a materialistic rut, and to seek other perspectives. The figure on the card is that of a man suspended by one leg, hanging upside down as he serenely contemplates the universe. He has apparently abandoned the things of this world in search of spiritual enlightenment. Astrologers associate the Hanged Man with the sacrificial, psychic, spiritual and illusory planet Neptune.

Trump 13, Death: Perhaps the Hanged Man of the previous card was contemplating his own mortality, the ultimate transition, the final letting-go. In Trump 13, the Fool learns the lesson from the New Testament that, unless the grain of wheat falls into the ground and dies, it cannot grow. This is a card about transition, transformation, renewal, death of the old, purification, and significant change. Astrologers associate the Death Trump with the mysterious, secretive, healing, sexual, evolutionary, regenerative sign Scorpio, the Scorpion.

Trump 14, Temperance: Having confronted death in Trump 13, the Fool emerges with a sense of integrity, perspective, balance, and moderation. He has learned the virtue of Temperance. Astrologers associate Temperance with the wise, tolerant, and independent sign Sagittarius, the Archer.

Trump 15, the Devil: Despite the maturity the Fool has reached in Trump 14, he is not immune to having to confront his personal demons. The Devil Trump is about the various chains that bind us and inhibit our development. These bonds come in many forms: ignorance, unbridled passions, obsessions, materialism, fanaticism, excessive spirituality, petty attachments, poor impulse control, negative thinking, co-dependency, wrong beliefs, and self-imposed doubts and uncertainties, to name a few. Astrologers associate the Devil card with the ambitious, determined, aspiring sign Capricorn, the Goat. Jungians relate the Devil card to the archetype of the Shadow, the dark side of ourselves.

Trump 16, the Tower: A lightning bolt strikes the tower out of the blue, destroying part of its structure, setting it ablaze, and casting its inhabitants to the ground. With the Tower Trump, the Fool again learns that drastic change can disrupt the life cycle without warning. Perhaps the Tower card is advising the Fool to break from the bondage symbolized by the Devil card, to face the truth and get on with his development. Astrologers associate the Tower Trump with the fiery, energetic, warlike planet Mars, but the suddenness of the disruption shares many of the characteristics of the planet Uranus, the Awakener.

Trump 17, the Star: Following the disruption of the Tower card, the Fool sees a ray of hope in the Star Trump. If he has learned his lessons of the Devil and the Tower and cast aside the chains that bound him, the Fool is now ready for further enlightenment and development of his special talents. Astrologers associate the Star Trump with the humanitarian, visionary, altruistic sign Aquarius, the Water Bearer.

Trump 18, the Moon: It is difficult to see things clearly by the light of the moon. In the Moon Trump, the Fool learns to deal with illusion, deception, obscurity, lack of clarity, hidden forces, basic instincts, moodiness, cycles, intuition, melancholy, mental unrest, and the repressed contents of the personal unconscious. Astrologers associate the Moon Trump with the imaginative, psychic, impressionable, gullible, and mystical sign Pisces, the Fishes. Jungians connect the Moon card with the archetype of the Great Mother.

Trump 19, the Sun: After wandering in the moonlight, the Fool is born again in the dazzling radiance of the sun. He feels invigorated, goal-oriented, and full of zest and optimism. He has gained a respect for his inner child and has the courage to express his true self. His conscious planning and individual effort are now rewarded with success. Astrologers assign the Sun Trump to the masculine, dynamic and energetic sun, the source of energy in our solar system.

Trump 20, Judgement: Awakened by the light of the Sun, the Fool is now able to hear the trumpet of the Judgement card sounding the call of the Self to spiritual rebirth and the healing of the psyche to resurrection. Astrologers associate the Judgement card with the transforming planet Pluto, god of the underworld.

Trump 21, the World: The Fool completes the cycle. The circular wreath surrounding the figure on the World Trump symbolizes the completion of the journey, the achievement of wholeness, the actualization of the Self. Astrologers associate this final card with the planet Saturn, the planet with the outermost orbit of the seven known planets in ancient times, end of the visible solar system, symbol of structure and stability.

～

Having reviewed the archetypal journey of the Fool, let us now consider each Major Trump in detail.

The Fool: 0 (or 22)
Le Mat, El Loco

Upright: The beginning of a journey. A leap into the unknown.

Key Words and Phrases: Innocence. Spontaneity. The new-born baby archetype. Potential. A fresh start. A new chance. A novel experience. A new way of perceiving the world. An opportunity. An important decision. A surprising solution. The start of an adventure. Significant and unexpected circumstances. Time for a change. Originality. An open mind. Optimism. Childlike wonder. Naiveté. Sprightliness. Purity of action. Freedom from bias. A new phase of life. Excitement about discovery. A carefree attitude. Surprise. Being born again. Trusting with faith. Freedom from inhibition. Enthusiasm. Taking a risk. Trust in a higher power. Confidence that you are headed in the right direction. Creative non-conformity. Leaving the past behind to start something new. An unexpected influence. Homosexuality. Bisexuality. Zero is the number of pure potential. All things are possible. To boldly go where no man has gone before.

Situation and Advice: The Fool appears when you are about to embark on a new phase in your life. An unexpected opportunity may appear out of the blue, or you may be called upon to make a major decision that will lead you down new paths. This new beginning could lead anywhere and you may need to go with the flow. A new relationship may be about to start, or an unconventional person may enter your life. The people you meet now may be participants in a new cycle of personal or professional growth. The Fool may also represent a bisexual or homosexual person who will influence the situation.

This card suggests the need to take a risk with childlike optimism and innocence. Because a novel point of view may offer a surprising resolution to a problem, you should remain open to new ideas. The Fool may signify a period marked by nervous energy, lack of clarity, and uncertain conditions. Sudden developments may catch you off guard and leave you feeling somewhat confused until you regain your bearings. You are now capable of much originality. You would be wise to leave the past behind and get on with starting something new. It would be a mistake to cling to traditional and outworn methods because the collective unconscious is advising you to start a new life cycle. On occasion the Fool will signify embarking on an actual journey, especially if other travel cards appear upright in the spread (such as the Chariot, the Wheel of Fortune, the World, Six of Swords, Eight of Wands, or Knight of Wands).

People: A newborn. A child. Those who are starting anew. Mystics. Dreamers. Innocents. Adventurers. Visionaries. Travelers. Wanderers. Innocent or inexperienced people.

Eccentric, independent and unconventional people. Bisexual or homosexual individuals. Adolescents. Someone about to make an important decision or begin a journey. Those who herald the beginning of a new phase in your life.

◐

The Fool Reversed: Foolishness. Fear of the unknown.

Key Words and Phrases: Impulsiveness. Poor judgment. Risk. Jadedness. Naiveté. Inexperience. Gullibility. Unfounded optimism. Irresponsibility. Lack of foresight. Frivolity. Unexpected problems. Lack of follow-through. A cliffhanger. Wasting energy. Excessive conformity. Lack of perspective. Poor decisions. Head in the clouds. An obsession. Throwing caution to the winds. Playing with fire. Look before you leap.

Situation and Advice: When reversed, the Fool warns against taking risks unless you carefully consider the situation. You may feel like you are standing at the edge of a cliff about to fall off. You may be foolishly obsessed with your own point of view. Remember Emerson's saying that a foolish consistency is the hobgoblin of little minds. Your current situation causes you to fear the unknown or what the future may bring. Avoid excessive optimism and blinding yourself to the downside risk of a venture. An impulsive decision or an unwise gamble will work to your detriment. Unexpected problems may arise. You may be in a precarious situation brought on by your own or someone else's folly. Your judgment may be faulty, or you may not be receiving sound advice. You must strive to keep matters in perspective. Someone around you may be making foolish decisions. You yourself may not be using prudent enough foresight to ensure genuine happiness. Someone may not be as loyal or committed as you believe they are. You or your partner may be fickle about the relationship. Remember that infatuation is not the same as love.

People: Gamblers. The foolhardy. The uncommitted. The reckless. Pollyanna.

The Magician: I
Le Bateleur, The Juggler, El Mago

Upright: Mastery of special knowledge. Focused energy.

Key Words and Phrases: The virile son archetype. Ability to achieve your goal. The cumulative result of disciplined training. Transformation through willpower. Ability to harness creative forces. Creative visualization. Ability to make decisions. Disciplined and creative action. New skills. Self-confidence. Creative power. Divination. Self-determination. Trial and error learning. Opportunities. Problem-solving ability. Legerdemain (sleight of hand). Adaptation to change. Virility. Being in the limelight. Marketing yourself. Self-employment. Dexterity. Medical expertise. Linguistic ability. Inventive ability. Making good use of available equipment. Creating new projects of lasting value. Action. Modern technology. The central nervous system. The lungs. The hands. The five senses. Androgyny. I am the master of my fate. I am the captain of my soul.

Situation and Advice: You are about to take advantage of the expertise you have gleaned from a period of disciplined training. You, or someone you trust, are able to use special skills and talents to achieve your goals. The time is right to initiate projects because you are master of your destiny. Any equipment you need will be at hand. Technical mastery of modern gadgets will assist you.

You are able to master new situations, take positive action and focus your attention to realize your potential. You are able to promote and market yourself to those who are interested in making use of your special skills and knowledge. Creative visualization would be beneficial at this time, as well as advanced training or education. Your skills at organization come in handy. In money questions, financial success is likely. The Magician tells you there is a way you can manipulate the forces of nature to achieve your goals. Special skills and technical expertise may be necessary for success. The Magician urges you to observe, experiment, remain adaptable, refine your skills, and learn about how to manipulate the world. In health matters, the Magician can represent a skillful physician or surgeon.

People: A son. A brother. A virile man. Those who manipulate the physical world. Politicians committed to the proper use of power. Writers. Magicians. Jugglers. Engineers. Inventors. Agents. Those who have technical expertise or are able to use many tools. Entrepreneurs. Alchemists. Teachers. Guides. Latency-age (aged five to puberty) children. Speakers. Linguists. Artists. Applied scientists. Medical specialists. Neurosurgeons. Artisans. Psychotherapists.

◐

The Magician Reversed: Blocked creativity. The Trickster.

Key Words and Phrases: Feigned expertise. Weakness. Indecision. Not seeing things for what they really are. Selfish behavior. Dithering. Frustration. Impotence. Delays. Reluctance to take a chance. Not using available equipment. Squandering energy or resources. Unrealistic goals. Making mistakes. Not learning from past mistakes. Overconfidence. Lack of dexterity. Failure of technology. Abuse of talents. Manipulation. Sexual inhibitions. Excessive arrogance. Lack of self-confidence or willpower. Avoidance of problems. Pooping out. Can't do anything right. A little knowledge is a dangerous thing.

Situation and Advice: For some reason you are not using your skills and talents to accomplish your goals. Your indecisiveness may be causing difficulties or delays. Perhaps you don't know enough to get the job done and need further training to perfect a skill. You may be pretending to know more than you actually do about a matter. Your lack of confidence may cause you to bypass important opportunities, or perhaps your overconfidence gets you involved in unrealistic schemes. Someone may be blocking your efforts or pulling the wool over your eyes. The Magician is a trickster, after all. Sometimes the Magician reversed refers to a sibling who is causing trouble for you.

If you asked about a relationship, you may be feeling sexually frustrated. Alternately, you may be involved with someone who is good in bed but who does not appreciate the enduring emotional aspects of a relationship. Examine your own behavior to see if you have been acting selfishly with little regard for the rights and needs of others.

Now is the time to apply yourself with special diligence to achieve success. The Magician reversed suggests feeling a lack of empowerment. You should avoid excessive materialism and narrow self-interest. You may be out of touch with your feminine intuitive side because of your excessive focus on manipulating the external world. This would not be a good time to give up a secure job in favor of self-employment.

People: Impostors. Those who manipulate appearances to gain power. Those who want only sex without love. Tricksters. Selfish people. Ineffectual or obstructive persons. Those unjustifiably overconfident of their own skills or knowledge. Self-proclaimed geniuses. Screw-ups.

The High Priestess: 2

Juno, The Papess, The Female Pope, La Sacerdotisa

Upright: Intuitive awareness.

Key Words and Phrases: The virgin daughter archetype. Mastery in the internal world. Inner space. Spiritual forces. Secrets. Matters not yet revealed. Love without sex. Spiritual enlightenment. Psychological insight. Inner illumination. Moral guidance. Looking within. Learning about feelings. Trusting your inner voice. The subconscious. Hidden issues. Early memories. Past conditioning. The messages of dreams. Hidden influences. Esoteric knowledge. Occult wisdom.

Help. Advice. Plumbing the depths. The invisible aspects of the universe. The female pope. Reflection. Meditation. Understanding of higher truths. Going with the flow. Unrevealed secrets. The unknown. The anima. Budding awareness of sexuality. Female mystery. Lesbian sexuality. Access to hidden knowledge. Learning. The power of silence. Unlocking of mysteries. Celestial mother. Hidden talents. Guardian of Hidden Wisdom. Body fluids. Digestion. Female issues. Life without men. Virginity. Decreased libido. Celibacy. Go with the flow.

Situation and Advice: Something is going on beneath the surface. Hidden knowledge needs to see the light of day. The High Priestess appears when you need to attend to your inner-most feelings and listen to your inner voice. Some aspect of your current situation deeply touches your unconscious mind. Now is a time to reflect, meditate, pray, and contact your inner self. Trust your feelings. Your dreams and intuitions give the best counsel. Past conditioning and early memories are affecting the current situation. You may have a strong interest in the occult, mysticism, divination, psychology, psychoanalysis, or any subject dealing with the hidden aspects of existence. At the same time your interest is sex is at a low.

An intuitive or psychic woman may come to your assistance. Someone who understands the inner workings of the mind or of your current situation may be of help. A secret or hidden aspect of your situation may be revealed. The High Priestess appears when you need to tap into your hidden potentials, psychological depths, or unseen talents to achieve success. Sometimes the High Priestess refers literally to book learning through further training or education.

People: A daughter. A sister. The vestal virgin. Single women. Devout persons. Those who want love without sex. Psychics. Psychologists. Counselors. Intuitives. Adepts. Idealized lovers. Sensitive people. Intuitive confidantes. Someone keeping a secret. Researchers. Initiates. Those who understand the inner workings of the matter inquired about. Luke Skywalker. The Fairy Godmother. The Virgin Mary.

◐

High Priestess Reversed: Not listening to your inner voice.

Key Words and Phrases: Misuse of intuition. Acting on bias or prejudice. Shallowness. Manipulativeness. Lack of emotional control. Being out of touch. Too little time for reflection. Ignoring your dreams and intuitions. Hysterical outbursts. Repressed feelings. Hidden enemies. Not following your hunches. Failing to use native talents. Fear of listening to your inner voice. Discounting the promptings of your heart. Emotional insensitivity or hypersensitivity. Secrets revealed. Nothing is hidden. Superficiality. Lack of forethought. Loss of virginity. Observing but not participating in the life force. Excessive reliance on external validation. Excessive reliance on analysis and rational thought. Increased interest in sex. It's right here in black and white. It just doesn't feel right, but I'll do it anyway. I only bet on a sure thing.

Situation and Advice: The High Priestess reversed suggests you are paying insufficient attention to your true needs and feelings. You may be overly intellectual or rational in your approach to problem solving. Alternatively, you may be acting out of bias or prejudice. Someone around you may be hysterical and emotionally out of control. You may be so preoccupied with the duties of your external life that you don't leave enough time for yourself. Your unconscious is trying to tell you something but you are unwilling to listen. You are out of touch with your feelings and with what is happening beneath the surface. Hidden knowledge will influence your decision; be sure to get all the facts before proceeding. You may be feeling emotionally sensitive or need to deal with someone who is highly overwrought. Your strong sexual desires may impair your judgment. Don't say yes when you mean no.

People: Manipulative people. Secret enemies, especially women. A cruel female. Emotionally troubled persons. Shallow or superficial individuals. The mentally ill. Self-destructive individuals. Promiscuous individuals.

The Empress: 3
L'Imperatrice, La Emperatriz

Upright: Mother. Fruitfulness. Abundance. Healing.

Key Words and Phrases: Queen of life. The mother archetype. Jung's anima archetype. The bed of life. Fruitfulness. Prosperity. Creativity. Productive action. Fecundity. Nurturing. Healing. Love. Harmony. Union. Synthesis. Sensuality. Continued growth. Material comfort. Status. Social standing. A beautiful home. A luscious garden. Abundance. Physical love and affection. Feminine sexuality. Marriage. Gain. Fertility. A good harvest. Pregnancy. Creativity. Maternal instincts. Willingness to help others. Birth. Motherhood. Grounding in the life process. The successful results of hard work. The passage from one stage of growth to another. Fulfilled potential. Royalty. Good fortune. Mother Earth. Mother Nature. Go forth and multiply.

> The more remote and unreal the personal mother is, the more deeply will the son's yearnings for her clutch at his soul, awakening his primordial and eternal image of the mother for whose sake everything that embraces, protects, nourishes, and helps assume maternal form, from the Alma Mater of the university to the personification of cities, countries, sciences, and ideals.
>
> —C. J. Jung, *CW* 13:147

Situation and Advice: The Empress is a card of good fortune suggesting female creativity, fertility, sexuality, and generativity. Now is the time to express your creative instincts in productive action. Any kind of artistic endeavor will prosper. Your career may involve you with beauty, sensuality, or providing material comforts. Your hard work now pays off with material success. Sexual relationships are satisfying. This card may indicate marriage, pregnancy (especially with the Three of Cups), or childbirth. If you are expecting a child, all will go well. The fruits of your labors are realized. You are able to surround yourself with beauty and material comforts. You are able to share your feelings and to give and receive love.

People: A mother. A wife. A woman of importance. A maternal, nurturing woman. A helpful woman. A woman of influence. A pregnant woman. An earth mother. A regal woman. A female employer. Royalty. A woman who owns land. Creative people. A parent. Women of power and authority. An important woman who enters your life. For a man, the woman of his dreams.

The Empress Reversed: Blocked development.

Key Words and Phrases: Failure to thrive. Stagnation. Problems with a pregnancy. Undeveloped creativity. Refusal to grow. Foolish satisfaction with the present. Excessive preoccupation with material comfort. Disregarding opportunities. Birth control. Infertility. Impotence. Abortion. Miscarriage. Sterilization. Lack of children. Promiscuity. Sex without love. An unwanted pregnancy. Financial hardship. Trouble. Poverty. Illness. Greed. Excessive materialism. Physical discomfort. Lack of productivity. Wasted energy. Depression. Despair. Suffering. Neglecting the wisdom of the heart.

Situation and Advice: Generally you are feeling blocked and unable to create. Your level of material comfort may be low, or you may be selfishly hanging on to your material possessions instead of sharing with loved ones. Greed may be creating problems in your relationships. Your mood may be depressed or despairing. Money may be tight and you may be feeling impoverished and unable to make ends meet. An unsatisfactory relationship may involve sex without love. The Empress reversed sometimes indicates sexual problems or an unwanted pregnancy. This card can be a warning to avoid unsafe sexual practices. It can also refer to problems with a pregnancy and a possible miscarriage. You may discover you are unable to conceive or decide you do not want any more children.

People: A woman who has had a miscarriage. Promiscuous people. Nonproductive people. Icy people. Emotionally unstable people. Prostitutes.

The Emperor: 4

L'Empereur, El Emperador

Upright: The father. Order. Control. Power.

Key Words and Phrases: The world of grownups. Masculine power and control. Self-assertion. Status. Dealing with authority. Temporal force. A man of influence. The outer world. The structures of society. The order we impose upon the world. Royalty. The drive for achievement, success, respect, and stability. The impulse to create something of lasting value. Regulation. Dominion. Rational thought. Mind over matter. Domination of the world. Ambition. Security.

Structure. Strength. Exuberance. Fearlessness. Firmness. Stability. Leadership. Law and order. Wisdom. Logic. Head over heart. The spirit of the law. The Freudian superego. Jung's animus archetype. Self-control. Completion. Achievement. Recognition. Ruler. Becoming your own person. Material wealth. A job promotion. Establishing a project on a firm foundation. Rational understanding. Government. Facing the music.

> The father represents the world of moral commandments and prohibitions, although, for lack of information about conditions in prehistoric times, it remains an open question how far the first moral laws arose from dire necessity rather than from the family preoccupations of the tribal father. . . . The father is the representative of the spirit, whose function is to oppose pure instinct.
>
> —C. J. Jung, CW 5:396

Situation and Advice: The Emperor suggests that you have the ability to use rational thought and direct action to achieve worldly success. You may receive a job promotion in recognition of your excellent organizational skills. You may need to deal with an important rival or with someone in authority. This is a card of respect, stability, solidity, governance, and rationality. It shows you becoming your own person as you establish yourself in the world.

Now is the time to act responsibly and organize a structured, stable environment. A mentor or helpful partner may assist you. Your status in society is likely to be an issue. The Emperor suggests an overemphasis on domination in romantic relationships that leads to excluding sensitivity and affection. In stressful spreads this card warns against excess and suggests a possible confrontation with the rules of society.

People: A father. A husband. A person of power or high position. A man of importance. A paternal man. A man of influence. An opponent. An important rival. A helpful man. The president. An employer. A land owner. Someone in power. A secure, stable business person. An organizer. A mentor. A company you work for. Men of authority. The upper classes. Royalty. Those who are direct and forceful. Political leaders.

◑

The Emperor Reversed: Lack of progress.

Key Words and Phrases: Refusal to grow up and enter the adult world. A wimp. Running away from problems. Lack of control or discipline. Tyranny. Abuse of power and authority. Insubordination. Immaturity. An inferiority complex. Problems accepting authority. The Peter Pan syndrome. Rebelliousness. Dependency. Abrasiveness. Belligerence. Coarseness. Impatience. Indecisiveness. Unreliability. Laziness. Narrow mindedness. Being excessively logical to the exclusion of feelings. An arbitrary decision. Following the letter rather than the spirit of the law. Burdens. Excessive responsibilities. Lack of direction. Remaining tied to the parents' apron strings. All head, no heart. I don't want to grow up. Who will take care of me? Screw you. Me Tarzan, you Jane.

Situation and Advice: Something is hampering your progress at this time. You may be viewing matters too much with your head rather than your heart. Your rigid adherence to principle may actually violate the spirit of the law. Perhaps you are in a situation where you feel incompetent or inferior. You may feel tempted to escape or run away from your problems. An immature man may be causing trouble. The Emperor reversed may reflect a refusal to accept legitimate authority while preferring childlike dependency or irresponsibility. You need to grow up and stop living in the world of childhood. There is something excessive or exaggerated about your behavior. Perhaps you are bullying others or acting in a tyrannical manner. A current romantic relationship may be marked by domination-submission, master-slave, or sado-masochistic themes. If you asked about work, you probably will not receive a promotion at this time.

People: An immature man. A coward. A tyrant. A bully. One who abuses power and authority. A weak or ineffectual person. A wimp. Someone subject to parental authority. One who is dependent and a burden to others. A mamma's boy or girl. Someone who refuses to grow up. A rebel without a cause.

The Hierophant: 5

The Pope, the Pontiff, Jupiter, The High Priest, El Sacerdote

Upright: Tradition. Convention. Orthodoxy.

Key Words and Phrases: The high priest archetype. Conventional wisdom. An official ceremony. The establishment. Moral requirements. Spiritual growth. Wise counsel. Professional advice. A bridge. Prayer. Spiritual authority. Divine law. A higher authority. A repository of ancient teachings. Moral development. Seriousness. Celibacy. Platonic relationships. Teaching. Learning. Seeking advice. Preference for tradition. Conformity. Conservatism. Established codes of behavior or belief. External authority. Jung's process of "persona identification," the adoption of a social mask. The search for spiritual truth. Man's search for meaning. Organized religion. Theological doctrine. Schools. Places of worship. Structured environments. Traditional institutions. The establishment. The "system." The Ivy League. Celestial father. The search for meaning. Religious ceremonies. Attendance at a wedding or a religious service such as a confirmation or Bar Mitzvah. Rites that link an individual with the traditions of a community. A mighty fortress is our God. Simon says . . . The Church teaches. According to conventional wisdom . . .

Situation and Advice: The Hierophant may indicate a spiritual search for meaning. The focus is on moral development. A wise guide or established teacher may appear to help you in your spiritual search. You may participate in a rite or ceremony which links the individual with the traditions of a community. You may visit a place of worship, perhaps to attend a wedding. Now is a time to heed conventional wisdom. The Hierophant can represent any expert consultant who renders professional advice. You may wish to consult an established expert for help with your situation. Someone in authority may intercede on your behalf to get you what you want. In questions of romance, the Hierophant suggests a very traditional or Platonic relationship.

People: The Pope. The clergy. Justice of the peace. Those connected with ceremonies. Gurus. Educators. Teachers. Students. Advisors. A helpful and wise person. Mentors. Professionals. Doctors. Marriage counselors. Arbitrators. Attorneys. Consultants. University officials. Spiritual leaders or counselors. Figureheads. A person who passes on his or her knowledge and understanding to a new generation. One who is serious in his or her intentions. Conformists. Conservatives. Traditionalists.

◑

The Hierophant Reversed: Breaking with convention.

Key Words and Phrases: Unorthodox approaches. New Age beliefs. Bad advice. Closed-mindedness. Dogmatism. Stubbornness. Scandal involving the clergy. Materialism. Extremism. Vengefulness. Secretiveness. Rigid orthodoxy, or else excessive nonconformity. Rejection of tradition. Putting up a mask. Misrepresentation. Propaganda. Misleading information. Extreme conformity to convention. Lack of originality. Religious extremism. Fanaticism. The Inquisition. The failure of conventional wisdom. The need for original methods and unorthodox solutions. If God wanted us to fly, he would have created us with wings. The clothes make the man. Don't judge a book by its cover. Up the establishment.

Situation and Advice: In its positive aspect, the Hierophant reversed may indicate you need to try an unconventional approach to solve your current problem. Traditional wisdom may not be a reliable guide at this time. You may need to break the conventional mold to get out of a rut. Dare to be different. To succeed, be innovative in your thinking. Set aside your mask and let yourself and others see how you truly feel about the matter.

In its negative aspect, the card may imply you are being too fanatical in your thinking and too dogmatic in your assessment of events. Are you applying the positive attributes of the Hierophant (traditional wisdom and conventionality) in an upside-down way? Are you behaving in an obsessive-compulsive or passive-aggressive manner? Have you put up a mask that hides your true feelings, not only from others but also from yourself? Too much nonconformity can be a handicap. Traditional or established methods may not produce the desired results. The advice you now receive may be unhelpful or misleading. A religious ceremony or wedding may be called off. If you asked about a romantic relationship, marriage is not a wise move at this time.

People: Those involved with New Age beliefs or religions. Rebels. Eccentrics. Innovators. Superstitious people. Someone impressed by appearances. Intolerant or dogmatic individuals. Obsessive-compulsives. Passive-aggressive individuals. The bride left at the altar.

The Lovers: 6

L'Amoureux, The Lover, Los Enamorados

Upright: Choice.

Key Words and Phrases: Union. Sharing. Trust. Duality. Short trips. Health. Healing. A romantic meeting. Sexuality. Attraction. Romantic love. Sexual adjustment. A partnership. A new relationship. A major choice. An important decision. A fork in the road. An ordeal. Temptation. Being put to the test. Reviewing an important relationship. Thoughts of love and marriage. Choosing one of two divergent paths. A love affair or relationship with a trial or choice involved. The power of love. The desire to share your life with another person. Commitment. Engagement. Marriage. The tree of life. Torn between two lovers. The road less traveled. I can't get you out of my mind. Until death do us part.

Situation and Advice: The Lovers card often appears when you are faced with a crucial life decision and must choose which path to follow. It can herald a romantic adventure, often with a trial or a choice involved. Commitment, sexual adjustment, love, and marriage may occupy your thoughts. You may be preoccupied with the progress of an important relationship. When the Two of Cups upright also appears in the spread, you are probably dealing with a significant love relationship.

This card cautions you to consider carefully all the ramifications of a major decision before making a final commitment. Somehow you are being put to the test before you can enter the next stage in your development. You are at a fork in the road. You may be about to enter into a new relationship or partnership. You may need to choose between two potential partners. You may find yourself buying new clothes or otherwise improving your personal appearance to attract new love into your life. Short trips and communications are also likely.

In the Waite deck, the Lovers card portrays the Archangel Raphael, patron saint of healing, as the background figure. In the Robin Wood deck, the two lovers stand beneath the tree of life. The Lovers card can signal a need for healing, either physical or spiritual. This is a good time for a heart-to-heart talk about an important relationship with a trusted advisor or friend. In a health reading, the Lovers card is a sign of spiritual protection and recovery.

People: Partners. Lovers. Couples. Business partners. Twins. Someone on the horns of a dilemma. Healers. Good friends. Romeo and Juliet.

○

The Lovers Reversed: A bad choice.

Key Words and Phrases: Failing a test. The end of love. Inconsistency. Freedom at all costs. Fear of commitment. Impatience. Wanderlust. Refusal to make an important choice. An ill-considered decision. Fickleness. Infidelity. An immature attitude toward love. Hedonism. Sex without love. Marital problems. A troubled or unhealthy relationship. Health problems. Illness. Irresponsibility. Dislike. Disharmony. Not getting together. Bluntness. Hurt feelings. Disunion. Indecision. Opposition. A troubled relationship. Separation. Parting. Disjunction. Divorce. Quarrels. Disagreements. Inner conflict. Opposition from others. An alliance ruptured by outside forces. Isolation. Feeling cut off from another. Love is blind. You don't care about me anymore. Love 'em and leave 'em. A lover in every port.

Situation and Advice: You may have hurt someone's feelings, or vice versa. Perhaps a chance to get together or an invitation fell through and the people involved are questioning each other's affection. Maybe you are involved in a separation or the end of a love affair. If you asked about marriage, you may despair ever finding a suitable partner and fear living your life alone. Concerns about your sexual adjustment may occupy your mind. Perhaps you are involved in an unhealthy relationship. Your fear of commitment may be creating problems in your love life. You must learn to take responsibility for your behavior and the choices you make. Someone around you may be opposing a decision you have made. If you are facing a major decision, seek expert advice and choose carefully to avoid future regrets. Sometimes this card signals the onset of a problem with health.

People: Those faced with an impossible choice. Separated persons. Opponents. The uncommitted. Those involved in unhealthy relationships. Don Juan. Sexual deviants.

The Chariot: 7

Le Chariot, El Carro

Upright: Progress through balancing opposing forces.

Key Words and Phrases: Clear purpose. Determination. Being able to carry on. Initiative. Self-assertion. Willpower. Control. Conquest. Success. Dominion. Centeredness. Inner peace. Triumphant progress. Single-mindedness. Ambition.

Mastery. Courage. Skill. Energy to fight for a goal. Great effort. Achievement. The drive for success. Self-control. Sense of purpose. A journey. News. Winning. Victory resulting from personal effort. Honors. Recognition. Control over conflicting forces. Inner struggle. Self-discipline. Conflict of interests. Ability to stay on top. Steering a middle course. Balancing conflicting emotions. Triumph over obstacles. Charging ahead through struggle and conflict. Coming out on top. Strength of will. Going with the flow. Transportation. Communications. Vehicles. A new car. I am the master of my fate, I am the captain of my soul.

Situation and Advice: The Chariot suggests a need to stay centered and take control of competing forces to carry on. You are capable of a calm sense of command, provided you steer a middle course between conflicting thoughts, feelings, and wishes. At the same time you may feel unable to speed up the outcome, so the best course of action is to go with the flow of the forces you have set in motion. You may find yourself struggling to assert yourself because you need to resolve a set of conflicting interests. You will be able to stay on course after making a firm resolution. Your strategy should be to move forward with determination and a clear sense of purpose. You will conquer your difficulties and emerge victorious. Generally whatever situation you asked about will resolve itself in your favor. Your strength of will and sense of purpose will enable you to come out on top. The Chariot can literally mean travel, buying a car, or treating yourself to a new means of transport.

People: Military persons. Messengers. Professional drivers. Motorists. Chauffeurs. Travelers. Jockeys. Those involved with transport. Victors. Those at peace with themselves.

●

The Chariot Reversed: Out of control.

Key Words and Phrases: Reckless action. Feeling overwhelmed. Failure. Overweening ambition. A misdirected sense of purpose. Imbalance. Unfairness. Lack of direction. Scattered energy. Plans fall through. Too narrow a focus. Too rapid a pace. Restlessness. Obstacles. Struggle. Conflict. Wrong use of energy. Pressures. Wastefulness. Indulgence. Inconsiderateness. Resentment. Unnecessary force. Bossiness. A domineering attitude. A smothering relationship. Insecurity. Suspicion. Anxiety. Moodiness. Rigidity. Repression. Character defects caused by the failure to integrate conflicting emotions. Difficulties with travel or transport. A trip delayed or canceled. An automobile accident. Car problems. It's bigger than both of us.

Situation and Advice: You are feeling out of sorts, uncentered, and not in control of your destiny. You may have strayed off the path you set for yourself some time ago. You need to resolve a situation involving conflicting forces. You feel pulled in two directions and need to find a middle course. Perhaps you have taken on too many projects and cannot balance all the competing demands on your time. Taken literally, the Chariot reversed can mean problems with travel or transport, or the need for car repairs.

People: Those involved in conflict. Unbalanced persons. Reckless drivers. Stranded motorists. Impulse-ridden individuals. Machiavelli.

Strength: 8*

La Force, The Enchantress, La Fuerza

Upright: Moral force.

Key Words and Phrases: Self-confidence. Inner strength.
Action. The power of conviction. Patience. Wisdom.
Assertiveness. Gentle force. Ability to overcome problems
through willpower. A strong position. Self-discipline. Faith in
your own abilities. Heroism. Protection. Nonviolence.

*In some decks, Strength is number 11.

Courage. Energy. Strength. Virility. Vitality. Healing. Good
health. Recovery after illness. Potency. Empowerment. Self-
reliance. Gentleness. Endurance. Taming the beast within.
Harnessing instinctive desires. Proper channeling of libido.
Reconciliation. Diplomacy. Tact. Beauty and the Beast.
Patience is a virtue.

Situation and Advice: You will need to rely on inner
strength, patience, and gentleness to solve your problems.
Now is a time to have faith in yourself. Your position is
strong and you are able to confront someone who has been
pushing you around. You can channel your animal passions
constructively to achieve good health and success. A tactful,
diplomatic approach leads to success. If you asked about
health, you can expect healing and renewed vitality.

People: Athletes. Weight lifters. Gymnasts. Those who work
with animals. Healers. People of calm conviction. Arbitrators.
Those who are at home with their sexual and instinctive
appetites. Those who have come to terms with the Shadow
aspect of their personality.

◑

Strength Reversed: Weakness. Sickness.

Key Words and Phrases: Impotence. Being bullied. Self-
doubt. Fearfulness. Depression. Diffidence. Timidity.
Insecurity. Concession. Giving in to base urges. Inability to
cope. Lack of confidence. Unassertive behavior. Unhappiness.
Giving in to fears. Lack of self-discipline. Worry. Dependency.
Self-defeating behavior. An overbearing attitude. Arrogance.
Insolence. Abuse of power. Despotism. Vanity. Chauvinism.
False sense of power. Lack of conviction. A caricature of inner
strength. Excessive aloofness. Rebelliousness. Fanaticism.
Anarchy. Conflicting interests. Feeling worn down.
Immunodeficiency.

Situation and Advice: You may be feeling weak, ill, vulnerable, depressed, and overwhelmed by your current situation. This is not a time to force an issue. The Strength card reversed suggests a need to come to terms with your inner demons. You may be depending too much on other people, or possibly on drugs or alcohol, to steer your life. Alternatively, someone may be bullying you or pushing you around. You need to assert your inner strength with conviction to feel empowered and self-reliant. Perhaps you need to reassess your situation because you are trying to accomplish a goal that is currently beyond your abilities. To make progress, you need to come to terms with guilt, self-doubts, and fears. The Strength card reversed sometimes literally indicates fatigue, physical weakness, or illness, and the need to take better care of one's health. Currently, you may also have contact with sick people.

People: Frail or weak people. Invalids. Sick people. Immunosuppressed individuals. Dependent people. Jekyll and Hyde personalities. Those dominated by their animal passions. Substance abusers. Cowards. Wimps.

The Hermit: 9
L'Ermite, The Wise Man, El Ermitaño

Upright: Searching within.

Key Words and Phrases: Contemplation. Meditation. Becoming centered. The need for psychological space. Contact with the Source. Quiet study. Self-discovery. Withdrawing from society. Keeping to yourself. Patience. Discretion. Prudent reflection. Time spent alone. Thoughtful planning. Seeking sensible advice. Deliberation. Attention to details. Inner guidance. Counseling. Self-examination. Reassessment. Discovery. Wisdom. Forethought. Old age. Sanctuary. The process of searching for deeper truths. Inner understanding. Pondering life's mysteries. Withdrawal from daily routine. The search for mystical enlightenment. The need for solitude and introspection. A quiet spell. Patient waiting. Being attuned to the spiritual dimensions of the universe. The wish to bring knowledge to light. Attending to your mental health. Atonement. The sounds of silence. The answer lies within. I need some space. The currents of universal being flow through me. Keep it quiet. Patience is a virtue.

Situation and Advice: Now is a time to withdraw voluntarily from the world to seek truth in solitude. You must reunite with the Source. You need to rest and think silently about your situation. Meditation, patient contemplation, and calm reflection are in order. This is a time of patient waiting and keeping to yourself. Sometimes counseling will aid in your search for self-understanding. Take time to consider matters carefully. Be patient as you strive to make a prudent decision. Most likely the answer lies within, but if you are feeling stuck seek sensible advice from a wise and more experienced person. This is also a good time to take up the serious study of a subject that interests you.

People: A spiritual advisor. A wise person. A teacher or mentor. Gurus. Hermits. Monks. Cloistered nuns. The elderly. Seekers of wisdom. Those who need a rest to gather their thoughts and reassess their situations. Those who wait patiently. Those in a period of preparation. People in voluntary isolation. A prudent counselor.

◐

The Hermit Reversed: Wisdom spurned.

Key Words and Phrases: Excessive isolation. Enforced silence. Exile. Loneliness. Lack of human contact. Foolish or excessive self-reliance. Withdrawal from others. Feeling rejected. Self-absorption. Fear of intimacy. Focus on externals. Rejecting good advice. Imprudence. Rashness. Disregarding wise counsel. Feeling isolated. Bereavement. Rejection. False pride. Lack of communication. Aloofness. Suspicion. Self-pity. Nervousness. Worries about health. Whining. Complaining. Skepticism. Escapism. Victimization. Confusion. Self-deception. Being your own worst enemy. I'd rather do it myself. I did it my way. Nobody loves me. I am a rock, I am an island.

Situation and Advice: You may be so caught up in doing things your own way that you reject good advice or input from other people. Your tendency to cut others out of your life may leave you feeling lonely and rejected. Such character traits may even lead to the breakup of a relationship.

People: Asocial people. Self-absorbed, ignorant or stupid people. Exiles. Lonely people. Irresponsible, foolish people. Those who refuse to see the truth. Someone who is distant or aloof from others. Extremely self-contained or isolated people. Schizoid or paranoid characters.

The Wheel of Fortune: 10

La Roue de Fortune, La Rueda de la Fortuna

Upright: A change for the better.

Key Words and Phrases: Good luck. Advancement. Opportunity. Important developments. Improvements. Rapid change. The upside of a cycle. Fate. Destiny. Progress. New doors open. The ups-and-downs of fortune. Tao. A fortunate turn of events. A lucky break. The end of one phase and the start of a new one. Improving circumstances. Gambling. Games of chance. Lady luck. A new vehicle (new wheels). Karma. Everything changes. You cannot step into the same river twice.

Situation and Advice: You are entering a new cycle involving a fortunate set of circumstances that promise beneficial change and continuing progress. Forces in motion stimulate change and growth. Rapid changes offer new opportunities to improve your life. A chance circumstance may bring an end to past difficulties and herald a period of good fortune and success. You may need to make an important decision that will influence the unfolding of events in your life. A new chapter in your life is about to begin. You are ending one phase and starting something new. The finger of fate works in your favor. Sometimes the wheel refers literally to a new vehicle coming into your life.

People: Gamblers. Speculators. Lucky people.

◑

The Wheel of Fortune Reversed: What goes up, must come down.

Key Words and Phrases: Failure. Hapless circumstance. Bad luck. A turn for the worse. Unexpected setbacks. Stagnation. Deterioration. A negative twist of fate. The downside of a cycle. Misfortune. Disappointment. Jogging in place. Stuck in a rut. Feeling out of sync. A dead end. Going downhill. Resistance to beneficial change. It will get worse before it gets better. What did I do to deserve this? Without rhyme or reason. The fickle finger of fate.

Situation and Advice: Circumstances take an unexpected turn for the worse. Hopes and wishes go unfulfilled. Your life appears to proceed without rhyme or reason. You are entering the downside of a cycle and a period of disappointment before things look up again. This is not a good time to take significant risks. You need to wait for a new turn of the wheel of fortune. It may help to check your astrological transits and progressions for some insight into your current run of bad luck.

People: Losers. The unlucky. The hapless.

Justice: 11*
La Justice, The Balance, La Justicia

Upright: Being judged. A fair outcome.

Key Words and Phrases: Legal affairs. Equilibrium. Harmony. Restoration of balance. Fairness. Arbitration. Neutrality. Impartiality. Maintaining a proper balance. Order restored. Prudent money management. Strategy. Accountability. Integrity. Examination of conscience. Carefully

*In some decks, Justice is number 8.

considered choices. Clear vision. A sense of proportion. The power of intellect. Rationality. A just outcome. The right decision. Clear-cut perspective. Intervention of the law. Decisions needed to maintain justice, law, and order. A trial. A court case. Dealings with the law. Litigation. Contracts. Binding agreements. Settlements. An apology. A marriage contract. A divorce agreement. Powers that enforce justice. Virginity. Testicles and erect phallus. Justice will prevail. Put yourself in my shoes! Crowley's "The Woman Satisfied."

Situation and Advice: Justice usually appears when you must weigh many factors to make a reasoned and thoughtful decision. This card cautions you to deliberate carefully and wisely before reaching any conclusions. It is a card of calm and balance. You would do well to examine your conscience and consider the other person's point of view before making a moral choice. Issues of fairness are prominent.

Justice may also indicate involvement in legal proceedings in the near future. Legal matters will proceed in a fair and dispassionate manner. Justice will prevail in the end, especially if the Judgement Trump also appears upright in the spread. An impartial third party may assist in bringing about a fair outcome. If someone has wronged you, you may receive an apology soon. If you have acted unjustly, you are about to face the consequences.

People: Arbiters. Lawyers. Judges. Witnesses. Legal authorities. The court. Someone who must make a decision. One who apologizes.

◐

Justice Reversed: Being judged unfairly.

Key Words and Phrases: Unfair treatment. Injustice. Delayed justice. Equivocation. Lack of commitment. Not getting what you deserve. Imbalance. Excess. Loss. False accusations. Refusal to apologize. The wrong decision. Unfairness.

An unjust outcome. Bigotry. Bias. Prejudice. Abuse. Conflict. Taking sides or taking advantage of others. Not weighing both sides of an issue. Imbalance. Fence sitting. Partiality. False accusations. Vindictiveness. Legal problems and entanglements. Illegal actions. Red tape. An unjust court decision. Failing an examination. Nepotism. Separations. Protracted litigation. Laziness. Manipulation. Peace at any price. Combativeness. Abrasiveness. Cruel and unusual punishment. Taking the law into your own hands. Abuse of legitimate authority. Lawlessness. Overconfidence. Police brutality. Getting away with murder. Two wrongs don't make a right. I'll never admit I was wrong. Humpty Dumpty sat on a wall . . . .

Situation and Advice: There may be a delay in receiving what you truly deserve. You may be in a situation where you feel you are receiving unfair or prejudicial treatment. Perhaps you are the victim of false accusations, or you have falsely accused another. Someone involved in making a decision about you could be prejudiced in the matter. Your own overconfidence or lack of commitment may be working against you. You may need to stop sitting on the fence and make a firm decision to pursue your goal.

A person in authority may be abusing his or her power. An apology may be in order but not forthcoming. Do not take the law into your own hands because only further injustice will result. You need to stop sitting on the fence for fear of upsetting others. If you are involved in a lawsuit or arbitration, the outcome may be costly or unfavorable to you (especially if the Six of Wands reversed appears in the spread). If you are taking an examination or somehow being judged, the results may not reflect what you truly know, perhaps due to some unfair aspect of the situation or perhaps due to your inadequate preparation.

People: False accusers. Those who discriminate against or treat others unfairly. Those who refuse to apologize for past wrongdoings. Manipulators. Mobs. Fence sitters. Biased individuals. Bigots. Corrupt judges. Bad cops. Looters. Vigilante groups.

The Hanged Man: 12
Le Pendu, El Colgado

Upright: Suspension. A new perspective.

Key Words and Phrases: Reversal. Slowed action. Limbo. Taking your time. A testing period. A lesson to be learned. Cosmic consciousness. Enlightenment. A unique viewpoint. A new angle. Dancing to a different drummer. Spiritual attunement. Selflessness. Sacrifice. Commitment. Dedication. Flexibility. Adaptability. Daring to be different. Breaking with the past. Readjustment. Voluntary sacrifice to obtain a higher good. Stasis. Calm. In slow motion. An apparent standstill. At a crossroads. Reflection. Serenity. Higher wisdom. Mysticism. Devotion. Unexpected domestic or career changes. Let go and let God. A foot in both doors. I can see the Promised Land. Naked we come into the world and naked we leave the world. What makes him tick? To thine own self be true.

Situation and Advice: Now is a time to pause and suspend activity. You need to reevaluate your attitudes, goals, and priorities while remaining true to your spiritual values. Time appears to be moving slowly and you may feel like you are in a state of suspended animation. This is a testing period and there is a lesson to be learned. You are in the midst of a major transition and feel caught between the old and the new. You are capable of unselfish dedication to a significant project or ambition. Yours is a unique perspective that others may not appreciate or understand.

Perhaps you must let go or make a sacrifice to achieve a greater good. You may join a group of people who have made similar sacrifices. You need to give up the old to make way for the new. You may relinquish a selfish desire out of love and commitment to another person. You may get out of a relationship because you realize it is detrimental. Time spent in contemplation, rest, relaxation, and reflection is well worth it. You need to reconnect with the spiritual dimension of life. Perhaps you've been worrying excessively and need to contact a higher power. Other people are unlikely to understand where you're coming from.

People: Those who selflessly dedicate themselves to a goal. Someone who withdraws from life to meditate. Someone who dares to be different. A hospital patient. A spiritual person. A saint.

●

The Hanged Man Reversed: Useless sacrifice.

Key Words and Phrases: Materialism. Refusal to make necessary sacrifices. A martyr complex. False security. A bad investment. A poor financial decision. Lack of commitment. The triumph of selfishness. Dissatisfaction. Depression. Ennui. Apathy. Lack of effort. A sense of futility. Stuck in the status quo. Refusal to break with the past. Lack of spiritual attunement. Excessive conformity. Soul murder. A false self. Denying an important part of yourself. Keeping up with the Joneses. The end of indecision.

Situation and Advice: For some reason you are being untrue to your Self. Perhaps you are sacrificing part of your life for no good reason. You may be living up to someone else's expectations and denying your own inner needs and values. Are you playing the martyr role in a relationship? Such behavior can only lead to a sense of futility and a reluctance to commit yourself to a worthwhile goal. You may be unwilling to make a sacrifice for a higher good. Are you afraid to upset those around you by marching to your own drummer? Remember Emerson's saying that a foolish consistency is the hobgoblin of little minds. You may need to turn your world upside down to achieve enlightenment. Don't squander your energies on useless projects. If you asked about a financial matter, beware of making a bad investment or of following a questionable fiscal course at this time.

On a positive note, a period of suspension or being in limbo may be coming to an end. If you have been able to reset your priorities and rediscover your direction in life, you are now ready for decisive action.

People: Martyrs. Selfish people. As-if personalities (those who define themselves in terms of the wishes of others). The uncommitted.

Death: 13
La Mort, The Reaper, La Muerte

Upright: Major transformation.

Key Words and Phrases: Necessary and profound change. Liberation. The dawning of a new era. Leaving the past behind. The end of a cycle and the start of a new one. Entering on a new way of life. Death of the old self. Empowerment.

Rebirth. Renewal. Sudden inevitable change. Transition. Cleansing. Purging. Revitalization. Stripping away the worthless matter. Liberation through purgation. Grieving the loss of a former lifestyle. Inevitable endings. Change of status. Marriage. Divorce. Starting or leaving a job. Leaving home. Relocation. The end of a relationship. Loss of virginity. Spiritual regeneration. The shedding of outmoded attitudes. Reincarnation.

Situation and Advice: Death is Trump thirteen, a number associated with death since the use of the lunar calendar in which the thirteenth month was the time of death and regeneration. A major change is about to take place. Transformation is imminent. The Death card often appears when you are facing significant life events like marriage, divorce, leaving home, relocating, career moves, or parenthood. A momentous alteration in your life structure is about to occur. A situation is coming to an end and a new era is dawning. Now is a time to rid yourself of attitudes and situations you have outgrown to pave the way for a new stage in life. A loss is possible. All that is useless or outmoded must be discarded. This is a time of endings and new beginnings; as the New Testament reads, "Unless the grain of wheat falls into the ground and dies, it cannot grow." You must let go of old unproductive ways. Sometimes this card means literally the death of someone you know.

> Men fear death, as if unquestionably the greatest evil, and yet no man knows that it may not be the greatest good.
>
> —William Mitford

People: Those undergoing major life changes. Agents of change. Undertakers.

◐

Death Reversed: Resistance to necessary change.

Key Words and Phrases: Inertia. Bullheadedness. Being at a standstill. Obsessions. Stagnation. Immobility. Fear of change. Fear of releasing an outmoded situation or attitude. Clinging to the moribund past. Taking an extreme position. Refusal to change. Obstinacy. Decay. Turning your back on the future. Depression. Being in limbo. Being forced to give up what you would not let go voluntarily. Loss of friendship. A birth.

Situation and Advice: When Death occurs in the reversed position, you are clinging to an outmoded situation, relationship, or attitude that really should be discarded. Your fear of change rivets you to the past and hinders your growth. What are you afraid of? Your resistance to necessary change makes the experience more painful when it inevitably occurs. It is better to take the bull by the horns than to undergo such changes involuntarily.

People: Those who cling to the past for fear of change and transformation.

Temperance: 14
The Angel of Time, La Templanza

Upright: Moderation. Self-restraint. Blending.

Key Words and Phrases: Modulation. Prudence. Tolerance. A middle course. A balanced viewpoint. A sense of proper timing. Fairness. Absence of prejudice. Not taking an extreme position. Compromise. Descent of spirit into matter. Discretion. Intermingling. Fruitful combination. The right mixture. Artistic creation. Compatibility. Calm capability. Merging of diverse forces. Equilibrium. Composure. Tranquillity. Peace. Morality. Harmonious balance. Coordination. Patience. Forgiveness. Accommodation. Adaptation. Wise management. Frugality. Mercy. A balanced expression of sexuality. Reasonableness. Compassion. Friendship. Forgiveness. Cooperation. Reconciliation. Gentleness. Purification or cleansing of the soul. A mixed marriage. Interracial harmony. Time heals all wounds. Everything in moderation. Take it easy! One day at a time. Nothing in excess. We are all God's children. Without regard to race, color, or creed.

Situation and Advice: A sensible intermingling of diverse elements brings forth a new creation. You may establish a friendship or relationship with someone of a different race or culture. You are able to cooperate harmoniously and patiently with others. Issues of prudence versus excesses in behavior, including sexual activity, may be on your mind. You can now blend varied ingredients into a harmonious mixture. Moderation and wise management are the keys to success. You need to slow down, reevaluate your position, and remain open to compromise. Old wounds heal with the passage of time. A temporary separation is possible.

People: Spiritual healers. Adepts. Artists. Protectors. Managers. Biracial persons. Partners in a mixed marriage. Civil rights workers. Chefs. Good cooks. Alchemists. Mediators.

◑

Temperance Reversed: Extremism.

Key Words and Phrases: Fanaticism. Immoderation. Sexual excesses. Lust. Lack of balance. Pressures. Refusal to compromise. Overreaction. Overdoing it. Discord. Wasted energy. Lack of control. Obsession. Excessive ambition. Impatience. Volatility. Moodiness. Unbridled passions. Lack of restraint. Inappropriate behavior. Fickleness. Frivolousness. Scattered energies. Impulsiveness. Conflict of interests. Indecision. Imbalance of mind and emotions. Haste makes waste. Outlandishness. Impropriety. Closed mindedness. Stress. Poor judgment. The clash of opposites. Immorality. Wantonness. Going overboard. Gluttony. Overindulgence. Pigging out. Trying to combine inharmonious elements. A repulsive mixture. Forcing a situation. Unsafe sex. Throwing caution to the wind. Eat, drink, and be merry, for tomorrow you may die. Everything in excess.

Situation and Advice: You have been exhibiting a lack of moderation and are now facing the consequences. Your failure to control your appetites may have harmful results. Issues of sexual fidelity may be a problem in a close relationship. Your obsession with a goal may lead you to take extreme measures to achieve your ends. Your refusal to compromise causes problems.

People: Gluttons. Wastrels. Extremists. Those unable to curb their appetites. Nymphomaniacs. Addicts. Alcoholics. Women who love too much. Those who engage in compulsive sexual activity.

The Devil: 15

Le Diable, The Black Magician, El Diablo

Upright: Bondage. Self-imposed limitations.

Key Words and Phrases: The power of negative thinking. Finding it hard to let go. Pessimism. Refusal to leave a bad situation. Excessive dependency. Unnecessary guilt. Heavy commitments. Confronting your personal demons. Darkness. The need to see things clearly. Excessive attachment to material goods. Vanity. Selfishness. Unhealthy attachments. Greed. Lust. Powerful sexual urges. Inhibitions. Fears. Hang-ups. Self-doubts. Hopelessness. Oppression. Ties that bind. Unhappy choices. Feeling stuck in a confining situation or relationship. Co-dependency. Enslavement. Imprisonment. Indulgence. Addiction. Caught in a vice of your own making. Obsession with power, sex, or money. Sadism. Cruelty. A conflict between money and spiritual well-being. Primitive urges. Uncontrolled passions. Addictions. Perversions. Sexual instincts. Repressed fears. One's Achilles' heel. Jung's concept of the Shadow. For what shall it profit a man if he shall gain the whole world and lose his own soul? (Jesus). The Devil hath power to assume a pleasing shape (Shakespeare).

Situation and Advice: You are feeling trapped in an oppressive situation that may be of your own making. Perhaps you are overburdened by some heavy commitment. Are you refusing to leave a problematic relationship? Are you finding it hard to let go when you know you should? When the Devil appears in a reading, you need to review your bondage to material goods, unbridled passions, harmful relationships, and financial security. Your fearfulness and negative thinking are hampering your life.

Take a good look at reality. How are you enslaved in your life? Are you caught in a web of unhealthy attachments? Are you acting out of greed and fear of material loss? Are you using money to buy love? Are you remaining in a relationship you know is harmful? Are you trapped by material success? Are you obsessed with wealth or sexual conquests? Do drugs, alcohol, or some other appetite control your life?

The Devil warns against using your power or influence to enslave or manipulate others. You are caught in a prison of your own making and it is time to face your fears and inhibitions. Your hopelessness and belief that you are unable to change is stifling your growth. Why do you believe your fate is to suffer? Confront your Shadow to allow personal growth to continue (the Jungian Shadow refers to the dark side of ourselves—our fears, hang-ups, and most difficult aspects of our personalities—that we must confront and come to terms with before becoming integrated and whole).

People: Those overly concerned with money. Those involved in unhealthy attachments. Greedy, miserly people. Those ruled by their animal passions. Destructive people. Battered women and battering men. Those whose lives are closely connected with slavery or bondage.

◑

The Devil Reversed: Release from bondage.

Key Words and Phrases: (+) Confronting one's fears. Release from bondage. Removing the chains. Co-dependent no more. The power of positive thinking. Cutting the ties that bind. Overcoming temptation. Seeking enlightenment.

(–) Indecision. Rigidity. Excessive ambition. Immoderate greed. Instability. Clinging. Dependency. Feeling at the end of your rope. A smothering relationship. Abuse of power. Perversity. Dehumanization. Using people for selfish ends or material gain. Absolute power corrupts absolutely.

Situation and Advice: In its positive aspect, the Devil reversed indicates that the chains have dropped from your neck. You have confronted your false values and self-imposed limitations. You are no longer dominated by your obsessions. A burdensome commitment is coming to an end. You are now ready to live freely and independently, no longer clinging to toxic relationships, to lust for money and power, or to the power of negative thinking. You are ready to break free of an oppressive situation.

In its negative aspect, the Devil reversed indicates that you may be acting in a self-centered or greedy fashion. You may need to choose between money and happiness. Your desire for material gain or power may have become an obsession. It is possible that someone is controlling or manipulating you. You are prone to depression now unless you can break free of the ties that bind you. Many of your inhibitions are self-induced and you have been unwilling to face up to them. The negative meaning of the Devil reversed warns against engaging in the baser forms of sexual expression. You feel hopelessly trapped in an unbearably burdensome situation.

People: (–) Sadistic, controlling and manipulative individuals. Spiteful people. Misers. Sex offenders.

(+) Those who have confronted their fears and are free.

The Tower: 16

The House of God, The Lightning-struck Tower,
La maison de Dieu, La Torre

Upright: A bolt from the blue. Collapse of a structure.

Key Words and Phrases: Collapse of an old way of life.
Modification. Disruption. Shock. Havoc. Awakening.
Instability. A jolting insight. A shocking revelation. A traumatic
experience. Major transformation. A crisis point. A surprise.
Unavoidable change. Release from bondage. Structural flaws.

The death of an illusion. Liberation. Breaking free. Shocking spiritual enlightenment. Purging. Rapid change. Darkness dispelled. Piercing to the quick. Disturbing news. An illuminating flash that sets you free. Eliminating what is worthless. Release from self-imposed captivity. Tumult. Disappointment. Shattering false beliefs. Collapse of plans. Breaking down outmoded forms. Demolition of useless structures. Confronting shame and guilt. Casting off false values. A moment of truth. Destruction of something corrupt. Separating the chaff from the wheat. Freedom. Enlightenment. Social conventions that bind you. A new job. A change of residence. A disturbing incident. Separation. Divorce. An accident. Problems with property. Bankruptcy. Loss of security. Earthquakes. Natural disasters. In medical readings, a stroke or sudden attack. Hospitalization (especially together with the Four of Swords, which indicates recuperation is necessary). No pain, no gain. I see the light. Some day you'll thank me for this. Aha! You can't go home again. Back to the drawing board.

And the walls came tumbling down.

—The Battle of Jericho

Situation and Advice: The appearance of the Tower in a spread often heralds swift, shocking, and dramatic change. The usual structures of your life begin to crumble, and you must deal with the collapse of an old way of life. You may find yourself suddenly selling your home, moving to a new residence, changing jobs, pursuing a new career, entering psychotherapy, or significantly altering important relationships. The point of such change is to help you learn an important truth about yourself and act accordingly. The upheaval associated with this card involves a moment of truth that forces you to rid yourself of false life structures and identify what you truly value. The more entrenched you are in a phony lifestyle, the more disruptive this change will be. Now is a time to rid yourself of binding social conventions and false beliefs that hinder your growth. The structures imprisoning you must be shattered before you can achieve enlightenment. Occasionally this card portends a theft, job loss, family quarrels, or trouble with property. The old order must dissolve to make way for the new. Unsound structures will come tumbling down.

People: Aggressive, energetic people who challenge your world-view. Those who traumatize or cause disruption. Someone who has suffered a stroke. Victims of natural disasters.

The Tower Reversed: A shock.

Key Words and Phrases: (+) The trauma is over. The change has happened. Things will never be the same. Time to pick up the pieces and start anew.

(−) Self-imposed captivity. Continued oppression. Unalterable circumstances. Inability to change. Restriction of freedom. The bondage of the flesh. Imprisonment. Disruption. Breakdown. Chaos. Upheaval. Catastrophe. Freedom at a price. Tyranny. Injustice. Failure to live up to expectations. Give me liberty or give me death. Stone walls do not a prison make, nor iron bars a cage.

Situation and Advice: In its positive aspect, the Tower reversed indicates that a shocking or disruptive influence is coming to an end. You are now able to pick up the pieces and start anew.

In its negative aspect, you may feel burdened by injustice or unfairness in your life's circumstances. Structures or relationships you have taken for granted may be suddenly shattered or lost. You feel boxed in, hampered, confined. Literal imprisonment is a rare possibility. You feel stuck in a negative situation with no exit. You must now face problems that could have been avoided. You experience the consequences of past mistakes.

People: Those in a state of shock.

The Star: 17

L'Etoile, La Estrella

Upright: Hope.

Key Words and Phrases: Inspiration. Luck. Tranquillity. Optimism. Trust. Enjoyment. Confidence. Faith in the future. Comfort. Relief. Renewal. Happiness. Promise. Help. Protection. Restoration. Spiritual love. Selflessness. Heavenly light. Illumination. Reflection. A special talent. Harmony.

Enthusiasm. Creativity. Fertility. Charisma. Grace. Beauty. Peace. Refreshment. Balance. Poise. Emotional and spiritual riches. Inner guidance. A sense of direction. Expanded horizons. Inner healing. Renewed health. Guiding light. Higher knowledge. Special talents. Occult understanding. Expansion of knowledge. Ability to plan for the future. Meditation. Learning astrology. Spiritual growth. Faith. Contemplation. Aid from many sources. Help from above. Astrological insight. Education. Heaven on earth. When you wish upon a star. As above, so below.

> The heavens declare the glory of God; And the firmament sheweth his handiwork.

—Psalm 19

Situation and Advice: The Star is a very positive card. Now is a time to rely on your intuition, inner wisdom, and guidance. Consulting your horoscope is also likely to be beneficial. The Star is a card of hope, protection, promise, joy, inspiration, good fortune, and spiritual happiness. Your guardian angel is watching over you. A desired response or result is on the way. This is a good time to exert yourself because you can achieve your ideals. Often the Star card is urging the querent to develop a special talent. A young woman may light up your life.

People: A guardian angel. A female child. A young woman. Those who render assistance. Astrologers. Astronomers. UFO buffs. Healing agencies. ET.

◐

The Star Reversed: Difficulty accepting help being offered.

Key Words and Phrases: (+) Hope. Faith in the future. Unjustified pessimism.

(–) Delays. Disappointment. Disillusionment. Pessimism. Poor judgment. Unfulfilled hopes. Fleeting happiness. Missed opportunities. Haplessness. Disquiet. Loss. Anxiety. Ill health. Rigidity. Self-doubt. Distrust. Obstinacy. Egotism. Aloofness. Rejecting spiritual guidance. School problems. The glass is half-empty.

Situation and Advice: The Star retains much of its positive meaning in the reversed position. You may, however, may be unaware of the spiritual riches that surround you. As a result, there may be a delay in your plans or some difficulty with a venture. A pessimistic attitude or lack of confidence may get in the way of happiness. You are focusing on the glass being half-empty rather than half-full. Your skittishness may cause you to overlook promising opportunities. There is cause to have faith in the future. You may be having a hard time accepting the help being offered. You may be blind to your own acres of diamonds.

In an otherwise negative reading, the reversed Star may indicate a loss of hope, depression, and possible illness (especially when many Swords occur in the reading).

People: Those who have trouble accepting help. Pessimists.

The Moon: 18

La Lune, La Luna

Upright: Deep instinctual forces. Self-deception.

Key Words and Phrases: (+) The pull of the Moon. Our roots in the animal kingdom. Past conditioning affects present behavior. A time to be passive and receptive. Intuition. Strong emotions. Secret truths. Psychic awareness. Mediumship. The uncanny. Dreams. Imagination. Fantasy. The netherworld. The mother. The female archetype. Change. Mystery. Bewilderment. The oceanic feeling. The creative potential of the unconscious mind. Fiction. Creative writing. Acting. Work involving illusion. The entertainment industry. Wildlife. The wilderness.

Travel. Everything in our transitory world is but a resemblance (Goethe). O Swear not by the moon, the inconstant moon, that monthly changes in her circled orb (Shakespeare).

(–) Moonlit fantasy. Escapism. Confusion. Deception. Trickery. Insincerity. Slander. Lies. Betrayal. Muddled thinking. Infidelity. Craftiness. Fear. Deceit. Uncertainty. Insecurity. Fluctuation. Illusion. Lunacy. Doubt. Indecision. Bad dreams. Apprehension. Unforeseen or unpredictable dangers. Neuroticism. Overwhelming emotion. Troubled imaginings. Negative moods. Depression. Hidden enemies. Self-undoing. Gynecological problems. Things are not what they seem.

Situation and Advice: According to tradition, the Moon warns of deceit, lies, dishonesty, confusion, peril, self-deception, and moonlit fantasy (what we think we perceive by moonlight often looks quite different in the light of day). Some of these meanings are inherent in the Moon card's astrological association with Pisces and the horoscopic twelfth house of confinement and undoing, which also refers to psychic awareness, spirituality, and concern for those less fortunate.

The Moon card suggests you are entering a period of fluctuating moods and uncertainty during which you must confront unconscious forces in order to proceed. That which has been invisible or secret is coming to the surface. You can make good use of your creative talents in writing, art, drama, acting, psychology, or psychotherapy. Travel, especially over water, is possible. You notice how ingrained patterns from the past are affecting your current behavior. Expect the uncanny.

You should attend to your dreams, feelings, hunches, and intuitions now. It is important to become aware of what lies beneath the surface or buried in the past. Your gut feelings may be more reliable than logical analysis. Awareness of the psychological dimensions of human existence now plays an important role in your life. The Moon card asks us to reflect on our primitive origins in the animal world and in the collective unconscious. If your question was about being deceived, the Moon card suggests that you are the victim of false information and double dealing. Something is happening behind the scenes that will eventually come to light. The Moon can also signify that your mother or a mother substitute is about to figure prominently in your affairs.

People: (+) Mothers. Women. Travelers. Artists. Psychics. Creative writers. Oceanographers. Veterinarians. Actors. Poets. Star-crossed lovers. Psychotherapists. Psychologists. Visionaries. Those in touch with the unconscious mind. Animal lovers.

(–) Liars. Con men. Impostors. Embezzlers. Someone who pulls the wool over your eyes. Impractical dreamers.

◐

The Moon Reversed: Step into the light.

Key Words and Phrases: (+) Beneficial changes. Clear thinking. Seeing things as they really are. Shedding light on the matter. Confusion ends. Hidden matters come to light.

(–) Lunacy. Misunderstandings. Escapism. Ambiguity. Unclear thinking. Being in the dark. Deception. Victimization. Untruths. Misperception. Daydreaming. Illusions. Confusion. Vague fears. Worries about health. Problems involving women. Primitive responses. The dark side of the unconscious. Unsettling emotions. Covert motives. Self-doubts. Hidden fears. Dark secrets. A warning of danger. A test of faith.

Situation and Advice: It is time to step into the light. Make no major decisions until this period of confusion ends. You will soon be able to see more clearly in the light of day. In the process you may need to confront your own monsters from the Id. Some matter that was difficult to comprehend now becomes clear. You may become aware of a secret enemy or of some clandestine threat to undermine your well-being. With an otherwise negative spread, you would do well to guard against theft, sabotage, underhanded tactics, misunderstandings, and the excessive use of drugs or alcohol. Check to see how your mother is doing.

People: (+) Those who have dealt with confusion and now see things clearly in the daylight.

(–) Emotionally troubled or mentally ill individuals. Devious and deceptive people. Crooks. Secret enemies. Subversives. Deceivers. Liars.

The Sun: 19
Le Soleil, El Sol

Upright: Success. Fulfillment.

Key Words and Phrases: Giver and sustainer of life. Vitality. Pleasure. Ambition. Confidence. Optimism. Exuberance. Achievement. Affirmation. Empowerment. Masculine energy. A time to take charge. A prosperous development. Illumination. Truth. Logic. Clear thinking. Warmth. Friendship. The power of positive thinking. Pure rational thought. Joy. Satisfaction. Creative self-expression. Hope.

Enrichment. Self-control. Blessings. Spiritual victory. Acclaim. Display. Attainment. Opportunity. Energy. Spontaneity. Creative inspiration. Public recognition. Celebration. Good health. Virility. Happiness. Prosperity. Rationality. Academic honors. Scientific achievement. Invention. Marriage. Children. Emotional well-being. The dawning of a new day. Summertime. Hot weather. Enjoyment of outdoor activities. A birthday party. On a clear day you can see forever. You light up my life. You are my sunshine. It feels great to be alive. And a good time was had by all.

Situation and Advice: A ray of sunshine enters your life. This is a time of hope, joy, celebration, success, optimism, achievement, good fortune, health, and happiness. Time spent with good friends or children is rewarding. Students do well on tests. Other examinations turn out favorably. You are capable of conscious, rational, and thoughtful solutions to problems. You feel vital, healthy, and alive. A literal interpretation of this card is a trip or a vacation to enjoy the outdoor sunshine or a day at the beach.

People: Children. Babies. Fathers. Sun bathers. Inventors. Cheerful people. Decisive men. Leaders. Kings. Prominent people. Scientists. Academicians. Apollo. Virile men.

◐

The Sun Reversed: Delayed or partial success. Vanity. Boasting. Ostentation. Arrogance. Egotism. Problems of narcissism. Excessive concern with external appearances. Negative thinking. Failure. Pessimism. Depression. Ill health.

Key Words and Phrases: (+) Delayed but eventual success. Lesser joys. Modified happiness. Partial success. Arrogance about one's success. The Sun is such a positive card that even in its reversed position it does not entirely lose its favorable meaning. It can still represent success, but only after delays or obstacles, and is not as intensely auspicious as the upright card. The Sun reversed can also signify the seeking of success for the wrong reasons or the desire to appear prominent and/or accomplished without truly earning one's success. Keeping up with the Joneses. Me, me, me. A fly in the ointment.

(–) However, in an otherwise negative spread, the sun can have an unfortunate connotation. Failure. Uncertainty. Unhappiness. A clouded future. Problems with children. Marital difficulties. Plans that fall through. Gloom. Loss. Loneliness. Depression. Lack of energy. Unclear thinking. Feeling unappreciated. Disagreements. Misunderstandings. Cancellations. Hopelessness. Lack of purpose. Illness. Poor health. Sunburn. Broken engagements. Difficulty getting pregnant. Misjudgment. Learning disabilities. Problems with examinations. The approach of darkness. Nightfall.

Situation and Advice: Even in its reversed position, the Sun remains a positive card. You may experience a delay or an obstacle before achieving the success promised by this card. Another possibility is that what you desire may be unattainable or unrealistic. You may achieve only partial success. Even if you get what you want, you may not feel satisfied with the outcome. Sometimes the reversed Sun card indicates arrogance based on letting success go to one's head. Are you seeking recognition without the willingness to truly earn your success? Are you letting your accomplishments go to your head?

In an otherwise negative spread, the Sun reversed will indicate problems that are annoying but not overwhelming. For a while you may feel like you have a perpetual dark cloud over your head. You may feel unloved or unappreciated. Your pessimistic outlook may be adversely affecting your health. Pregnancy and dealings with children may be a source of concern. You may be going through a rough time in your marriage or love life. Students may not do as well on exams as they would like to. You may be plagued by a sense of failure. You may be suffering from some minor health problems. Are you filling your mind with negative affirmations?

People: Those with a gloomy disposition. Arrogant or boastful people. Egotists. Those overly concerned with superficial appearances. Pessimists.

Judgement: 20
Le Jugement, El Juicio

Upright: Summing up. Rebirth.

Key Words and Phrases: A developmental milestone. A momentous choice. The ending of a phase of life and the assessment of its worth. Judging or being judged. Growing up. A change of position. The end of an era. The end of a situation. A rite of passage. A career change. A promotion. Resurrection. The need to evaluate or be evaluated. Rejuvenation. The Phoenix rising from its ashes. A ponderous decision. A call to action. Renewal. An identity crisis. A time for evaluation. A new direction. Readjustment. Transition. Awakening. Metamorphosis. Breaking with convention. Major changes. A mandatory choice that will change life for the better. Cleansing. Purification. Regeneration. A new life. New opportunities. Self-appraisal. Self-improvement. Final reckoning. Transformation. Healing. Breaking free of old habits. Revitalization. A favorable legal decision. Balancing accounts. A clean slate. A final examination. Commencement. Graduation. As you sow so shall you reap.

> Earth to earth, ashes to ashes, dust to dust; in sure and certain hope of the Resurrection to eternal life.
>
> —1662 Prayer Book

Situation and Advice: A cycle is ending and you must prepare for a new stage of growth. You are reaching a milestone in your development. You may be faced with a crucial decision that will alter your life's course. If you make this decision with full awareness of its potential for transformation, the outcome will be beneficial. Now is a time of major changes and improvements, a kind of rebirthing process. If you are contemplating a career change, you will achieve success. In matters of health, healing and recovery will take place. If involved in legal matters, they will be decided in your favor. If a student, you will pass your examination. If you asked about a medical examination, the results will be favorable.

This is the end of a cycle, a time of renewal and awakening, and a time to reap the rewards of past actions. The time has come to wipe your slate clean and prepare for a positive new beginning. You are able to see things more clearly now.

People: Judges. The Supreme Court. Executioners.

◑

Judgement Reversed: An unwelcome transition. A negative assessment.

Key Words and Phrases: An unwanted termination. Disappointment with a past situation. Delay. Indecision. Fear of change. A forced ending. Being found wanting. A major unwelcome change. Avoiding a necessary decision. The

Phoenix does not rise. Procrastination. Remorse. Regret. An unhappy ending. Lack of purpose. Refusal to let go. Ignoring a call for action. Avoidance of challenge or growth. Loneliness. Fear of death. Separation from a loved one. Disillusionment. Loss. Failing an examination. A disappointing legal decision. Feeling in a rut. Refusing to face the facts. Shame. Self-pity. Illness. Negative karma.

Situation and Advice: You must now face the consequences of a poor decision you made in the past. Alternatively, you may be avoiding an important decision because you fear the changes it will create in your life. Perhaps you have reviewed an entire phase of your life and now realize it has not been worth it. You may have outgrown a relationship, job, situation, or limiting structure but feel reluctant to let go.

Even though you don't feel ready, you may need to terminate some aspect of your life. Circumstances, illness, or even a death may separate you from a loved one. Perhaps a job or career matter has put distance between you and a significant other. A relationship may be coming to an end and you may be reluctant to close the final chapter. You can't postpone facing the facts forever. As difficult as it may seem, you need to let go of the past to get on with your life.

Major unwelcome changes may be out of your control. A legal decision or examination result may not be in your favor. Sometimes Judgement reversed indicates health problems, especially trouble with eyesight or hearing. If you asked about the results of a medical examination, be prepared for upsetting news. In relationship questions, Judgement reversed can symbolize separation or divorce. If you asked about a legal matter, the reversed Judgement card suggests that it will not be decided in your favor (especially if the Six of Wands reversed, indicating delays caused by treachery, appears in the spread). In its reversed aspect, the Judgement card is advising you to take account of negative karma and learn from your past mistakes. You may need to cut your losses and proceed in a more constructive direction.

People: Those involved in unwelcome endings or unwanted major life changes. Those learning the lessons of negative karma. Students who fail exams. Losers in a lawsuit.

The World: 21
Le Monde, The Universe, El Mundo

Upright: Reaching a natural conclusion.

Key Words and Phrases: The end. The last of the Major
Arcana. Fulfillment. Attainment. Culmination. Harmony.
Well-being. The end of a phase and starting something new.
Unity. Elation. A journey's end. Ecstasy. Reaching your goal.
Receiving a prize. Completeness. Wholeness. Oneness. A job

well done. Admiration. Beauty. Completion of a cycle. Success. Triumph. Freedom. Liberation. Peace. The joy of life. An ideal state of being. Affirmation of life. Cosmic flow. The promised land. Expanded horizons. The end of the rainbow. A pleasant surprise. Completion of a cycle. Enlightenment. Greeting each day enthusiastically. Ideal environmental conditions. Physical and emotional health. Spiritual well-being. The best possible outcome. Travel. A journey. Change of job or residence. Readiness to start again. Commencement. Graduation. A peaceful death at the end of a long and fulfilling life. All's well that ends well. Somewhere over the rainbow. The party's over. It's time to call it a day.

Situation and Advice: You have reached the final stage in your striving to reach a goal. All is well and success is at hand. Everything is progressing smoothly according to plan. You will receive what is rightfully yours. You feel whole and complete. You have reached the promised land. After this period of completion, you will begin a new life cycle and need to cope with fresh experiences. As you end this phase, you prepare to start something new. Travel over long distances is a possibility now.

People: Winners. Achievers. World travelers. Those involved in international affairs. Those who have satisfactorily reached their goals.

◐

The World Reversed: Stagnation. Unfinished business.

Key Words and Phrases: Imperfection. Delayed success. Failure to complete a cycle. Frustration. Obstacles. Pending completion. Loose ends. Fear of change. Stasis. Running in place. Stuck in a rut. Lack of commitment. Quitting too soon. Not finishing what you start. Insecurity. Resistance to change. Unwilling to face the future. Stubbornness. Lack of application. Keeping your blinders on. An unsatisfactory outcome. Pooping out. Travel postponed. You're not there yet. Farther to go.

Situation and Advice: You are finding it difficult to reach your goal because you have not taken care of necessary unfinished business. As a result, you feel like you are in a rut and unable to bring matters to a satisfactory conclusion. Issues seem to drag on without resolution. You feel bored, stagnant, and ineffectual. You are tempted to quit a task rather than bring it to completion. You are resisting change and do not feel ready to deal with new experiences. You need to step back and look at the entire picture so that you can tie up the loose ends and achieve your goals.

The World reversed can sometimes indicate that a trip you were planning will be delayed or that you may simply repeat an old itinerary.

People: A jack of all trades and a master of none. One who stays voluntarily in a rut. Those who do not finish what they start. Losers.

∾

Chapter Five

The Minor Arcana or Pip Cards

Pips are the dots or markings on cards that indicate their numerical value. The Pip cards refer to common feelings and routine events of daily life. They sometimes describe characteristics of people we meet or aspects of our own personalities. Usually the Pip cards depict situations or emotions we are currently facing or are about to confront.

The meanings of the Pip cards are derived from numerology and the ancient concept of the four elements. Each suit represents one of the classical elements: Air = Swords, Earth = Pentacles, Fire = Wands, and Water = Cups (see table on page 24). The ten cards in each suit follow a sequence of numerological meanings:

1: The seed or root of the element.

2: Balancing duality; pure manifestation.

3: Blending, creation, and fertilization.

4: Establishing foundations.

5: Upsetting the prior stability.

6: Re-establishing harmony.

7: Loss of stability brought on by new awareness.

8: Mastery and autonomy; acknowledgment of error.

9: Completion, crystallization, fulfillment, peak experience.

10: Ending, final transformation, preparing for a new cycle.

The Personal Year Number

Another helpful numerological concept is the idea of a personal year number. This is found by adding all the numbers in your birthdate for the current year. For example, if your birthday is November 29, then your personal year number for 1995 would be 11 (November) + 29 + 1995 = 2035. This number is further simplified as 2 + 0 + 3 + 5 = 10, and then the 10 = 1 + 0 + 1. The number 1 implies that the personal year from 11/29/95 to 11/29/96 will be an important time of new beginnings. During a one personal year, people often change jobs or residences or begin a new relationship. An emphasis on the number one in a spread would have the same significance.

~

Wands
Batons, Staves, Scepters, Rods, Staffs, Clubs

Element: Fire

Astrological Signs: Aries, Leo, Sagittarius

Season: Spring (the season initiated by cardinal sign Aries)

Traits: Energetic. Cheerful. Outgoing. Vital. Enthusiastic. Fun loving. Active. Resourceful. Fond of travel. Inspirational. Creative. Entrepreneurial. Having leadership ability. Impetuous. Ardent. Sporting. Full of life. Restless. Impulsive. Pioneering. Enterprising. Sprightly. Shallow.

Occupations: Entrepreneurs. Salespersons. Teachers. Preachers.

Key Words and Phrases: The thrusting phallus. Power. The spark of life. Career. Commerce. Business opportunities.

Travel. Work. Negotiations. A busy time. New ventures. New projects. Enterprise. Action. Enthusiasm. Energy. Force. Renewal. Faith. Bursting forth. Creativity. New life. Growth and development. Passion. Spirit. Distinction. Hope. Ambition. Winning and losing. Games of competition. Politics. Desire for growth. Inspiration. Day-to-day matters.

People: Fair, blonde, or red hair. Dark or light eyes. Fair or freckled complexion.

Pentacles
Coins, Deniers, Disks, Diamonds

Element: Earth

Astrological Signs: Taurus, Virgo, Capricorn

Season: Winter (the season initiated by cardinal sign Capricorn)

Traits: Resourceful. Service oriented. Dutiful. Practical. Down-to-earth. Realistic. Plodding. Insensitive. Pragmatic. Efficient. Sensible. Decent. Reliable. Persistent. Thorough. Materialistic. Money-minded. Dull. Studious. Educational. Taciturn. Unimaginative. Selfish.

Occupations: Bankers. Business people. Accountants. Property managers. Builders. Farmers. Students. Laborers. Construction workers.

Key Words and Phrases: The material world. Business. Possessions. Money. Property. Inheritance. Real estate. Wealth. Material resources. Savings. Talents. Training. Education. Study. Time. Profit and loss. Giving and receiving. Tangible reality. Matter. The physical body and its state of health. Fiscal affairs. Work. Values. Skills. Management. Results. Financial security. Practicality. Construction. Material goods. Nature. Feces. Domestic matters. Emotional security. Sensual pleasure. Salt of the earth.

People: Brown or dark hair. Dark eyes. Dark complexion. People of darker-skinned ethnicity.

Swords
Epees, Spades

Element: Air

Astrological Signs: Gemini, Libra, Aquarius

Season: Autumn (the season initiated by cardinal sign Libra)

Traits: Mental. Communicative. Detached. Aloof. Impersonal. Impartial. Intellectual. Cool. Calculating. Discerning. Serious. Analytical. Head over heart. Strong-minded. Determined. On the go. Truth seeking. Piercing to the quick. Insensitive to or uncomfortable with feelings. Avoids intimacy. Interested in abstractions. Aggressive. Spiteful.

Occupations: Intellectuals. Journalists. Communicators. Travelers. Arbitrators. Professionals. Doctors. Lawyers. Judges. Paid advisors. Enforcers of the law. Military leaders.

Key Words and Phrases: Strife. Tension. Upset. Conflict. Struggle. Hostile forces. Communication. Travel. Powerful ideas. Worries. Important decisions. Major choices. Truth. Justice. Intelligence. Foresight. The piercing phallus. Obstacles. Disagreements. Worries. Troubles. Sorrows. Problems. Stress. Pressure. Boldness. Courage. The mind. The mental aspects of life. Thought. Mental activity. Reason. Logic. Detachment. Moving on. Separations. Broken relationships. Unkempt promises. Confusion. Sarcasm. Threats. Danger. Animosity. Irritability. Problems. Arguments. Contention. Loss. Disappointment. Setbacks. Legal action. Ill health. Sickness. Surgery. Cutting. Overwork. Accidents. Death.

People: Brown or black hair. Light eyes. Olive complexion.

Cups
Coupes, Hearts

Element: Water

Astrological Signs: Cancer, Scorpio, Pisces

Season: Summer (the season initiated by cardinal sign Cancer)

Traits: Emotional. Artistic. Creative. Sensitive. Nurturing. Tender. Pleasant. Touchy-feely. Relationship oriented. Kind. Friendly. Companionable. Romantic. Impressionable. Emotional. Imaginative. Caring. Compassionate. Empathetic. Intuitive. Psychic. Responsive. Aesthetic. Weak. Unreliable. Tearfully sentimental. Angry. Resentful. Emotionally intense. Concerned with the needs of others.

Occupations: Counselors. Artists. Musicians. Psychics. Those who work with feelings. Welfare workers.

Key Words and Phrases: Emotions. Moods. Affections. Love. Caring. Romance. Relating. Emotional problems. Matters of the heart. The vagina. The womb. Partnership. Relationships. Sensitivity. Receptivity. Feelings. Imagination. Sex. Happiness. Intuition. Art. Creativity. Dreams. Fantasy. Visions. Comfort. Satisfaction. Harmony. Children. Family.

People: Light brown, blonde, or gray hair. Blue, light, or hazel eyes. Medium or fair complexion.

~

Aces
Ones

Key Words and Phrases: Seeds. New beginnings. The creative principle. The start of anything. The root force. Births. New projects or ventures. Fresh ideas. New challenges. Initiation. Incitement. Innovation. Inspiration. Vitality. Potential. Leadership. Initiative. Independence. Something new. Early stages of action. Raw energy. Creative power. Upsurge of energy. The number one.

God said, 'Let there be light,' and there was light.

—Genesis

Corresponding Major Arcana Card: The Magician.

Situation and Advice: The Ace of each suit gives birth to the remaining cards of that suit. As the first cards of each suit, Aces represent each suit's root forces and are associated with the number one. There is a correspondence between the number one and the signs Aries and Leo. The Sun rules Leo and is exalted in Aries. The Sun symbolizes traits like leadership, force, strength, energy, initiative, ambition, courage, independence, originality, and managerial ability. Negative traits include being bossy, arrogant, bullying, and domineering. All of the Aces reversed denote a selfish use of the energy of the card.

The prominence of Aces in a reading suggests new beginnings, ambitions, fresh opportunities, and the planting of seeds, which anticipate long-range development. This is the right time to begin a new venture. You might become involved with someone new or rejuvenate an existing relationship. Aces can signify a time to initiate plans for a major move or a career change.

Aces represent the beginning of a cycle. It is a time to seek out opportunities and broaden your horizons. The yang energy of the number one is helpful for promoting new projects. Be prepared to make independent decisions and to take chances to get ahead. Yang energy suggests that males may figure prominently in the matter under scrutiny.

Personal Year: During a one personal year we begin a new nine–year cycle. This is a time for leadership, independent decision making, advancement, progress, and pushing to achieve our goals. We are able to pursue opportunities and start new ventures. There is a danger, however, of rash and impulsive decisions.

Ace of Wands
Rearing to Go

Upright: New life.

Key Words and Phrases: Start of a new venture or enterprise. Energy. Birth. Force of the element fire. The power of inspiration. A turning point. New experiences. Fresh ideas. New beginnings. Inspiration. Innovation. Optimism. Forward looking. Invention. Confidence. Enthusiasm. Drive. Virility.

Sperm fertilizes egg. An upsurge of creativity. The waxing of creative energy. Starting over. Forces set in motion. Creativity. Fertility. Conception. Growth. Procreation. Male potency. Driving force. Putting ambitions into action. The phallus. Sexual passion. An exciting opportunity. Success in a new venture. Initiative. Energy directed toward a worthwhile project. News of a birth. An important business communication. Good news. This could be the start of something big.

> The force that through the green fuse drives the flower
> drives my green age . . . .
>
> —Dylan Thomas

Situation and Advice: You may be starting a business or an enterprise. You have energy at your disposal to lay new foundations and begin something promising. You are open to new interests. Something happens to stimulate your career. This is a time of initiation, invention, and creativity.

People: Pioneers. Inventors. Entrepreneurs. Adventurers. Initiators. Those who create.

◐

Ace of Wands Reversed: Can't get going.

Key Words and Phrases: Unfulfilled promises. Thwarted growth. Dashed hopes. Delays. Difficulties. Trouble getting started. False starts. Abortive attempts. Cancellations. Wasted energy. Frustration. Misdirected force. Selfishness. Lack of motivation or initiative. Unproductiveness. Impotence. Infertility. Sterility. False hope. Poor planning. Miscarriage. Abortion. Not even trying. Futility. Inhibited progress. Ineffectiveness. Powerlessness. Being unyielding. Being too demanding. A lack of ideas. Pessimism. All talk, no action. Promises, promises, promises!

Situation and Advice: A venture that looked promising may fail to materialize. A promise you were counting on may fall through. A project begun with enthusiasm may not have the energy to sustain itself. You may be feeling frustrated, impotent, or powerless to accomplish your goals. Your own unyielding or selfish behavior may be the root of the difficulty.

People: Those who promise but do not deliver. Unambitious, unproductive, impotent people. Stubborn, unyielding people.

Ace of Pentacles
Firm Financial Foundations

Upright: A windfall. A helping hand.

Key Words and Phrases: The beginning of fiscal improvement. A tangible beginning. The power of solidity and security. Force of the element earth. Comfort. Prosperity. Sensual enjoyment. Physical matters. Energy for material achievement. A salary increase. Financial good fortune. Winning.

Early stages of material comfort. The birth of prosperity. A new opportunity. The start of a successful venture. Flow of capital. Money coming in. Purchases. Property matters. Material gain. Financial advantages. Success. Recognition. A promotion. Career change. Reward for hard work. A new beginning with firm foundations. Fertility. The good things in life. Good health. Pennies from heaven. Everything he touches turns to gold.

Situation and Advice: You are now able to start a business venture that promises monetary gain. Receipt of money or a gift is possible. A financial enterprise begun now will eventually lead to prosperity and material security. Money will become available if you need it to start a new material venture. You will be rewarded for hard work. If a student, you may be receiving your degree soon. You may soon need to deal with important correspondence or legal documents. Often the Ace of Pentacles represents the early stages of contact with a person or persons who will open the door to future financial opportunity. If you asked about romance, the Ace of Pentacles promises a secure relationship full of sensual pleasure and sexual fulfillment. The Ace of Pentacles is favorable for all matters related to the body, one's health, and tangible physical reality.

People: Helpers. Hard workers. Sensualists. Those at home with their physical natures. Body builders. Laborers.

◑

Ace of Pentacles Reversed: Flawed financial foundations.

Key Words and Phrases: Delayed income. Inadequate payment. Material loss. Misuse of money or possessions. Pooping out. Bad investments. Failed promises. Insecurity. Money problems. Poor planning. Flawed start of a venture. Plans fall through. A false start. Greed. Miserliness. Discontent.

Possessiveness. Materialism. A rash decision. A poor choice. Carelessness. Over-indulgence. Putting all your eggs in one basket. A stitch in time saves nine. Haste makes waste. I want what I want when I want it. The check is in the mail. I'm pooped.

> A horse, a horse, my kingdom for a horse.
>
> —Shakespeare, *Richard III*

Situation and Advice: Something is likely to go wrong with a new venture you have recently begun. Desired or promised results are unlikely to materialize. A loss is possible. You may receive less money than expected, or payment may be delayed. Circumstances surrounding health, job, money, or business matters seem to work against you. Excessive greed or materialism may cause problems. Perhaps you jumped too quickly to a decision without doing sufficient homework. A contemplated investment may not pay off. Sometimes the reversed Ace of Pentacles indicates fatigue, health problems, or pooping out. It can also reflect a cynical, puritanical attitude which interferes with sensual pleasure.

People: Those who fail to carry through on promised actions. Hasty, greedy people. Misers. Cynics. Puritanical persons. Emotionally insecure people.

Ace of Swords
The Power of Intellect

Upright: A sense of power. Strength in adversity.

Key Words and Phrases: Great force at your disposal. Force of the element air. The power of intellect. Freedom. Determination. Mental energy. Courage. Fresh ideas. The power of words. Something good emerging from evil circumstances. Beginnings of success. Right timing. Inevitable and radical change. Concentrated energy. Surmounting obstacles. A focused mind. Logic. Order. Discipline. Strength of purpose. Balanced action. Rationality. The power to think things through. Hitting the mark. Justice. The law. Legal matters. Authority. Willpower. Needed surgery. Medical incisions. Blood tests. Injections. Every cloud has a silver lining. The pen is mightier than the sword. Think before you act. Mind over matter.

Situation and advice: The Ace of Swords may appear at the start of an intellectual enterprise. Because Swords relate to strife, conflict and difficulty, this card suggests the beginning of a promising venture that develops out of adversity. The traditional meaning of this card is "strength in adversity"—out of evil something good emerges. You have the discipline and determination to overcome obstacles and difficulties. From the inevitable and sometimes painful variations of life, something positive will emerge. Great strength and force is at your disposal. You are able to focus your mind and concentrate your energies toward pursuing a goal. Your capacity for logic, balance and order are needed. Sometimes this card indicates recourse to the law for the resolution of conflict. In a medical reading, the Ace of Swords can refer to the need for injections, cutting, or surgery.

People: Champions. Logical authoritative persons. Dominating persons. Those who work in the legal system. Those who struggle for a cause. Surgeons and medical specialists. Those who cut for a living. Sharp-tongued individuals.

◑

Ace of Swords Reversed: Throwing your weight around.

Key Words and Phrases: Threats. Excessive force. Heavyhandedness. A hollow victory. Cutting words. Sarcasm. Bullying. Opposition. Victimization. Delay. Bad timing.

Obstacles. Illusions. Unclear thinking. Needless severance. Lack of planning. Abuse of power. Misdirected energy. Unnecessary cutting. Destructiveness. Wantonness. Chaos. Exploitation. Domination. Injustice. Unfairness. Problems with authority. Legal difficulties. Misuse of intellect. Disregarding the feelings of others. Getting cut. Self-mutilation. A sting operation. Problems with a medical injection or surgery. Haste makes waste. He who lives by the sword, dies by the sword. Might makes right. Pierced to the quick. Up yours!

Situation and Advice: You may be involved in an exploitative situation. Perhaps you are applying more force than is needed to achieve your objectives. Be careful not to come on too strongly, and don't burn your bridges behind you. There is a tendency to cut things out of your life unnecessarily when the reversed Ace of Swords appears. Remember, you can catch more flies with honey than with vinegar. You may need to extricate yourself from a relationship in which you are being treated cruelly or unjustly. You may be the one to sting or get stung at this time. In health readings, this card can indicate being cut by a sharp object as well as problems with injections or surgery.

People: Bullies. Self-mutilators. Exploiters. Victims. Jack the Ripper.

Ace of Cups
The Stirrings of the Heart

Upright: New love.

Key Words and Phrases: Emotional renewal. An upsurge of new feelings. Force of the element water. The power of imagination. Emotional and spiritual nourishment. Love. Happiness. Friendship. Kindness. Peace. Sensitivity. Contemplation. The start of a creative enterprise. Art. Poetry.

Joy. Ecstasy. Abundance. The first stirrings of love. Tender feelings. Falling in love. A new relationship or revival of an old one. Compassion. Social life. Partnership. A positive work relationship. Health. Romance. Marriage. A loving union. Fertility. Pregnancy. Childbirth. Motherhood. Engagement. A gift. Spiritual love. Psychic ability.

Situation and Advice: The Ace of Cups indicates a new beginning in your emotional life. You may be entering into a new relationship that can lead to marriage, lasting friendship, or a close emotional tie. If you asked about pregnancy, motherhood could be in the offing. If you are already engaged in a close relationship, this is a time for emotional renewal. You may receive a gift from a close friend of loved one. You are about to be blessed with love and happiness.

People: Lovers. Artists. Psychics. Compassionate persons.

◑

Ace of Cups Reversed: Nobody loves me.

Key Words and Phrases: Unrequited love. Loss of love. A broken heart. Rejection. Extinction of love. The end of an affair. Problems in a relationship. Conditional love. Avoidance of emotional attachment. Loneliness. Grief. Loss. Separation. Tears. Depression. Sadness. Sorrow. Distress. Woe. Egotism. Self-centeredness. Manipulation. Sex without love. Infertility. Not ready for love. Delay in starting a relationship. Marital problems. Unhappiness. Toying with someone's emotions. Lack of emotional fulfillment. Feeling jerked around emotionally.

Situation and Advice: The Ace of Cups reversed indicates unhappiness in your emotional life. Perhaps you are recovering from some loss, separation, or disappointment in a relationship. You may now realize that a friendship will not turn into a love relationship. Someone may be toying with your feelings, or you may be emotionally jerking someone else around. Your special someone may be more interested in sex than long-term commitment. A sense of feeling unloved, manipulated, or emotionally deprived often accompanies this card.

People: Those who have been scorned or rejected. Unhappy, grieving individuals.

~

TWOS

Key Words and Phrases: Formation. Duality. Balance. The relationship between two objects, ideas, or persons. A fork in the road. Competing or combined forces. The need to reconcile opposites. Conflict. See-saw. Creativity not yet fulfilled. Nurturing. Partnership. Reflection. Deciding between two alternatives. A dilemma. The need to make a choice. Which way do I turn?

> God created man in His image. In the image of God He created him. Male and female He created him.
>
> —Genesis

Corresponding Major Arcana Card: The High Priestess.

Situation and Advice: The number two is associated with the Moon and the sign Cancer. People born under Cancer are often shy, reticent, gentle, imaginative, impressionable, sensitive, emotional, and receptive. They are often involved in the helping and healing professions and in charities or community service work. Cancer natives are fond of music, poetry, history, feeding, painting, dance, and drama. They need to guard against being gullible, emotionally imbalanced, and overly sensitive.

A prominence of twos in a spread suggests the need to make a choice. Often this decision requires cooperation, teamwork, patience, balance, tact, nurturing, and diplomacy. The foundations laid by the aces of the suits need to be nursed along because they are just now beginning to take hold. A gentle rather than aggressive approach is more likely to succeed. Many short trips are likely.

The number two represents a yin energy which promotes cooperation, partnership, friendship, and receptivity. Yin energy often refers to females who may figure prominently in the matter inquired about. This is a time of waiting for the seed planted during the number one period to germinate. Think twice about making any major life changes when twos predominate.

Personal Year: A two personal year heralds a time of patience, waiting, slow development, cultivation, steady movement, balance, and harmony. Cooperation with others is a keynote. Partnerships and associations are favored. Love, romance, and parenthood often mark the two personal year. Metaphysical interests, religious activities, creative hobbies, and writing all prosper. The two year is a time to cultivate projects initiated in the previous one personal year. This is usually not a year to make major life changes.

Two of Wands
Opportunity

Upright: Off to a good start. A period of waiting.

Key Words and Phrases: The early stages of an enterprise. The need to wait to see how matters will develop. Not much actively happening. A cooperative venture. Collaboration. Completion of the first stage of a project. Sincere effort. Faith in the future. Transition. Achievement. Ambition. Pride.

Ownership. Partnership matters. A joint creative endeavor. Gratuity. Energetic involvement. Growth. Initiative. Preparation for success. Unfulfilled potential. The possibility of prosperity through hard work. A new outlook. A new business partnership. Successful negotiation. Foresight. Headed in the right direction. Waiting for a reply. Relocating. A move. Travel. Where do I go from here?

Situation and Advice: The Two of Wands often signifies a waiting period during which you may feel restless as you prepare for a change. You are at the early stages of a new enterprise and you may feel uneasy about any further progress. Most likely there is little actively happening now. Chances are that you are at the stage of considering a project, a trip, or an activity with a partner. You may be anticipating a response to a business proposal or to a job or a school application.

Now is a time for dealing with problems energetically. Any negotiations you are involved in should go well, but you must actively assert yourself. This is a time to take charge of your life. You have the ability to overcome obstacles. Take command of your creative energies and make solid plans to pursue your goals.

Success results from your hard work. You will achieve your goals if you proceed according to plan. Moving to a new home or business location is possible. You may also receive some job-related gratuities. You may need to attend to important correspondence or contract matters. This is one of the cards that indicates the possibility of travel.

People: An enterprising person. A business partner. A proud person. Someone involved in negotiations. Someone waiting for an answer. A traveler.

Two of Wands Reversed: Anticlimax.

Key Words and Phrases: Misgivings about a venture. Delays. Pooping out. Losing interest. Lack of activity. Going the wrong way. Feeling overwhelmed or disillusioned. Unable to marshal your energies. Potentials not realized. Partnership difficulties. Differences of opinion. The dissolution of a business partnership. Disagreements. Failed negotiations. Misplaced values. Self-doubt. Excessive pride. Inattention to detail. Abuse of wealth or power. Problems with property matters. Bad news. A trip postponed or canceled. Nothing happening.

Situation and Advice: Matters may not work out the way you have planned. You may be doubting your own commitment or enthusiasm for a project recently begun. You may receive bad news, perhaps about the unfortunate outcome of negotiations. Chances are you will feel disillusioned because matters do not work out the way you had hoped.

Excessive pride, your own or someone else's, may be causing difficulties. If you own or manage property, expect problems to arise. Your dissatisfaction and sense of futility may lead to arguments with associates or even to the dissolution of a partnership. If you are contemplating a joint venture with other people, the Two of Wands reversed warns you to consider the matter carefully.

People: A wimp. An incompetent partner. One who doubts his or her own abilities. A proud person who causes trouble.

Two of Pentacles
The Ups and Downs of Fortune

Upright: Juggling finances. The need for flexibility.

Key Words and Phrases: Balancing multiple obligations. Walking a tightrope. Pulled in many directions. Coping with the variations of daily life. Monetary fluctuations. Working two or more jobs. Splitting up resources. A balancing act. Working hard to make ends meet. Creative financing. Resources spread thin. Skillful manipulation. Juggling many projects at once. Multiple responsibilities. Need to make a decision. Good news. A gift. A change of job or environment. A new relationship. Sailing off. Movement or travel that alters your life. A journey. Everything changes. Easy come, easy go. Taking from Peter to pay Paul. Go with the flow. Time is money.

Situation and Advice: You are trying to juggle several tasks at the same time. Perhaps you no longer enjoy your work as much as you used to because it has become a duty or obligation. Are you working to please others and neglecting yourself? You need to schedule your time wisely. Your finances are in a state of fluctuation and you must do a monetary balancing act. As a result, a new enterprise may have a hard time getting off the ground. You may be feeling spread thin and need to borrow from Peter to pay Paul. Money you thought was there is not, but other money becomes available. You may need to divide joint resources with a partner.

You may have to work hard for little reward and may be preoccupied with monetary matters. You need to make a decision that will ease the tension in your life. Perhaps a change of job or environment will improve your situation. Now is a time to be adaptable and "go with the flow." A trip may be in the offing. Your skill at handling multiple obligations will lead to success. Good news or a gift may be on the way.

People: Those who must juggle many obligations. A Jack of all trades.

◑

Two of Pentacles Reversed: Feeling overwhelmed by complexity.

Key Words and Phrases: The juggler can't hold on to his money. Unable to maintain balance. Bucking the tide. Instability. Disequilibrium. Disorganization. Wastefulness.

Inflexibility. Moodiness. Restlessness. Indecision. Aimlessness. Debt. Unwise spending. Mishandled finances. Inadequate effort. Complications. Poor concentration. Lack of focus. Bad news. Opposition. Discouragement. Spread too thin. A trip is canceled or postponed. Unable to hold it all together. Up in the air. Coming apart at the seams. A partner keeps too many joint resources. Buying too much on credit. Red tape. Biting off more than you can chew. My eyes are bigger than my stomach. I owe my soul to the company store. I just can't take it anymore.

Situation and Advice: You may be feeling overwhelmed by your many obligations. Life is full of complications and endless details just now. You may be up to your eyeballs in red tape. It is difficult to muster the tenacity of purpose to accomplish your goals and deal with opposition. Perhaps you've bitten off more than you can chew and are feeling spread too thin. You need to narrow your focus and concentrate on a single task at a time. A partner may have appropriated too many of your joint resources so that money is not available when you need it. On the other hand, you may have mishandled your own finances through unwise spending or the excessive use of credit. Now you're having trouble paying the piper.

As difficult as it may seem, you must be flexible and force yourself to go with the flow. Review your goals and be sure you have the requisite skills and dedication before proceeding any further.

People: A scatterbrain. An impulsive, immature person. One who is spread too thin. Rigid, inflexible persons. Those who have charged their credit cards to the limit.

Two of Swords
Stalemate

Upright: A tense situation. An impasse.

Key Words and Phrases: A tight rein over the emotions. Feeling deadlocked. Feeling uncertain about which way to go. Suspended action. Indecision. Stalemate. Paradox. Inaction. Staying put. Strain. Opposition. Delay. Waiting. Aloofness. Antagonism. Quarrels. A truce in a struggle. A difficult decision. Feeling overwhelmed by too many factors. A precarious balance. Suppressing your feelings. Going nowhere fast.

Unable to make a move. Perfectly balanced. Keeping the lid on emotions. An agreement. A settlement.

Situation and Advice: You are on the horns of a dilemma and cannot see clearly which path to choose. You don't know whether to follow your head or your heart. You feel immobilized by indecision, as if you have reached a stalemate or an impasse. You feel a need to keep a tight rein on your emotions. You may be using all your intellectual defenses to avoid facing your feelings about an issue. You are taking a passive stance of waiting for something new to happen before making a decision. You may be burying your head in the sand rather than taking action. However, you can't hold out forever. You must confront issues directly because problems won't go away if you pretend they don't exist. You must face what you really want or feel. Sometimes this card can mean reaching a settlement or agreement.

People: Someone who can't decide or who is suppressing important emotions. Feuding parties.

◑

Two of Swords Reversed: Renewed action.

Key Words and Phrases: The stalemate is over. The decision is made. Movement. Change. Able to make decisions. Release. The early consequences of a choice. Resumption of movement. Taking the lid off. Facing your feelings. Emotions break through to the surface. The ripple effect.

Situation and Advice: You have recently made a decision, or perhaps circumstances made the decision for you. Now you must wait to see how matters will unfold. The tension has been broken. Strong emotions have come to the surface and can now be dealt with head-on. The stalemate is over and changes are on the way. Your life can now go forward.

People: Someone who has recently made a decision of uncertain outcome.

Two of Cups
Mutuality

Upright: A happy union.

Key Words and Phrases: Sharing. Warmth. Attraction. The early stages of a harmonious relationship. Romance. A love affair. A happy atmosphere. Mutual exchange. Rapport. Friendship. A balanced partnership. A business deal. Balanced give and take. Cooperation. Reciprocity. Kindness.

Affection. An end to hostilities. Understanding. Emotional equilibrium. Harmony. Union. Mutual respect. Finding common ground. Reconciliation. Commitment to a relationship. Platonic love. Entering into a contract or agreement. Getting engaged. Marriage. I love you.

Situation and Advice: The Two of Cups suggests the continuance of a harmonious relationship. If you've been involved in a dispute, you are able to find common ground and reach a compromise between opposing viewpoints. Now is the time to cooperate and reason with others. A resolution of problems and a reconciliation is possible. You may find yourself deciding to enter into a contract or a binding agreement. If you asked about a relationship, the Two of Cups promises harmony, understanding, friendship, and the possibility of romance. An engagement or marriage are possible outcomes. A spirit of cooperation pervades the work environment. A thoughtful gift may be on the way.

People: Couples. Partners. Friends. Lovers. Colleagues.

◐

Two of Cups Reversed: The end of a relationship.

Key Words and Phrases: Rejection. Parting. Disillusionment. Breakup of a partnership. The dissolution of a contract or a binding agreement. A troubled relationship. Incompatibility. Lack of compassion. Unrequited love. The departure of a loved one. Distrust. Infidelity. Arguments. Misunderstanding. Disagreement. Conflict. Inconsiderate behavior. The violation of a trust. Imbalanced give and take. A broken agreement. Disharmony. Resentment. Hatred. Contention. Disputes. Inequity. Separation. Divorce. Breaking up is hard to do. Parting is such sweet sorrow. I hate you.

Situation and Advice: You may be concerned about a separation from someone you care about. Perhaps you are involved in a situation of broken trust, rejection, inconsiderate behavior, hurt feelings, or a partnership that has not lived up to expectations. An atmosphere of disharmony surrounds you. Someone may be resenting another's selfishness and an argument may ensue. One partner may be doing all the giving and the other partner all the taking.

People: An ex-partner. One who violates another's trust. Someone who takes without giving.

~

Threes

Key Words and Phrases: Creation. Growth. Development. Increase. Flowering. Expansion. Regeneration. Fertilization. Exploration. Moving out into the world. Initial completion. Enthusiasm. Preparation. Perspective. A first stage of growth is achieved. Intermingling of opposites to produce a third independent entity that can reconcile the differences. Sperm unites with egg. Three is a number intimately linked with the human genitalia.

> Then God blessed them and said to them, 'Be fruitful and multiply; fill the earth and subdue it.'
>
> —Genesis

Corresponding Major Arcana Card: The Empress.

Situation and Advice: The number three is associated with the Major Arcana card the Empress, and with the planet Jupiter and the signs Sagittarius and Pisces. Jupiter is a planet of luck, fun, friendliness, broadening horizons, communication, salesmanship, publication, self-expression, creativity, optimism, growth, expansiveness, pride, ambition, broad perspective, travel, higher education, and independence.

Negative aspects of Jupiter include wastefulness, sloth, vanity, superficiality, over-inflation, and exaggeration.

A prominence of threes in a spread suggests a period of personal growth, creativity, expansion, self-promotion, self-expression, popularity, and self-improvement. Creative projects will be successful. A job promotion is likely. Threes are associated with career success, personal recognition, advancement, and promotion. Long-distance travel is possible. Romance is in the air. On the negative side, there is a possibility of overwork, extravagance, wastefulness, scattered energies, nervous tension, and emotional upset now.

As an odd number, three participates in the yang vibration. Threes in a spread often suggest the need to get out, have fun, and socialize more. This is a good time to promote yourself through writing, lecturing, or broadcasting.

Personal Year: A three personal year is a time for fun and enjoyment. Creative self-expression, procreation, self-promotion, salesmanship, writing, lecturing, teaching, socializing, taking courses, communicating, love affairs, and creative endeavors are all favored. The danger of a three year is one of overextension, over-commitment, wastefulness, scattered energies, and extravagance.

Three of Wands
Birth of an Enterprise

Upright: The successful birth of an enterprise. Cooperation.

Key Words and Phrases: Brisk business. A new project. Initial success. Favorable early returns. Help in putting plans into action. Sharing creative energies. Exchanging ideas. Opportunities. Setting goals for the future. Satisfaction, yet more to be done. New ideas on the way. News about work.

Teamwork. Negotiations. A new project. Sending or shipping goods. Showing your wares. A new job. Helpful advice. Family support and assistance. Seeds begin to sprout. Partnerships begin to prosper. Work-related travel. It's looking good. The ships are coming in.

Situation and Advice: Business matters are active and thriving. You have completed the first stage of a project, but there is more to do. You can count on teamwork and cooperation. You feel a sense of both accomplishment and challenge as you prepare to enter the next phase of your enterprise. Opportunities abound, and a new job is possible. Business-related news arrives. You may travel or correspond in connection with your work. This is a good time to publicize your creative accomplishments. You may find yourself shipping your goods and products to a distant location. Someone may offer helpful information or assistance. Take the opportunity to cooperate with others if you wish to lay the groundwork for future development.

People: Merchants. Those involved in commerce. Producers of goods. Co-creators. Authors. Corporations.

◑

Three of Wands Reversed: Attainment slips away. Lack of cooperation.

Key Words and Phrases: Overconfidence. Unrealistic plans. The stunted growth of an enterprise. Pipe dreams. Arrogance. Too proud to accept help. Wasted effort. Delays. Setbacks in a creative project. Blocked creativity. Timidity. Disappointment. Goals are hard to reach. A promising venture fails to deliver. The ships are not coming in. Opposition. Carelessness. Misinformation. Stubbornness. Unhelpful alliances. Dissolution of achievements. Come down from your pedestal.

Situation and Advice: For some reason you are unable to put your money where your mouth is. Perhaps an offer of help has not materialized or is not in your best interest. A recently launched venture may not be developing the way you had hoped. Perhaps your plans are unrealistic, or you may lack the energy and resources to transform your ideas into reality. Did you set your goals too high? Are you afraid to pursue them? Is there a lack of cooperation? Are all the members of your team playing for the same goal? Has someone you admired let you down?

People: Timid, unrealistic people.

Three of Pentacles
A Job Well Done

Upright: Beneficial use of talents.

Key Words and Phrases: Early stages of accomplishment. First rewards. Employment. Work involving status. A chance to earn money. Superior ability. Professional growth. Increased status. Competence. Sincere effort. High standards. Expertise. Craftsmanship. Doing a job the right way. Success through skill. Job satisfaction. Diligence. Attention to detail. Improvement in work conditions. Advancement. Recognition. Approval. Upgrading social status. Honor. Good grades in school. Certification. Progress. New learning. Fraternal efforts. Confidence. Payment or acclaim for a job well done. Desire for social status or approval from others. Earning a degree. Work done for others. Assistance from others. Making improvements to home or property. Possible change of residence. Off to a good start.

Situation and Advice: The Three of Pentacles is a card of developments occurring on the physical plane. The situation could involve your money, job, education, physical health, a house, or a project that will produce tangible results. You will be rewarded for doing a competent job and making use of your skills, knowledge, and talents. You are off to a good start and could become recognized as an expert in your field. You will have an opportunity to earn money professionally for what you know. You desire status, recognition, or approval from others, and you feel a sense of accomplishment for a job well done. A promotion is possible. You may apply your talents to improving your home or property, which may involve painting or redecorating. If a student, you will receive good grades or complete your degree. In questions about romance and relationships, this card suggests too little emotional involvement and too much emphasis on materialism, status, social considerations, and family pressures.

People: Hard workers. Talented individuals. Craftsmen. Careful, diligent, competent workers. Perfectionists.

◐

Three of Pentacles Reversed: Problems with or at work.

Key Words and Phrases: Lackluster performance. Lack of direction. Job dissatisfaction. Goofing off. Lack of ambition.

Delays. Disappointment. Paltry effort. Boredom. Half-hearted effort. Inexperience. Lack of knowledge. Inadequate skills. Inferior ability. Ignorance. Missed opportunities. Inadequate equipment. A thankless task. Insufficient materials. Criticism for a poor performance. Poor grades in school. An unhappy job situation. Being overqualified for a job. Lack of respect. Excessive concern with recognition, approval, or social status.

Situation and Advice: The Three of Pentacles reversed suggests that you need to learn more, work harder, and acquire new skills to complete an important project. Be careful not to miss valuable opportunities because you are afraid to take a risk. Others may take you to task for not knowing what you are doing and producing inferior results. Although you are working hard, you may feel undervalued or else dissatisfied and bored with your work. Perhaps you are focusing more on gaining approval and recognition than on doing a job well. An excessive concern with upgrading your social status may be blocking genuine relationships with others.

People: Goof-offs. Unskilled workers. A pretentious novice. A poor worker. Social climbers.

Three of Swords
Heartache

Upright: Necessary cutting. A bleeding heart.

Key Words and Phrases: Stormy weather for the emotions. Loss. Woe. Emotional pain. Love lost. A bleeding heart. Difficulties in a relationship. Turbulent emotions. A narcissistic injury. Irritability. Quarrels. Conflict. Misunderstanding. Alienation. Disharmony. Upheaval. Neurotic behavior.

Sorrow. Hurt. Misfortune. A surgical operation. Severance. Upsetting changes. Feeling under the weather. Stress. Tension. Illness. Weeping. Grieving. Mourning. Darkness before the dawn. Depth of feeling. A rift. Separation. Divorce. Rejection. Abandonment. Loss of a lover. Tears. Miscarriage. Heart trouble. Abortion. Funerals. Obituaries. Death. Painful news. Pierced to the quick.

Situation and Advice: The Three of Swords suggests you have something to mourn or cry about. You are experiencing stress or sadness because of an emotional hurt that may involve separation from a loved one. It is important to put your sorrow in perspective. You may need to let go of a relationship or situation that only brings you anguish. This card may herald a period of illness or feeling under the weather. It is a card of severance and necessary cutting, and sometimes indicates a need for major surgery or dental treatment. Take care not to alienate loved ones simply because you are feeling tense and irritable.

On occasion, the Three of Swords will indicate a loss through death. Usually, death is shown in a spread by the appearance of many cards signifying death; for example, the Tower, Death, many sword cards, many reversed cards, et cetera. Often, however, when the Three of Swords appears, you will learn of the death of someone you knew.

People: The forlorn. Grief-stricken persons. Irritable, stressed-out people. Those with heart disease.

◐

Three of Swords Reversed: The pain is ending.

Key Words and Phrases: Recovery. The worst is over. The separation has occurred, but the hurt lingers on. Less harsh severance. Dwelling on past hurts. Lingering regret and depression. Minor surgery.

Situation and Advice: The heartache is ending. You have been involved in a painful situation that is in its final stages. The suffering has been unbearable and will linger for a while longer. There is nothing you can do to resurrect the lost relationship. Now that the worst is over, recovery can take place. If a separation does occur, it will not be as painful as when the Three of Swords falls upright. In health readings, minor surgery or dental treatment may be indicated.

People: A rejected lover.

Three of Cups
Celebration

Upright: A time to rejoice. Having fun.

Key Words and Phrases: Joy. A joyful occasion. Satisfaction. Reunion. Uniting with others. Family gatherings. Happy hours. Hobbies. Things done for enjoyment. The satisfaction of initial completion. Festivities. A party. Abundance in family life. Good fortune. Happiness. Plenty for all. Playfulness. Hospitality. Freedom from want. Celebration of bounty. Reaping your harvest. Sharing good times.

Conception. Gestation. Pregnancy (especially if the Empress, suggesting fertility, appears upright in the spread). Birth. Achievement. Healing. Renewed health. The early stages of happiness. Beginning of a new lifestyle. Marriage. Marital status. A wedding. Divorce. Something's coming. Something good. If I knew you were coming, I'd have baked a cake. Eat, drink, and be merry.

Situation and Advice: There is something to celebrate; now is the time to have fun. Get ready for a party, wedding, graduation, promotion, birth, or some other joyful occasion. You will be sharing happiness with others. This is a time for celebration, but there is still work ahead. If you asked about marriage or pregnancy, expect a favorable outcome. The Three of Cups often means that marriage (or divorce that will make a new marriage possible) is on your mind. In a health reading, the Three of Cups promises renewed health and recovery after illness. In career questions, the Three of Cups suggests a hobby rather than a profession.

People: Party-goers. Hobbyists. Those who entertain. Bartenders.

◑

Three of Cups Reversed: Too much of a good thing. Self-indulgence.

Key Words and Phrases: Overindulgence. Dissipation. Infidelity. Romance gone awry. Harmful excess. Addiction. Alcoholism. No occasion to join with others. Hedonism. Obesity. Promiscuity. Sex without love. Self-pity. Selfishness. Marital problems. Difficulties with a pregnancy. Infertility. Inability to have children. Exploitation. Taking advantage of others. Wallowing in emotions. No reason to celebrate. An invitation is withdrawn. A cancellation. You don't go to the party. The festivities are called off. Divorce. A sad social occasion. An unhappy ending. Illness. Poor health. Failure to use one's natural abilities. Abuse. It's my party and I'll cry if I want to. What's there to smile about?

Situation and Advice: The wedding is called off. A situation that might have caused joy now brings pain. Perhaps you will not be able to attend a celebration or reunion as planned. The Three of Cups reversed warns that you may be allowing excessive sensual pleasures to harm your well-being or health. We all have personal addictions that can lead to self-undoing. It is possible to have too much of a good thing, and there is a price to pay for overindulgence. You may also be having troubles in a romantic relationship. Perhaps you or your lover have lost interest or become unfaithful.

People: Selfish, spoiled, and overindulgent people. Addicts. Spoilsports. Unfaithful lovers. Those who are promiscuous.

~

Fours

Key Words and Phrases: Structure. Stability. Foundation. Order. Predictability. Solidity. Fixity. Tenacity. Entrenchment. Work. Reality. Organization. Manifestation. Practical attainment. Tangible results. Crystallization. Coagulation. Stagnation. Logic. Reason. Power and control. The material world. The physical universe.

> God made the two great lights, the greater light to rule the day and the smaller one to rule the night, and He made the stars. God set them in the firmament of the heavens to shed light upon the earth, to rule the day and the night and to separate the light from the darkness. God saw that it was good. And there was evening and morning, the fourth day.
>
> —Genesis

Corresponding Major Arcana Card: The Emperor.

Situation and Advice: The number four is associated with the Emperor card of the Major Arcana and with the planet Saturn and the sign Aquarius. Saturn is the planet of order, work, power, being in control, discipline, organization, structure, crystallization, solidity, foundations, practicality, patience, exactness, mathematical precision, economy, property, real estate, endurance, and lasting value. Negative traits of Saturn and Aquarius include being dogmatic, rigid, stubborn, repressed, melancholy and overly serious. Aquarians are progressive, humanitarian, independent, Bohemian, unusual, and somewhat eccentric.

A prominence of fours in a spread suggests a time to lay foundations for future success. Now is a period to work hard at organizing your business affairs and structuring your life. Saturn may make you feel restricted and burdened at times. You may be faced now with important decisions that require careful deliberation. There is the possibility of an illness or a need for rest and recuperation. The influence of Aquarius may bring unusual or eccentric people into your life.

Saturn is one of the astrological factors associated with karma. When fours predominate, you may need to pay a karmic debt. You do well to pay attention to details, exercise self-discipline, and approach life in an organized, systematic fashion. Major life changes should be undertaken only after careful deliberation.

Personal Year: A four personal year is a time to be pragmatic, orderly, systematic, and conservative. Four years are often marked by hard work to assure security and lay firm foundations. There may be a general feeling of restriction and limitation throughout the year. Property matters, real estate, savings, budgeting, legal affairs, merchandising, self-discipline, and attention to details are all favored. The four personal year is usually not a time to make major career changes.

Four of Wands
Haven of Refuge

Upright: A well-deserved rest.

Key Words and Phrases: A special gathering to mark reaching a stage of development. Peace. A hiatus. The joy of achievement. A commemorative event. Contentment. Blessings. Harmony. A happy and secure home. Putting down roots. A sound business partnership. Buying a house.

Success. Laying the foundation for a marriage or a committed relationship. Moving to a new house. Fruition. A good harvest. Improvement. Prosperity. Enjoyment. Celebration. Productivity. Comfort. A creative pursuit. Satisfaction. Happiness. Holidays. Relaxation. Possible romance. Marriage. A honeymoon. Reward after labor. Semester break. Coming of age. A Bar Mitzvah or similar ceremony. A happy ending.

Situation and Advice: The Four of Wands is a positive, happy card depicting a time for rest and reward after a laborious task. An enterprise has reached a successful stage of development and it is time to celebrate this achievement. The roots you have laid are secure. You may be thinking about buying a house and putting down roots. A creative task is going well. You can enjoy the initial fruits of your labors before beginning a new round of work when the holiday is over. The Four of Wands may signify a special ceremony or celebration that marks a rite of passage, i.e., the achievement of one stage of development and embarking on a new one. In relationship questions, this card symbolizes the foundation of a committed and positive relationship and is one of the cards that traditionally signifies marriage.

People: Vacationers. Happy or contented people. Home buyers. Those involved with serving at social events like a bar mitzvah, graduation, et cetera.

◑

Four of Wands Reversed: Delayed but impending success.

Key Words and Phrases: (+) Similar in meaning to the upright card but to a lesser degree. Success but at a greater price than anticipated. Rest. A pause to relax. Improvement. Happiness after difficulties are overcome. Appreciation. Reward. Delayed but impending completion of a phase of a project. A non-marital commitment.

(–) Inhibition. Criticism. Insecurity. Poor service. Disappointment. Intolerance. Narrow-mindedness. Excessive conservatism. Holding back. Restriction. Disapproval. Problems with property. Dissolution of a partnership. The need to protect against loss of success.

Situation and Advice: Even in its reversed position, the Four of Wands is a generally positive card but there is a greater price to pay for success. A time of rest and reward for hard work is at hand. The Four of Wands reversed, however, may represent some form of obstacle or restraint that you need to overcome, or possibly some problems with property you own. If you are planning a social event, the service may be poor or the arrangements may not work out as well as you had hoped. You will need to expend more effort to achieve your desired goal.

People: Inhibited people. Those who provide poor service.

Four of Pentacles
Holding Tight

Upright: Maintaining the status quo.

Key Words and Phrases: Enrichment. Possession. Hard work pays off. Sound money management. Financial security. A solid financial foundation. A balanced budget. Ownership. Gain of money. Material acquisition. The power to acquire possessions. Sound business judgment. Holding on to possessions.

Seeking a guarantee. Buying a home. Conservative investments. Solid learning. Deeply ingrained beliefs. Passing an exam. Overcaution. A gift. An inheritance. Nothing ventured, nothing gained. You can't be too careful. Put it in writing.

Situation and Advice: The Four of Disks represents financial security. You may have a chance to enrich yourself and increase your assets. Sometimes this card warns of being too conservative or miserly because you fear taking a risk. Are you rigidly holding to deeply ingrained beliefs so that you are blindly maintaining the status quo? You may be afraid to let go of what you have carefully acquired. You must also learn to delegate rather than try to do everything yourself. Usually, however, the Four of Pentacles reveals a good business sense and a willingness to work hard for material gain. If your question was about finances, the Four of Pentacles assures security and material acquisition. If you asked about relationships, the Four of Pentacles warns that material interests are blocking your emotional growth.

People: Bankers. Wealthy people. Conservatives. Banks. Financial institutions.

◑

Four of Pentacles Reversed: Miserliness.

Key Words and Phrases: Greed. Unwarranted fear of poverty. Problems with the budget. Lack of financial security. Carelessness. Dissipation. Poor fiscal management. Loss of money. Trouble letting go. Failure to delegate responsibility. Inadequate payment for services rendered. Skimpy rewards. Delays. Obstacles. Envy. Fear of failure. Timidity. Suspicion. Defensiveness. Selfishness. Opposition. Lack of initiative. Unnecessary spending. Money problems. An unbalanced budget. Wastefulness. Lack of fulfillment. Failing an exam. I can't get no satisfaction.

So our Lord God commonly gives riches to those gross asses to whom He vouchsafes nothing else.

—Martin Luther

Situation and Advice: You may be having difficulty spending wisely, saving money, or balancing your budget. Concerns about security, financial or otherwise, preoccupy your mind. You may be holding tight when you should be letting go. An excessively defensive or timid attitude may be hampering your progress. Delays are possible.

People: Misers. Tightwads. Wastrels. Poor money managers. Powerless individuals. Mean-spirited, envious individuals. Scrooge. Ultra-conservatives. Those who worry too much about money.

Four of Swords
Respite

Upright: Recharging your batteries.

Key Words and Phrases: The need for rest and relaxation. A truce. The need for renewal. A slow period. Recuperation. Recovery. Repose. Time out. Retreat. Relief from stress. A welcome break. Convalescence. Inactivity. Regrouping. Withdrawal. A needed holiday. Repose. Solitude. Prayer.

Meditation. Introspection. Contemplation. Reevaluation. Calm before the storm. Recovery from an illness. A hospital stay. Involvement with hospitals. A doctor visit. A vacation. Travel. Peaceful surroundings. Getting away from it all. Give me a break. Let us pray.

Situation and Advice: Feeling stressed out? A temporary truce is in order. Now is the time to take a break and rest after a period of struggle or conflict. You need a period of renewal to calm your mind and rejuvenate your body. Now is a time to relax and regroup your forces. Some may seek solace in prayer and meditation. Obtaining distance from your daily routine will help put matters in perspective. Meditation will bring needed clarity to a situation. Perhaps you've been feeling harried and should take a day off from your daily routine. How about a vacation or a trip to get away from it all? If you have been ill, this is a time for convalescence. You may become involved with a hospital, either as a patient or a visitor.

People: Someone in need of a rest. A person recuperating from illness. A hospital worker. A visitor to a hospital. A medical patient.

◐

Four of Swords Reversed: Back into the action.

Key Words and Phrases: (+) No time to relax. Renewed action. The rest is over. A summons to action. Back to work. Healing. Recovery of previous functioning. Up and at 'em. Once more unto the breach!

(−) Illness. Isolation. Discontent. Withdrawal. Resentment. Rejection. Banishment. Loneliness. Indiscretion. Problems at work. Layoffs. Unrest. Opposition. Strikes. Boycotts. Riots. Confinement. Detention. Exile. Ostracism. Unpleasant surroundings.

Situation and Advice: In its positive aspect, this card means that the period of rest is over and it's time to get back into the action. You have taken a needed break and must now resume your activities. You feel refreshed and able to cope with life's stresses.

In its negative aspect, this card may herald problems in general, ill health, or a period of enforced isolation.

People: An unwelcome guest. An exile. A prisoner. An outcast. A striking worker.

Four of Cups
Discontent

Upright: In a shell. Dissatisfied.

Key Words and Phrases: Boredom. Weariness. Withdrawal. Social isolation. Declining social invitations. Reassessment. Reevaluation. Turning inward. Apathy. Walled off. Lost in thought. Silence. Distraction. Distance. Anticlimax. Something is missing. An empty feeling inside. Feeling in a rut. Resentment. Depression. Feeling jaded. Ennui. Introversion.

Looking within. Lack of motivation. Feeling fed up. Nobody understands me. The honeymoon is over. I never promised you a rose garden. The grass is greener on the other side. The winter of our discontent.

Situation and Advice: You may have withdrawn into yourself because of discontent with some aspect of your life. You have a sense of boredom or anticlimax. The honeymoon is over. Everything seems stale and unsatisfying. This is a time of needed reassessment. The danger of this position is that you do not see the good that surrounds you. In your withdrawn state you may reject help that is being offered. You may be feeling depressed, demoralized, and confused about your situation. The novelty has worn off and you are contemplating new sources of stimulation. You feel a sense of emptiness, as if something is missing from your life and you don't know what it is. Are you cutting yourself off from other people unnecessarily? The advice of the Four of Cups is not to rush but rather to take time to meditate and contemplate before proceeding.

People: Someone who is dissatisfied or must re-evaluate matters. Hermits. Recluses.

Four of Cups Reversed: The end of discontent.

Key Words and Phrases: (+) Renewed relationships with others. Something to look forward to. Accepting a social invitation. Motivation. Initiative. Socializing. Verve. Readiness for challenge and new opportunities. Revitalization. Feeling energized. Turning outward. Coming out of your shell. Letting down the wall. Satisfaction. No longer in a rut.

(−) Self-pity. Fatalism. Satiety. Excess. Apathy. Lethargy. Despair. Depression. Exhaustion. Lack of enjoyment. Lost opportunities.

Situation and Advice: In its positive aspect, matters are taking a turn for the better. You feel refreshed and await new challenges. Life is again satisfying after a period of boredom and discontent. You have something to look forward to. You may find yourself socializing and making new friends, perhaps as a result of attending a party or accepting an invitation. Now is a time to renew old acquaintances and to reassess what your relationships mean to you.

In its negative aspect, the Four of Cups reversed indicates you may be undergoing a period of significant depression. Don't let your self-pity get the better of you.

People: Those who are coming out of a rut or a period of withdrawal from social activity.

~

Fives

Key Words and Phrases: Upsetting the balance. Disrupted stability. Struggle. Uncertainty. Upset. Change. Disruption. Flux. A new cycle. Shifts. Adjustment. Adversity. Conflict. Strife. Disappointment. Loss. Missing out on something. Competition. Challenge. Difficulties. Problems. Study. Learning. Into every life some rain must fall.

Corresponding Major Arcana Card: The Hierophant.

Situation and Advice: The number five is associated with the Hierophant of the Major Arcana and with the planet Mercury and the signs Gemini and Virgo. Another name for the metal Mercury is quicksilver. Mercury symbolizes change, freedom of movement, adaptability, malleability, versatility, variety, travel, and learning. Mercurial people prefer intellectual work to manual labor. They need to guard against impulsiveness and a chameleon-like capacity to change their mind to fit any situation.

A prominence of fives in a spread suggests dramatic changes, often involving career advancement and travel opportunities. Some sort of public acclaim is also a possibility. Fives also signify adventure, challenge, and relocation. This is a time of high tension and nervous energy.

The number five represents a yang energy that is restless, volatile, and impetuous. This may be a time of hasty actions, adventurousness, excitement, freedom from past restrictions, hectic change, uncertainty, scattered energies, and creative opportunities. Writing, public speaking, advertising, travel, exploration, gambling, the arts, sales, and communication are all favored. Because of the restless nature of the fives, this is not usually a favorable time to make a major long-standing commitment.

Personal Year: The five personal year brings a release of the restrictions imposed during the four personal year. Five marks a year of significant changes and inner restlessness. Travel, freedom, new relationships, artistic expression, business expansion, pregnancy, variety, change, fluctuating finances, impulsive activity, and unusual happenings are all characteristic of the five personal year. Often the five personal year ends with an exciting new career opportunity.

Five of Wands
A Mock Battle

Upright: An exciting challenge.

Key Words and Phrases: External conflict. Struggle. Rivalry. The need to prove oneself. Male bonding. Same sex activities. Healthy competition. Assertiveness. Faith in one's ability to compete. Sowing your oats. Physical activity. Sports. Active games. Being one of the guys. Sparring. Obstacles.

A time for vigorous action. Success through formidable effort. Arguments. Strife. Agitation. Contention. Dissonance. Self-doubt. Quarrels. Rivalry. Squabbles. Legal problems. A fight without injury. Bickering. The martial arts. Annoying details. Minor irritations. A nuisance. Unexpected problems. A conflict of interests. Too many irons in the fire. The need to set priorities. War games. Testosterone. Hormones acting up. Territoriality. Delayed travel plans. The princess and the pea.

Situation and Advice: You may need to compete or face an exciting challenge to get what you want. Avoid passivity at this time. Success will come as a result of your assertive efforts to overcome nuisances and obstacles. Some of the strife may be due to your refusal to see the other person's point of view. Perhaps you have too many irons in the fire and are scattering your energy in too many directions at once; if so, you need to set priorities to avoid excessive stress.

The Five of Wands suggests that you will be dealing with contention and rivalry. Legal complications or problems are also a possibility. You may need to confront petty annoyances and difficulties. You are engaged in welcome competition. If your question was about romance, you may need to compete with another to win your lover's affections. If you asked about travel, expect a delay or some complication in your plans.

This card can simply indicate that you have a lot of energy to burn just now. You may need a night out with the guys or gals, as the case may be. Some may want to participate in karate or other martial arts. For example, on a day that I drew this card I arrived home from work to learn that my eleven-year-old son had cut open the heel of his foot while playing karate with a friend. My evening was spent taking him to the pediatrician.

People: Competitors. Sports teams. Open opponents. Martial arts enthusiasts. One who instigates contention.

Five of Wands Reversed: Squabbles. Relief after conflict.

Key Words and Phrases: (+) Healthy competition. Active games. Sports. Peace. Harmony. The struggle is over. The end of strife. Opportunities. Favorable changes. Freedom from bickering and conflict. A favorable legal decision (especially if another "positive legal" card, such as Justice upright or Judgement upright, appears in the spread).

(–) Internal conflict. Lack of faith in one's ability to compete. Unfair tactics. Legal battles. Bickering. Stress. Unhealthy competition. Hitting below the belt. Malice. Antipathy. Setbacks. Disagreements. Petty squabbling. Problems with travel plans. Trouble with contracts. Feeling overwhelmed takes a toll on your health.

Situation and Advice: In its positive aspect, the reversed Five of Wands means that the struggle is over and now is the time to proceed.

In its negative aspect, this card represents unhealthy competition, petty quarrels, unfair tactics, unwelcome challenges, malicious opposition, and nasty setbacks. Usually, the upright card shows healthy competition and the reversed card shows its opposite. The Five of Wands reversed may be advising you that the daily grind has been wearing you down and taking its toll on your health. Have you been scattering your energies in too many directions? Now is a time to set your priorities and deal more effectively with stress in your life. Relief is in sight.

People: Malicious or secret enemies. Underhanded opponents.

Five of Pentacles
Poverty

Upright: Down and out.

Key Words and Phrases: Loss. Disappointment. Misfortune. Troubles. Unemployment. Risky self-employment. Hardship. Lack of assets. Missing out on something. Feeling abandoned. Financial strain. Dwindling resources. Wasted talents. Sorrow. Uncertainty. Depression. Deprivation. Hard times. Overextension. Legal settlements. Lack of faith. Failure to pursue spiritual values. Neglecting the gift of faith.

Loneliness. Despair. Demoralization. Out in the cold. Feeling left out. Health problems. Need for reassessment. Money can't buy you happiness.

Situation and Advice: You may feel like you've been left out in the cold. You may be under strain financially and may have fallen on hard times. If financially secure, you are realizing that money can't buy you love. You may be overextending yourself. Now is the time to rid yourself of unnecessary expenditures and other confining situations in your life. This card raises the possibility that you are not putting your talents to good use. If you asked about a business venture, the Five of Pentacles warns you to avoid risks because loss of money is the likely outcome. A legal situation may result in financial loss. Your preoccupation with practical difficulties is preventing you from seeking spiritual guidance or comfort. If you asked about a love affair, don't count on its longevity.

People: The impoverished. The lonely. Those who are down and out.

◑

Five of Pentacles Reversed: Faith restored.

Key Words and Phrases: (+) A turn for the better. Spiritual awareness. Renewed faith. Improved working conditions. Better health. The end of poverty or unemployment.

(−) Unemployment. Frustration. Adversity. Despair. Money problems. Extreme poverty. Severe deprivation.

Situation and Advice: In its positive sense, the Five of Pentacles reversed means that the poverty and deprivation of the upright position is coming to an end. Health should improve. Problems involving money, income, and business begin to clear.

In its negative sense, the hardship of the upright card becomes more entrenched and chronic.

People: Those emerging from hard times.

Five of Swords
Empty Victory

Upright: One-upmanship. Negative energy.

Key Words and Phrases: Wounded pride. Humiliation.
Arguing. False pride. Taunting. Ridicule. Embarrassment.
Cunning. Gloating. Plotting. Turmoil. Underhandedness.
Betrayal. Malicious gossip. A dispute. An argument. Hostility.
Spite. Sabotage. A sneak attack. Insensitivity. Limitations.
Loss. Severing of ties. Failure. Misfortune. Defeat. Loss of
face. Cowardice. Negative thinking. Muddled opinions. Theft.

Not considering the consequences. Manipulation. Selfishness. A domineering attitude. Thoughtlessness. Tactlessness. Blaming. Destructive behavior. Revenge. Deceit. A funeral. It's not fair. Is that all there is? It's only important whether you win or lose, not how you play the game. Be careful—you just might get what you want.

Situation and Advice: The Five of Swords warns that you, or someone around you, may be acting in a negative or destructive manner. You may need to swallow your pride and admit your limitations before you can proceed. Your sense of ego may be preventing you from acknowledging that you have bitten off more than you can chew. Perhaps you are blaming others for your own mistakes.

You may be so concerned about winning that you ignore the consequences of your behavior. You may get something you thought you wanted only to realize it does not fulfill your desires. Spiteful or malicious actions will not produce the desired result. You may be listening to too many other people's opinions instead of reaching your own conclusions. You need the wisdom to accept the things you cannot change and to acknowledge defeat before moving on. You may have won a battle, but at what cost? As you emerge victorious, you ask yourself, "Was it worth it?"

You should also consider that someone near you may not deserve your trust. You may be the victim of nasty gossip or underhanded behavior. Someone may be working against your interests out of jealousy or spite. Any court cards that appear in the spread may provide further information about who is sabotaging your plans or attacking your reputation.

People: Those who lose face. Sore losers. Malicious gossips. Saboteurs. Troublemakers.

◐

Five of Swords Reversed: Vindication. Degradation.

Key Words and Phrases: (+) Being cleared of wrongdoing. The end of malicious gossip or slander. Treachery revealed.

(–) Similar to upright meaning but with a more negative connotation. Loss. Failure. Intimidation. Manipulation. Humiliation. Dishonesty. Illegal tactics. Underhandedness. Victimization. Spite. Deception. Weakness. Defeat. Unfairness. Egotism. False pride. Intrigue. Despair. A turn for the worse. Suspicion. Paranoia. A bad attitude. An exclusive focus on winning. It's mine, all mine!

Situation and Advice: In its positive aspect, the Five of Swords reversed suggests an end to the attacks and slander of the upright position.

In its negative aspect, the Five of Swords reversed suggests that you are dealing with a situation in which you are feeling humiliated, degraded, or victimized. Your self-esteem may be at a low because of a painful humiliation or defeat. Someone may be bullying you or acting maliciously and spitefully against you.

People: Bullies. Malicious enemies.

Five of Cups
Loss and Disappointment

Upright: Mourning.

Key Words and Phrases: Regret. Self-blame. Sadness. Brooding. An unhappy ending. Overturned emotions. Poor communication. Loss of trust. Emotional letdown. Betrayal in love. Exaggerated pessimism. Anxiety over separation. Salvaging what remains. The waning of love. Marital or family problems. A time of crisis in a love relationship. Breaking up. Feeling abandoned. Feeling scolded or punished. Separation. Divorce. Miscarriage. Unused talents. Something lost but something remains. No use crying over spilt milk. What's done is done. Let bygones be bygones. The glass is half empty.

Situation and Advice: You have suffered a loss or disappointment. You may feel abandoned or betrayed by a loved one. Not all is lost, however. Something remains to be salvaged from the situation. You can either focus on the glass being half-empty or half-full. If you are involved in a painful relationship, it is best to sever the emotional tie that has led only to regret and disappointment. You need to allow the grief work to proceed and also to revise your emotional priorities.

People: Someone who feels bitter, resentful, or burned out. A pessimist. A woman who has miscarried. A mistreated child.

◑

Five of Cups Reversed: The pain is ending.

Key Words and Phrases: (+) Hope. The rekindling of old love. Good news. Expectancy. Acceptance. New relationships. Opportunity. Renewal of old ties. Dealing constructively with misunderstandings. Recovery from past hurts. The glass is half full.

(–) A painful ending. Bereavement. Inevitable loss. Regret. The end of a valued relationship. Loss of love.

Situation and Advice: In its positive aspect, the Five of Cups reversed means that the emotional pain of the upright position is over. There is light at the end of the tunnel, and you are on the road to recovery from past hurts and losses. Someone from your past may renew your hope in the future. A lover may return from the past. The rapid changes in your emotional life can be a source of some discomfort. An old friend may reenter your life. Now is the time to clear up old misunderstandings or hurt feelings.

In its negative aspect, this card can represent the need to come to terms with the irrevocable ending of a valued relationship. It can symbolize bereavement, loneliness, and grief.

People: Old friends. Lost loves. A lover from the past.

~

Sixes

Key Words and Phrases: Harmony within flux. Justice. Equilibrium. Fairness. Balance restored. Peace. Appreciation. Reward. Values. Benefits from past behavior.

> God saw that all He had made was very good. And there was evening and morning, the sixth day.
>
> —Genesis

Corresponding Major Arcana Card: The Lovers.

Situation and Advice: The number six is associated with the Lovers card of the Major Arcana and with the planet Venus and the signs Taurus and Libra. Venus is a planet of harmony, love, romance, marriage, peace, beauty, luxury, the arts, music, cooperation, balance, and equilibrium.

A prominence of sixes in a reading suggests activities involving personal relationships, family, home, loved ones, creative ventures, education, love affairs, and romance. Marriage may be in the offing. Some creative or artistic endeavor is possible. There may be a chance to further your education and improve your career. Travel is not likely now.

The number six represents a yin energy that is pleasant, harmonious, settled, and peaceful. Sixes suggest the need to take into account the feelings and needs of others, and favor marriage and partnerships. Home, family, and the needs of children or elders may require your attention. Tact, forgiveness, and understanding are called for in personal relationships. If you have been having problems with a partnership, now is the time to resolve differences. If your question concerned indebtedness, you should be able to clear up the matter now.

Personal Year: Like the two year, the six personal year is a time of settled conditions, peace, and harmony. The focus now is on duty, relationships, home, family obligations, concerns about parents and children, education, schooling, clearing up financial problems, domestic issues, love, and marriage. There is a danger in a six year of getting overly involved in other people's affairs rather than minding your own business.

Six of Wands

Victory

Upright: The likelihood of success.

Key Words and Phrases: Triumph. Accomplishment. Acclaim. Appreciation. Vindication. The realization of an ambition. Wise decisions. Success. Self-assurance. Public recognition. Good news. Diplomacy. Conquest. Achievement. Resolution of problems. Reward. Fulfillment. Promotion. Honors. Winning. Applause. Encouragement. The right stuff.

Situation and Advice: The Six of Wands is a card of triumph and victory. You may receive recognition for your work or a promotion in your career. If a student, you may receive a scholarship or an academic honor. You will achieve a wished-for goal and your efforts will be rewarded. You have won a battle and will achieve the victory you deserve. Travel is possible. Problems will be solved. Agreements will be reached. Good news is on the way.

People: A victor. Someone who receives acclaim.

◑

Six of Wands Reversed: Victory eludes you.

Key Words and Phrases: Defeat. Delayed success. Not winning. Failure. Loss. Postponement. Triumph eludes you. Winning a battle but losing the war. A rival prevails. The other person wins. You're not up to the challenge. Red tape. Infidelity. Lack of communication. Misunderstanding. Playing second fiddle. Feeling unimportant. Better luck next time. I get no respect!

Situation and Advice: Some money or recognition you have been expecting is delayed or will not come through. You do not win this time around. You're not up to the challenge or you just don't have what it takes. You may not be able to reach a necessary agreement. There may have been a misunderstanding or a failure of communication. If your question was about competitive employment, there will either be a delay or someone else will get the job. If you asked about a relationship, you may feel like your needs are not being met. Perhaps your partner is not treating you with enough respect and you are feeling unimportant as a result. It's no fun always being in the back seat. The Six of Wands reversed sometimes means infidelity in a marriage, but this can simply take the form of one spouse putting a hobby or other interest ahead of his or her partner.

People: Losers. Those whom victory eludes. Rivals. Football, golf, et cetera, widows.

Six of Pentacles
Generosity

Upright: Getting what you deserve.

Key Words and Phrases: Helping others. An act of charity. Repayment of debts. Return on investments. Gratitude. Material gain. Sound money management. Giving of your talents, time, or money. Loans. Grants. Prizes. Bonuses. Shared wealth. Charity. Gifts. Appreciation. Financial assistance. Extra money. Receiving money owed. Your work pays off.

Equitable distribution of assets. Fair financial dealings. Enjoying the fruits of your labors. Profits. Teaching your skills to others. Mentoring. Helping others. Shared prosperity. A business opportunity. A promotion. A bonus.

Situation and Advice: The Six of Pentacles suggests a gift, the receipt or loan of money, or the chance to participate in a business opportunity. Someone owing you money is likely to pay up now. You will be dealt with fairly. Financial assistance is in the near future, and you will receive what is rightfully yours. You may also be in a position to offer monetary assistance or training to others. A friend may ask you for a loan. You may help someone find a job or improve their career status. Perhaps you are starting to save for your children's education or for your own future goals. You may be able to assist someone in the development of their talents. You might be in line for a promotion or financial reward. This is a time for generosity, sound investing, and sharing your wealth. You delight in being of assistance to others. A little extra money is on the way. Ask and you shall receive.

People: A mentor. A buyer. A philanthropist. An almsgiver. A wise investor. One who loans money. Someone who saves for a rainy day. A benefactor. Someone who renders service. A charity.

◑

Six of Pentacles Reversed: Loss of goods or property. A loan comes due.

Key Words and Phrases: Refusing to share. Withdrawal of financial support. Unfair business dealings. Dishonest bookkeeping. Unpaid bills. Money problems. Bad debts. Greed. Selfishness. Stinginess. Miserliness. Inequity. Unpaid debts. Wasteful spending. Loss through theft or carelessness. Not receiving money owed. Envy. Jealousy. Lack of recognition. A low rate of interest on an investment. Excessive self-interest. Lack of foresight. Imprudence. Lack of charity. Biting the hand that feeds you. Money with strings attached. Illegal money transactions. Laundered money. Why should I give you anything? Ask not what you can do for your country, ask what your country can do for you.

Situation and Advice: The Six of Pentacles reversed often suggests a loss of money or property due to carelessness, dishonesty, or lack of prudence. Someone may refuse to pay a debt or return a favor, or a loan may come due, leaving you financially strapped. Sources of financial support may dry up. You may not be able to get what is rightfully yours. Sometimes this card indicates an actual theft. A money manager may be involved in unethical or underhanded dealings. Material misfortune may result from the selfish actions of others. This card may also warn the querent about a lack of charity and generosity of spirit. If you are involved in a financial transaction, beware of devious schemes and misrepresentation in agreements.

People: Indentured servants. Those who owe money. Beggars. Thieves. Wastrels. Tightwads. Money launderers. Crooked money managers. Those who depend on others for basic necessities. The prodigal son. Those who spend only on themselves.

Six of Swords
Leaving Your Troubles Behind

Upright: Brighter days ahead.

Key Words and Phrases: Moving away from stress and troubles. Release of tension. A welcome transition. A reconciliation. Seeking calmer waters. Tranquillity and peace of mind restored. Easing of tension after a period of stress. Smooth sailing. Moving away from conflict or difficulties. Swimming with the current. Going with the flow. Travel. Relocation. Removal. A journey. A trip abroad. A welcome passage. Dealings with those from a distance. Increased knowledge. Release from a stressful situation. A beneficial change. Severing of ties. A change of attitude. A death that puts an end to suffering. Moving from a destructive to a constructive situation. The worst is over. Like a bridge over troubled waters . . . .

Situation and Advice: You are leaving behind a period of strain, worry, and anxiety. You are entering a more tranquil time in which your peace of mind will be restored. Sometimes a trip will relieve tension and reinstate balance and harmony. You may have the opportunity to travel or you may receive a visitor from afar. You are open now to new learning. This is a time to review past difficulties with an eye to assuring a better future. An event may relieve you, or someone close to you, of suffering. You are now able to leave a destructive situation or behavior pattern behind.

People: Travelers. People on a cruise. Those emerging from a period of suffering. People from or at a distance. One who helps in times of need.

◑

Six of Swords Reversed: Rough waters ahead.

Key Words and Phrases: Unable to leave your troubles behind. Delay. Postponement. Stuck in a negative thought pattern. Not accepting help offered. Unable to leave a troubling situation. Bucking the tide. Paddling upstream. Lack of progress. Feeling trapped or stressed. At a standstill. One problem after another. Fleeting relief. The easy way out. Unable to put the past behind. In a rut. Feeling unable to see your way out of your present predicament. Not facing reality. A trip is canceled or postponed. A change in travel plans.

Returning from a journey. Out of the frying pan and into the fire. Burying your head in the sand.

Situation and Advice: Try as hard as you might, you just have not been able to put your troubles behind you. You feel stuck and unable to move out of a difficult predicament. You may have sought an inadequate solution to your problems. Perhaps you have elected the easy way out or have simply buried your head in the sand. You need to face reality and confront your difficulties. You need to traverse a lot of rough water before your life can settle down again. Sometimes this card can literally signify a change of travel plans or the cancellation of a journey.

People: Procrastinators. Lazy people. Those traversing rough waters. Those arriving from a trip.

Six of Cups
The Good Old Days

Upright: Nostalgia.

Key Words and Phrases: Innocence. Reviewing childhood memories. Revisiting scenes of childhood. Sharing. An honest talk. Rekindling love. Renewing old ties. Harmony restored. Thinking about old times. A lover from the past. An old fling. Old friends. Karmic ties. Happy memories. Anniversaries.

Emotional renewal. Unearthing buried emotional treasures. Warm get-togethers. Celebrations. Gifts. Sentiment. Family values. Enjoyment of home and family. A trip to visit family. A job offer. A move. An inheritance. Dealings with children.

Situation and Advice: You may have the opportunity to renew an old acquaintance. Perhaps you will attend a family gathering or a school reunion. Someone from the past may reenter your life. Your thoughts turn to childhood memories and valued aspects of your early home environment. Some matter with roots in the past comes to fruition. The Six of Cups often advises that it is important to recover and deal with old memories.

An old lover may appear on the scene. An old friend may bring news that leads to a job offer or a change of residence. Children may play a significant role in your life at this time. You will need to review some aspect of your past life, perhaps during an honest talk with a trusted advisor. You may have occasion to use old skills that have lain dormant for a long time.

People: Old friends. Those who are like family to us. Childhood friends. Children. Former lovers. Those connected with one's past.

◑

Six of Cups Reversed: Clinging to the past.

Key Words and Phrases: Unwilling or unable to adapt to present circumstances. Dwelling on the past. Unable to cut the apron strings. Unproductive nostalgia. Seeking old forms of security. Vanity. Suffering from reminiscences. Not being given credit due. Ghosts from the past live on in the present. Skeletons in the closet. Clinging to outmoded customs and beliefs. Unwilling to try something new. The need to look to the future. I don't want to grow up.

Trust no Future, howe'er pleasant! Let the dead Past bury
its dead! Act—act in the living Present! Heart within, and
God o'erhead!

—Henry Wadsworth Longfellow

Situation and Advice: Some aspect of your family ties or
past relationships is holding you down. Are you still holding
on to mommy's apron strings? A matter from the past may
come back to haunt you. You may still be feeling the reper-
cussions of an old love affair in your present life. Something
you've been expecting may be postponed or delayed. You
need to give up old ties or own up to some past indiscretion
to get on with your life. Feelings and values rooted in your
early family or past relationships may be blocking your
progress. Dwelling on past achievements may be keeping you
from pursuing new accomplishments. Are you clinging to
outmoded beliefs and values? It's time to live in the here and
now with an eye to the future. Worries about children may
preoccupy you at this time.

People: Rip Van Winkle. Those living in the past. Mama's boys
and girls. Old fuddy-duddies.

~

Sevens

Key Words and Phrases: Choice. Wisdom. Fate. Divine
order. Dispassionate awareness. The need to make decisions.
Harmony dispelled. Spiritual development. Morality. Divine
justice. Mysticism. Magic. Change. A turning point. Rebellion.
Eccentricity. Intuition. The completion of a phase or cycle.

God blessed the seventh day and made it holy because on it
He rested from all His work of creation.

—Genesis

Corresponding Major Arcana Card: The Chariot.

Situation and Advice: The number seven is associated with the Chariot card of the Major Arcana and with the planet Uranus and the lunar sign Cancer. Uranus is a planet of abstract thought, theory, intellect, analysis, astrology, technical advances, independence, and the dispassionate search for truth. Cancer is a water sign related to our feeling nature. The planet Neptune, associated with meditation and respite, is exalted in Cancer.

A prominence of sevens in a spread suggests an original analytical approach to learning. Any travel now would be welcome and enjoyable. Work in the sciences, technology, or with computers is favored. You may have the opportunity to do some writing, research, or occult study. The focus now is on independent self-discovery and inner growth. Relationship issues and career matters take a back seat to self-awareness.

The number seven represents a mental yang energy. On the seventh day God rested, and sevens in a spread often point to a need for rest, solitude, retreat, meditation, and reflection. Otherwise, tension, overwork, worry, feelings of restriction, and nervous strain may result. The focus now should be on spiritual growth rather than materialistic ambitions. This is a time for analysis, reflection, and meditation rather than action.

Personal Year: Because seven is a spiritual number, the seven personal year is a time for reflection, rest, meditation, retreat, soul searching, inner awareness, reevaluation, and spiritual development. Any kind of research and metaphysical interest is favored. This is a great time to use the Tarot to foster spiritual awareness.

Seven of Wands
Holding Firm

Upright: Holding your own. A position of advantage.

Key Words and Phrases: Taking a stand. Holding firm against opposition. Struggling to stay on top. Success in a competitive undertaking. Matters coming to a head. Keeping your ground. Maintaining your position. Having an advantage. Feeling undaunted. Courage. Strength in adversity.

Holding a superior position. Self-confidence. Assertion. Successful competition. Steadfastness. Devotion. Challenge. Confrontation. Disputes. Opposition. Fights. An embarrassing situation. A conflict or struggle. A career change. Inner strength. Coping successfully. Learning. Teaching. Writing. Lecturing. Determination. Perseverance. A sense of purpose. Persevering despite adversity. Taking the bull by the horns. Having the advantage in a situation. Keep a stiff upper lip. When the going gets tough, the tough get going. I'd rather fight than switch. Against all odds. A head above the rest. One day at a time. We shall overcome.

> Here I stand. I can do no other. God help me. Amen.
>
> —Martin Luther

Situation and Advice: A situation of conflict is coming to a head, and you are able to view the matter from a superior vantage point. You may feel pressured as you enter this time of confrontation, challenge, and opposition. You will need to call on your reserves of strength and courage to prevail. You must summon your inner strength and determination to overcome the odds and face the competition. You have the advantage even if you don't realize it.

Perhaps a prior achievement has placed you in a competitive situation. To achieve success you will need to take a firm stand and defend your position. If necessary, you will be able to hold your own in an argument. Your devotion to your cause will win the day. You have the strength and tenacity to face the competition that is entering your life or business ventures.

Do not give up the struggle. If you make the effort, you will achieve victory. The best strategy is to tackle one problem at a time. Your hard work and thoughtfulness will pay off. This is a time to be especially observant. If your question was about career, you will be able to make a successful career move. You may be entering a period of new learning. You may be asked to teach or write about what you know.

People: Those who have the advantage. Those who keep their ground in a struggle. Those who make things happen.

◑

Seven of Wands Reversed: Feeling daunted.

Key Words and Phrases: Retreat from confrontation. Feeling vulnerable or overwhelmed. An inferior vantage point. At a disadvantage. Fighting a losing battle. Giving up in the face of opposition. Chickening out. The other team wins. Running from problems. Lack of assertion. Embarrassment. Passivity. Uncertainty. Timidity. Shame. Diffidence. Lack of confidence. Running from challenge. Anxiety about a decision. Fear of rejection. Wimping out. Cowardice. Fear of the future. Missed opportunities. Health problems. Not taking the bull by the horns. When the going gets tough, I get going. I'd rather switch than fight. His bark is worse than his bite.

Situation and Advice: The Seven of Wands reversed is an admonition to persist in pursuing your goals despite opposition. You can triumph if you do not retreat from confrontation. If you give up now, you may miss a valuable opportunity. The confrontation you fear is unlikely to take place. You need to confront your problems, not run away from them. Your diffidence and lack of confidence will only make matters worse. Are you afraid people will get angry with you if you assert yourself? So what if they do? Sometimes a good fight can clear the air. Why not take the bull by the horns and run with it?

In an otherwise negative spread, the Seven of Wands reversed suggests vulnerability and involvement in a losing battle. You might do best to cut your losses and withdraw from the battle.

People: A spineless wimp. Cowards. Those who let things happen. Those who are losing a battle.

Seven of Pentacles
Perseverance

Upright: Slow and steady growth. Taking stock of one's investments.

Key Words and Phrases: (+) Reevaluation of a project you have been working on for some time. Waiting for results. Hard work will eventually pay off. Patience. Persistent effort. Practical skill. Working hard. Established work. Reflecting on your gains. A waiting period. A plateau. Patience. Slow but steady progress. Attentive nurturing. Pausing to make a considered decision. Time for a change. Long-term projects. A lull during the development of an enterprise. Reflecting on what you have accomplished thus far. A time for assessment and future planning. A choice between risk and security. A welcome financial change. Waiting for results. Slowly but surely. You've come a long way, baby.

(–) Depression. A sense of failure. A feeling of wasted effort. Collapse of a project. Loss through speculation. Work done without pay. Premature cessation of effort. Something missing. Failure to pursue a profitable opportunity. Difficulty getting pregnant. Dissatisfaction. Imbalance. Malfunction.

Situation and Advice: In its positive aspect, the Seven of Pentacles indicates you may feel like you have been wasting time on a project, but this is not the case. You have reached a logical place to pause and assess the development of an ongoing project or enterprise. Your patient work is producing slow and steady growth. You have reached a plateau, but there is still much to do and your consistent effort will eventually pay off. Even though you do not yet see the final results, this is not the time to cease your efforts. The Seven of Pentacles advises you to reassess and reevaluate your progress, to decide what you still need to do to accomplish your goal, and to apply consistent effort until you succeed.

Your finances are taking a turn for the better. In the end your hard work will be rewarded. There is light at the end of the tunnel. Reflect on the words from the book of Genesis, "God blessed the seventh day and made it holy because on it he rested from all his work of creation."

In an otherwise negative spread, the Seven of Pentacles takes on a less favorable meaning. You may feel like abandoning a project you have labored long and hard to develop. You may realize that all the work you have done will not achieve your goals. Your health may be under par, perhaps due to a malfunction, a metabolic imbalance, or an infection.

People: A farmer. An investor. Someone who is making plans. The tortoise (of the tortoise and the hare). Patient workers.

◐

Seven of Pentacles Reversed: Giving up too soon.

Key Words and Phrases: Anxiety. Disillusionment. Depression. Loss. Demoralization. Despair. Wasted energy. Bad investments. Stuck in a dead-end job. Weariness. Going nowhere fast. Lassitude. Hopelessness. Success abandoned. Premature cessation of effort. Monetary lack. Worry about finances. Bankruptcy. Gambling losses. Hard choices. Fear of poverty. Abandoning an enterprise. Missed opportunities. Self-pity. Impatience. Rash decisions. Unwillingness to see matters through to completion. Petering out. Barrenness. Sterility. Illness. Malfunction. Infection. Imbalance. Patience is a virtue.

Situation and Advice: You may be going nowhere fast. You may be involved in a situation in which you have given up too soon out of a sense of hopelessness or despair. No doubt money worries are on your mind. Perhaps you have abandoned an enterprise because of financial problems. Have you borrowed too much on credit? Are your bills overwhelming you? Are you stuck in a dead-end job? Are you considering a bad investment? It is important to learn from your mistakes so you can do better next time. In your demoralized state, you also need to guard against health problems due to infection or internal malfunctioning.

People: Those who poop out. Quitters. Impatient persons.

Seven of Swords
Stealth

Upright: Doing the unexpected.

Key Words and Phrases: Guile. Circumspection. Cunning. Trickery. Cleverness. Duplicity. Escape. Putting something over on others. Insincerity. Taking advantage of someone. Thoughts about travel. A job or career change. Moving to a new location. The need for discreet management. Sabotage. Evasive or illicit tactics. Diplomacy. Discretion. Craftiness. Avoidance. Indirect action. Caution. Circuitous means. Brain over brawn. The need for professional advice. A unique worldview. Unfair acts. Illegality. A theft. A robbery. A rip-off. Feeling cheated. Bad luck. Guilt. Upset. Betrayal. Victimization. A dishonorable act. Self-defeating actions. A short trip. An elopement. Running away. Moving onward. Being your own worst enemy. Self-defeating behavior. Feelings of unease and escapism. Feelings of defeat or deception.

Situation and Advice: You may be feeling cheated or uneasy about something you have done. You may wish to escape or run away, but you need to avoid self-defeating actions. Do not become your own worst enemy. You will need to be diplomatic, crafty, or evasive to deal with the opposition and reach your goal. Be aware that others may be trying to put something over on you or may be damaging your reputation in devious ways. They may take advantage of the fact that you are preoccupied with other matters, or you yourself may strike when the opponent is looking the other way.

Your unique worldview and ability to do the unexpected can save the day. A plan you made may not work out as intended. Perhaps you will need legal or other professional advice. This card may indicate involvement in underhanded, deceptive, illicit, or sneaky endeavors. Sometimes an actual robbery or theft is indicated (especially if another "deception" card—like the Moon—appears in the spread), but more likely the damage you suffer comes from some form of words or communication. Be especially careful of what you say and of anything you put in writing at this time. A battle of wits may be forthcoming. Someone may be opposing your intellectual freedom and independence. This card may also indicate moving onward while leaving part of your life behind.

People: An ingenious person. A thief. A crafty person. A sneak. Someone moving from one place to another.

Seven of Swords Reversed: Appreciation.

Key Words and Phrases: (+) An apology. Good advice. Constructive criticism. Something of yours returns. Acting in your own best interests. Return of stolen goods. Give credit where credit is due.

(–) Indecision. Laziness. Pessimism. Chickening out. An unfinished project. Missed opportunities. Dwelling on past errors. Lack of skill or cunning. Dimwittedness.

Situation and Advice: If you've been robbed, the thief will not be able to hold on to the stolen goods. If someone has wronged you, expect an apology. You should appreciate any criticism you receive now because it is likely to be constructive. If something was taken unfairly from you, it may return now. Someone may offer assistance or helpful advice. This is a time to keep your wits about you if you wish to succeed. An overly conventional or unimaginative approach will get you nowhere.

People: Dimwits. Dingbats. Inept thieves.

Seven of Cups
Daydreams

Upright: Lack of focus. A sense of confusion.

Key Words and Phrases: Wishful thinking. Fantasy. Head in the clouds. Poor concentration. Uncertainty. A difficult choice. Not thinking clearly. Too many options. Can't decide. Muddled thinking. Scattered energies. Unrealistic expectations. Picking from among many alternatives. Illusion. Disorganization. Romanticism. Emotions dominate rational thought. Escapism. Inability to cope. Altered states. Visions.

A significant dream. Psychic impressions. Impracticality. Figments of the imagination. Longings. Confusing choices. Yearnings. An unwieldy imagination. A tough decision. Excess use of drugs or alcohol (especially if another "escapism" card—like the Moon—appears in the spread). Abuse. What do I do now? Castles in the air. What do I really want? You can't have everything! It's all a blur. Not seeing the forest for the trees.

Situation and Advice: You may be feeling stuck or confused about making a decision. The options may seem too numerous or too evenly balanced, or each option may involve some sort of trade-off. You can't have everything and you're not sure which way to go. Your heart urges you to go in one direction and your head says to go in another. You may not appreciate the ramifications of each choice before you. You need to focus and concentrate on a single goal to succeed. At this time your wishful thinking is your worst enemy.

Success will depend on your weighing matters carefully to reach a thoughtful and focused decision. The Seven of Cups warns that your thinking may be too muddled to make the best choice. Your expectations may be unrealistic and your imagination may be working overtime. You would be wise to take your time and seek more information. On the other hand, this is an excellent time for creative projects of any kind. Sometimes this card can herald a significant dream or psychic intuition. If so, be sure to listen to your inner voice.

People: Visionaries. Dreamers. Those with their heads in the clouds. Artists. Creative people. Those faced with too many options. Muddled thinkers.

◐

Seven of Cups Reversed: The fog lifts. Persistence is rewarded.

Key Words and Phrases: (+) Decisiveness. A realistic attitude. Determination. The need to make a definite decision. A good choice. Able to see the forest for the trees. A time for action. Head rules over heart. Clarity of thought. Cutting to the quick. Ease of decision making. Looking at things realistically. Perseverance wins in the end. Success comes the second time around. The need to try again. Back to basics. On a clear day you can see forever. I've made up my mind! Cut the crap. If at first you don't succeed, try and try again.

(–) Usually the reversed Seven of Cups indicates decisiveness and realism, but in an otherwise negative spread it can have the following meanings: Disillusionment. Total confusion. Self-deception. Bewilderment. Illusion. Flight from reality. Fantasy. Lost opportunity. Initial failure and the need to try again. False promises. Fear of success. Play it again, Sam. Say, what?

Situation and Advice: You may have been pondering a decision that you need to bring to closure. It has been difficult to choose among various options or course of action, and you may have been feeling disillusioned. Perhaps your emotions have been clouding the issue, or perhaps you have been scattering your energies rather than pursuing a determined course of action. Your first attempt at achieving a goal may have met with failure because you did not apply yourself wisely or with proper focus. You are now able to see past errors and false starts of previous attempts; this enables you to set your course more clearly to achieve your goal. You have overcome your confusion and have adopted a more realistic attitude.

You need to put matters in perspective and take a good hard look at the realities of the situation. You are now able to think clearly about the options and come to a reasonable and wise decision. You should focus on what is essential and persevere in following through on your good ideas. The Seven of Cups indicates that, if you set clear and specific goals, your hard work and diligent study will eventually be rewarded.

People: Those struggling to see matters clearly. Diligent students. Realists.

~

Eights

Key Words and Phrases: Power. Success. Regeneration. A fresh sense of direction. Completion of one stage of a project before moving on. Setting new priorities. Progression to a new phase of a cycle. New ways forward. Balance. Stability. Control. Reorganization. Enterprise. Executive ability. Harmonizing opposing forces. Death of the old to make way for the new.

Corresponding Major Arcana Card: Strength (or Justice in some decks).

Situation and Advice: The number eight is associated with the Strength card of the Major Arcana and with the planet Mars and the sign Capricorn, where Mars is exalted. Mars, the Greek god of war, symbolizes strength, leadership, self-reliance, impulsiveness, stamina, force, executive ability, and management. Capricorn is a sign known for ambition, hard work, organization, authority, structure, method, seriousness, perseverance, public status, and practicality.

A prominence of eights in a spread suggests a focus on karma, life structures, money, finance, and career. Themes of power, recognition, achievement, and paying off past debts come to the fore. You may receive a big break or make a major move now. In a positive spread, the eights sometimes indicate winning a sweepstakes or lottery. Significant changes in relationships may occur. You may move your home or otherwise change your living conditions now. Increased income from career and public acclaim may be indicated. Travel is unlikely.

The eight (consisting of two fours) represents a yin energy associated with personal power, advancement, reaping the harvest, material gain, and decisive yet tactful execution of personal plans. Like the four, eight is a karmic number sug-gesting you will now reap what you have sown. Also like the four, eights in a spread can symbolize real estate dealings and legal matters.

Personal Year: The eight personal year is a time of power and advancement in the external world. Business activities and partnerships, property and real estate matters, contracts, legal affairs, and material gain are all favored. Now is a time to reap what you have sown since the beginning of this nine-year cycle. Often changes of residence and alterations in long-standing relationships mark an eight personal year.

Eight of Wands
Speed

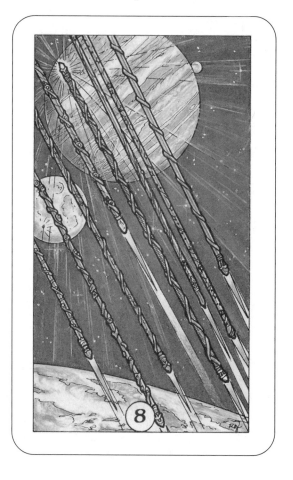

Upright: Full steam ahead.

Key Words and Phrases: Swift action. Forward motion. Smooth and rapid progress. Quick results. A fast pace. Travel without hindrances. Activity. Movement. The end of delays. Urgency. Excitement. Frenzy. Acceleration. New ideas. Mind broadening experiences. A job offer. Headway after a delay.

Quickness in approaching goals. Communication. News. Good messages. A journey. Vacations. Business travel. Sudden trips. Travel by air. Flying. Moves. Rushes of creative inspiration. Productivity. New friends. A sudden affair. Archery. Athletic ability. Physical exercise. All systems go! Everything's going my way.

Situation and Advice: All systems are go. You are moving rapidly toward achieving your goals. A period of stagnation or delay is ending. Favorable messages and fresh opportunities are coming in. There is excitement in the air as you make headway and launch new initiatives. Efforts to promote yourself succeed. You are full of energy and may start an exercise program for physical fitness. Your experiences also serve to broaden your mind. You may receive an urgent message. Sudden travel (probably by air) or a move is possible. If your question was about romance, the Eight of Wands suggests a sudden, passionate love affair. New friends enter your life.

People: Those on the go.

◖

Eight of Wands Reversed: Wasted energy.

Key Words and Phrases: Excessive speed. Hassles. Out of control. Being too pushy. Impulsiveness. Insecurity. Pressure. Haste. Ill-considered decisions. Precipitate actions. Too fast a pace. Theft. Opposition. Fights. Loss of a job. On strike. Upsetting news. Miscommunication. Embezzlement. Dismissal. Expulsion. Forcing an issue. Delayed news or messages. A trip canceled or delayed. A broken engagement. Problems with transport. Plans don't work out. A teenager being "grounded." Potential violence. You're acting like a chicken with its head cut off. Haste makes waste. I can't cope. Stop the world; I want to get off. What's your hurry?

Situation and Advice: You may be feeling overwhelmed by the fast pace of events. Perhaps you are in a dither and squandering your energy in fruitless directions. Your hasty actions don't get you where you want to go. Be careful not to force issues just now because you may precipitate violent opposition. Expect delays. Your plans may be canceled, especially if they involve travel. There may be problems with airplane flights or other forms of transport.

People: Those rushing fast to get nowhere. Pushy people.

Eight of Pentacles
The Work Card

Upright: Apprenticeship.

Key Words and Phrases: Talent. Education. Craftsmanship. Job training. Schooling. Study. Self-improvement. Learning. Acquiring skills. Enthusiasm about work. A labor of love. On-the-job training. Working hard to perfect a skill. Work-study programs. Absorption and pleasure in work. A new job. Material security. Good use of talents. A career change or promotion. A new field of work. Applied effort. Self-employment. A fulfilling hobby or avocation. Working on a project. Apprenticeship. Computer skills. Preparation for the future. Savings. Incremental gains of money. Cautious investing. Care with money. Learning to manage money. Income from the use of one's skills. Prudence. Diligence. Dedication. Perseverance. Also teaching, mentoring, tutoring, passing on skills and knowledge to others. If you're going to do a job, do it right.

Situation and Advice: The Eight of Pentacles suggests that your work will be fulfilling and enjoyable. You will use your skills wisely. If you are starting a new job, you will settle in easily and find the work absorbing. Your heart is in your work, and you may be up for a promotion. You have the opportunity to enter a phase of apprenticeship to develop your talents. Your time and effort will pay off. For some, the Eight of Pentacles will indicate starting over in a new career.

Now is a time to learn all you can about your profession. Do your homework. Take courses, attend seminars, and read books about your chosen field. You may have the chance to work with someone who can teach you new methods, or you may have the opportunity to teach others. You may not receive much financial reward now but the foundations you lay will pay off in career success at a later date. Wise money management is part of what you need to master. The Eight of Pentacles also symbolizes acquiring the latest information about modern technology and computers.

People: An apprentice. A good worker. A craftsperson. A computer whiz. A trade union. Also teachers, students, mentors, tutors. Those who train others.

Eight of Pentacles Reversed: Cutting corners.

Key Words and Phrases: Cheating. Pretending to know more than you really do. Fraudulence. Impatience. The easy way out. Misuse of skills. Shortcuts. Poor quality. A sense of entitlement. Tedious work. Lack of concentration. Fruitless labor. Lack of commitment. Self-criticism. Dishonesty. Devious business practices. Second-rate effort. False security. Unwillingness to learn. Kickbacks. Shoddy workmanship. Commercialism. Fraud. Dishonesty. Con games. Ripping off the system. Devious labor practices. Little reward. Jerry-rigged workmanship. Computer problems. Lack of work. Loss of a job. Unemployment. Feeling disenfranchised. Anger about the lack of opportunity. What they don't know won't hurt them! Slam, bam, thank you ma'am. I couldn't care less.

Situation and Advice: Your impatience or desire to take the easy way out may involve you in an unethical or unrewarding work situation. You may be dissatisfied with your job or may be actually unemployed. Perhaps you have lost a job because you are not working up to your potential. Maybe you were pretending to know more than you really do. If a student, you may be cheating on your exams.

In any case, problems regarding your work or lack of it preoccupy your mind and affect your behavior. Are you feeling disenfranchised and angry about the lack of opportunity in your life? Have you cut too many corners and produced a second-rate product? You may be suffering from a sense of entitlement, a belief that others should meet your needs rather than earning your own living. Consider the work you do. Are you involved in any devious or underhanded work practices? Are you making good use of your skills and talents? How does your effort at work make you feel about yourself? Are you proud of what you produce through the use of your skills and talents?

People: Those who pretend to know more than they do. Those who feel entitled to live off other people's labor rather than support themselves. Incompetent, lazy, or dishonest workers. Students who cheat on exams. Embezzlers. Con artists. Forgers. Swindlers. Insurance cheats. Income tax evaders. The unemployed. The socially disadvantaged. The disenfranchised.

Eight of Swords

Restriction

Upright: Feeling trapped.

Key Words and Phrases: An oppressive environment. Lack of empowerment. Blockage. Bondage. Forced restraint. A vicious circle. Lack of self-assertion. Isolation. Fear of the unknown. Inhibited energy. Inability to move. Feeling boxed in. Intellectual imprisonment. Caught in a vice. Holding yourself back. Blindfolded. Lacking confidence to proceed. A barrier. Problems with communication. Interference. Disappointment. Trapped by fear. Stuck in a difficult situation. Anxiety. Worry. Censure. Emotional pain. Hard times. Accidents. Deaths. Self-induced unhappiness. Confusion. Misunderstanding. Indecision. Paralysis. Fear of exercising your own power. Reluctance to assert yourself. Lack of faith in yourself. Negative feelings that hinder productivity. Illness. I keep running into a brick wall. Damned if you do and damned if you don't. Do not pass. Don't fence me in. Oh, the Boxes . . . And they're all made out of ticky-tacky and they all look just the same. This too shall pass. When I say 'no' I feel guilty.

Situation and Advice: Anyone who has seen the existentialist play *No Exit* will understand what this card is about. The Eight of Swords represents fear, blockage, limitation, and restriction that are often self-imposed. You feel boxed in, trapped, and unable to move. You may be acting as your own worst enemy because of your fear of the unknown and your reluctance to try something new or to assert yourself. You are stuck in a rut of your own making. Your ability to communicate may be temporarily impaired. You may be caught in a difficult situation from which there appears to be no escape. You feel boxed in and limited by circumstances; but the more important limitations are caused by your own refusal to open your mind to the truth of the situation. You must face your fears before you can make an important decision. With courage you can transcend your anxieties and resolve the problems that surround you. If you can't see things clearly, this is a time to seek wise counsel and heed sound advice. Sometimes the restrictions symbolized by the Eight of Swords are the result of an accident or a death that brings limitations in its wake.

People: Someone who feels trapped, restrained, or caught in a vice. A blind person. Someone in prison. Someone who feels confined by a relationship. One who is going in circles.

○

Eight of Swords Reversed: Release.

Key Words and Phrases: Removal of an obstruction. Unblocking something. A new beginning. Taking off the blindfold. Piercing the veil. Overcoming fear. Freedom from restriction. Breaking free. Relief. Cessation of interference. Free passage. Empowerment. Able to move again. Renewed faith in yourself. Productivity restored. Appropriate self-assertion. You're free to go. I can see my way out of this situation.

Situation and Advice: You are now able to break free of limitations and confront your fears and anxieties. The pressures you face are beginning to subside. You are able to see more clearly what surrounds you and to deal with factors that have been interfering with your progress. Having conquered your fears, you are free to start again. An obstruction is removed and there is free passage. Now is a time to be appropriately assertive and to refuse to accept the restrictions being imposed upon you by others.

People: Someone who has broken free of restraints or escaped from a confining relationship. A released prisoner.

Eight of Cups
A Change of Heart

Upright: Saying goodbye. Moving on.

Key Words and Phrases: Leaving. Walking away. Breaking loose. Going off into uncertainty. Arrivederci. A turning point. Withdrawing. Parting. Feeling disenchanted with a past situation. Disappointment. Leaving the past behind. Breaking away from dependent emotional ties. Turning your back on a difficult situation. Looking inward. Man's search for meaning.

Rejection of an outmoded lifestyle. Directing energies to a new interest. Abandoning previous concerns. Leaving home. Cutting the apron strings. Walking away from a difficult family situation. Searching for a new relationship. The quest for spiritual satisfaction. Leaving emotional matters behind. A job change. A relocation. Sayonara. Searching for the Holy Grail. A month's time.

Situation and Advice: You are leaving an unsatisfactory situation and moving on to something new. For some time you may have been disappointed with a former relationship or circumstance. You have gradually become aware that you are dissatisfied and have had a change of heart. Now you want to break loose and try something different. Perhaps you are seeking to fill a void in your life. It may be time to sever the old emotional ties and become your own person. Often the Eight of Cups suggests that matters will take one lunar cycle (a month's time) to work themselves out. Travel and a change of residence are possibilities.

This is a time to let go because old involvements simply will not work out. Reflect on what you have learned because you are maturing emotionally and it is time to pursue something more satisfying. You seek more meaning in your life. As you walk away from the past, a new relationship awaits you. The old books say that the Eight of Cups means assistance from a blonde woman. Who knows?

People: Seekers. Someone who is departing. One who is leaving an unsatisfactory situation behind. A helpful blonde.

◑

Eight of Cups Reversed: Refusing to move on.

Key Words and Phrases: (+) Feeling fulfilled and satisfied. Sticking with a good situation. Socializing. An enduring relationship. A difficult time is ending. Enjoying yourself. Seeking happiness. Going to a party. A new romance. Flirtation.

Friendship. A celebration. Returning to a former relationship. A month's time.

(–) Refusing to move on. Clinging to the past. Fear of the unknown. A wrong decision. Avoiding personal growth. Trouble making a commitment. Failure to grow beyond outmoded relationships and attachments. Accepting mediocrity. Pursuit of a false ideal. Abandoning a valuable relationship. Fear of intimacy. Turning your back on an important emotional alliance. Making a change you will later regret. The grass is greener on the other side. Don't toss the baby out with the bath water.

Situation and Advice: In its upright position, the Eight of Cups advises you to leave an unsatisfactory emotional situation behind and seek more fulfillment in your life. In its reversed orientation, the Eight of Cups may be telling you either that your current relationships are better than you think or that you are refusing to heed the advice of the upright card. You should appreciate what you've got before casting it aside.

You may be having trouble letting go of an unsatisfactory relationship. Are you about to settle for mediocrity? On the other hand, you may be leaving a perfectly good relationship behind for some neurotic reason of your own. You may not be taking the steps necessary to extricate yourself from a messy situation. It is possible that a change you are contemplating is the wrong move at this time. You may regret leaving your current situation or relationship.

In its positive aspect, the Eight of Cups reversed means you have succeeded in putting a difficult situation behind and are now ready to celebrate a new phase in your life. The reversed Eight of Cups sometimes heralds the start of a new romantic relationship or a change of residence. It can also represent something as concrete as going to a party or accepting a social invitation.

People: Those who toss out the baby with the bath water. A malicious blonde.

Nines

Key Words and Phrases: Nearing the end. The final stage. Attainment. Summing up before the completion of a cycle. Preparation for transition. Dreams. Bringing matters to a close. Creative energy. Compassion. Wisdom. Understanding. Service. Mysticism. Courage. Mastery.

Corresponding Major Arcana Card: The Hermit.

Situation and Advice: The number nine is associated with the Hermit card of the Major Arcana and with the planet Neptune and the signs Aries and Scorpio, which are ruled by Mars. Neptune is a planet of compassion, charity, selflessness, mysticism, understanding, and brotherly love, but also of confusion, fantasy, and self-deception.

The prominence of nines in a spread suggests the completion or ending of matters. You may be letting go of the past to make way for the future. Cars or appliances may break down. Sales are favored. Long-distance travel is possible. Your interests may turn to charitable or humanitarian causes.

Nines represent a yang energy associated with completions and endings. The focus now is on letting go and terminating properly. This is not a time to make binding commitments or to initiate new ventures.

Personal Year: The nine personal year marks the end of a nine-year cycle. It is a time of endings, terminations, and completions. Something is finishing to make way for a new cycle. Sometimes we receive public recognition during a nine personal year. Now is a time to clear the decks as we prepare to make major new changes in the coming one personal year. This is generally not a time to initiate a major commitment or significant new venture.

Nine of Wands
Strength in Reserve

Upright: Stand your ground. Defense.

Key Words and Phrases: Standing up for yourself. Activating one's defenses. Fortification. Guarding oneself. Protecting old wounds. Ability to resist an attack. Standing guard. Territoriality. A final challenge to overcome. Wariness. Protection. A defensive attitude. A strong constitution. The ability to recover from an illness. A healthy immune system. Resistance to illness or infection. Prior conflict. Protecting your rights. An unassailable position. A last stand. Another problem to overcome before victory. Inner strength. Determination. Perseverance. Necessary delay. The final hoop. On guard! It ain't over till it's over. If at first you don't succeed, try and try again. Leave well enough alone. If it's not broken, don't fix it. Don't change horses in mid-stream.

Situation and Advice: The Nine of Wands suggests a need to stand up for yourself. You have been hurt in the past and have therefore assumed a protective posture. You may be called upon to fight for your rights or to defend your reputation or a decision you have made. Although the situation looks demanding, you are on firm ground. Once you overcome this final challenge, you are on the way to success, so don't give up. Now is a time to remain watchful and stand firm for what you believe in. You have the strength in reserve to tackle any problem. This is not a time to make major changes in your position. You might be wise to leave well enough alone. You may need to resolve one final problem before you can achieve success. Your position is strong, and you have the courage and determination to achieve your goals when the time is right. Remember the boy scout motto: "Be prepared!"

In health readings, the Nine of Wands shows a strong constitution, able to recover from illness and to ward off the attack of pathological organisms.

People: A protector. A well-defended person. Military personnel. One who fights for his rights and reputation.

◑

Nine of Wands Reversed: Your defenses are down. Caught off guard.

Key Words and Phrases: Inadequate defenses. Not speaking up for yourself. Loss of rights. Carelessness. A foolish defensive position. Weakness. Cowardice. Illness. Injury. Poor defenses. A weakened immune system. Undermining. Inferiority. Impracticality. Refusal to compromise. Suspicion. Danger. Over-defensiveness. Fear of looking weak or helpless. Feeling overwhelmed. Adversity. Unrealistic plans. Loss. A snag. An obstacle. An impediment. Lack of preparation. An untenable position. Lack of initiative. Failure to defend. Refusal to take a stand. Obstinacy. Inflexibility. A wishy-washy attitude. Loss of tenure. Poor health. An indefensible position. Loss of status. Hitting below the belt. I wasn't looking. Not ready for prime time.

Situation and Advice: You may feel caught off guard by a situation that is out of your league and beyond your capacity to cope. You may have underestimated the strength of your opposition, and the challenges you must meet are harder than anticipated. Someone may be undermining your position and you fear a loss of status as a result. Have you boxed yourself in by adopting a foolish defensive posture? Are you now in an indefensible position? Did you take a stand on an issue not worth fighting for? Are you afraid to assert yourself regarding a matter you believe in? Your defenses appear to be down. Loss or illness is possible. In health readings, a weakened immune system and decreased resistance to disease are suggested.

People: Minor leaguers. Losers. Second string players. Those with an inferiority complex. Patients with poor immunity.

Nine of Pentacles
Self-Reliance

Upright: Relying on oneself. Being self-sufficient.

Key Words and Phrases: Self-mastery. Attainment. Gain. Desire for financial security. Money. Success. Material comfort. Leisure time. Fruitfulness. Cultivation. Self-worth. Well-being. Pleasure. Refinement. Prosperity as a result of past efforts. Solitary affluence. Well-deserved success. Fortunate property and real estate matters. Inheritance. Unearned income. Dividends. Possession. Ownership. Real estate investments. Improvements in land and property. Redecorating. Material security. Added income. Satisfaction. Self-employment. Mastery of one's resources. Self-control. The wise use of talents and resources. Taking good care of yourself. Material benefits. The capacity to be alone. Love of nature. Fondness of animals. Enjoyment of the outdoors. Gardening. Concern for the environment. Solitude. A feeling of incompleteness. Money can't buy you love. A garden of earthly delights. Save the whales. I can take care of myself.

Situation and Advice: This card depicts a woman in solitary enjoyment of the finer things in life as she surveys her luscious garden. She is reaping the benefit of the wise use of her talents and resources. She is alone and at peace with herself and her surroundings. She is in control of her thinking and of her destiny. She has a sense of self-worth and is able to manage her own affairs, but at the same time she may be experiencing a feeling of incompleteness.

The Nine of Pentacles represents the desire for financial security and carries the promise of physical comfort and material benefits. Management of real estate or property will go well. Outdoor activities bring much enjoyment. Plans to remodel or redecorate the home proceed smoothly. Property and real estate matters prosper. Psychologically, this card depicts what psychoanalyst D. W. Winnicott called the "capacity to be alone . . . one of the most important signs of maturity in emotional development." When this card appears in a reading, we should review how we spend our solitary time.

People: A wife. A self-sufficient or self-employed person. Someone concerned about the environment and the protection of other forms of life. A person of grace, beauty, skill, talent, and sound business sense. A wise property manager. Someone who spends much time alone. Animal lovers.

◑

Nine of Pentacles Reversed: Ill-founded success.

Key Words and Phrases: Scant financial yields. Unwise decisions. Dependency. Loss. Deprivation. Wastefulness. Theft. Rash decisions. Foolish actions. Entanglements. Suffering the consequences of poor choices. A guilty conscience. Illicit money. Pollution. Problems with property or real estate. Unexpected repairs. Financial setbacks. Problems with animals or pets. The burdens of wealth.

Situation and Advice: What passes for success is built on shaky foundations that may be about to give way. The crow is about to come home to roost. Beware of shady dealings that may compromise your integrity. There may be problems with property matters. A pet may need your attention.

People: Dishonest people. Those with a guilty conscience. Poor managers.

Nine of Swords
The Nightmare Card

Upright: Despair.

Key Words and Phrases: Sad, sleepless nights. Worry. Extreme stress. Upsetting premonitions. Threats. Guilt. Torment. Anxiety. Pain. Anguish. Depression. Feeling useless or overwhelmed. Demoralization. Brooding. Lack of confidence. Doom and gloom. Mental agony. Misery. Cruelty.

Spite. Slander. Sorrow. Hopelessness. Unhappiness. Crying spells. Accusations. Self-loathing. A guilty conscience. Illness. Surgery. Unfounded fears. A woman in pain. Female health problems. Possibility of a death. Nobody loves me. It's all my fault. I'm no good.

Situation and Advice: The Nine of Swords is the nightmare card. It shows a woman sitting in bed sleepless, holding her head in despair. Your sleep may in fact be disturbed as you struggle with some vexing matter. Someone's spiteful behavior may be causing you pain. You may be plagued by fear, guilt, doubt, and worries that are to a large extent unfounded. You are overly sensitive to criticism and the slights of other people. The difficulties you imagine may not appear so bleak when they see the light of day. Chances are you are dealing with a problematic situation or a difficult decision, but your worst fear is unlikely to materialize. The suffering you feel is the aftermath of previous difficult circumstances. Sometimes this card can literally mean that a woman around you is suffering mentally or physically and may need your assistance.

People: A worried or anxious person. An insomniac. Someone who is ill or facing surgery.

◑

Nine of Swords Reversed: The nightmare is over.

Key Words and Phrases: (+) Hope. Good news. Unfounded worries. Faith. Trust. Promise. A ray of sunshine. Help in the near future. The end of suffering. The period of stress and worry is over. A new dawn. Feeling useful again. Pleasant dreams. There is nothing to worry about. There's light at the end of the tunnel. Time heals all wounds. The nightmare is over.

Tomorrow is another day.

—Scarlett O'Hara

(−) Travail. Anguish. Isolation. Persistent sorrow. Seclusion. Depression. Despondency. Imprisonment. Slander. Spitefulness. Bereavement. Suicide. Death. Confinement. Institutionalization.

Situation and Advice: In its positive aspect, most often the appearance in a spread of the Nine of Swords reversed indicates that the nightmare is ending. You may still be suffering the aftermath of a trying situation, but the pain is mostly over. Your imaginings, however, are far worse than the reality of your situation. You have upset yourself unnecessarily by worrying without sufficient reason. You have let your negative thoughts and brooding run away with you. The Nine of Swords reversed is a hopeful card, counseling faith in the future and the promise of better days ahead.

In an otherwise very negative reading, however, the Nine of Swords reversed may simply reiterate the meaning of the rest of the spread. Your despondency has been prolonged and severe. You are too preoccupied with morbid worries and may be quite depressed. You are traversing a time of prolonged sorrow and despair. Usually, however, the reversed Nine of Swords carries a hopeful meaning.

People: (+) Those who have renewed hope for the future. Those who have been delivered from a nightmarish situation.

(−) Grieving people. The bereaved. Chronic insomniacs.

Nine of Cups
The Wish Card

Upright: Desires fulfilled.

Key Words and Phrases: Enjoyment. Contentment. Pleasure. Gratification. Comforts. Health. Happiness. Plenty. Smugness. Satiety. Satisfaction. Physical pleasure. Material happiness. A job well done. Financial well-being. Indulgence. A dream come true. A desired marriage. You get what you wish for. When you wish upon a star, your dream comes true. Eat, drink, and be merry.

Situation and Advice: When the Nine of Cups appears, especially as an outcome card, you will get what you desire. This card promises material benefits and physical luxury. It is a card of satisfaction and contentment, sometimes even smugness and overindulgence. This appearance of this nine can signal the end of a major phase of a project and the need to take a well-deserved holiday before proceeding. In marriage readings, it means you will marry the person you desire.

People: Those who get their wish. Someone who lives in the lap of luxury. An overly indulgent person. Those who are enjoying themselves. The Fairy Godmother.

◐

Nine of Cups Reversed: Smugness.

Key Words and Phrases: Not getting one's wish. Unrealistic desires. Too much of a good thing. Hedonism. Excessive preoccupation with sensual pleasure. Complacency. Vanity. Self-congratulation. Overindulgence. Extravagance. Superficial values. Greed. Shallowness. Emptiness. Financial loss. Deprivation. Lack of money. Seeking fulfillment from drugs or alcohol. Drug abuse. Gluttony. Abusing one's body. The culture of narcissism. Masturbation. Hedonistic self-centeredness. Superficiality in relationships. Unable to step into the other person's shoes. Lack of charity. Abuse. When you've got it, flaunt it. Mother's little helper. I can't get no satisfaction. We are the hollow men. Eat, drink, and be merry, for tomorrow you may die.

Situation and Advice: You may discover that getting what you wish for is not necessarily good for you. Sometimes this card reversed can indicate a health problem due to overindulgence or abusing your body. You may be feeling too smug and complacent for your own good. You may not get what you want. Greed may be a problem, and a financial loss is possible.

Your excessive preoccupation with gratifying your desires may be harming your personal relationships. Are you using drugs or alcohol to fill a void in your personal life? Is your hedonistic self-centeredness driving away those who love you? Do you close your eyes to the plight of those less fortunate than yourself? Does your value system revolve too much around self-stimulation? Can you care about anyone but yourself? Are you able to step into other people's shoes, especially those who are less fortunate than yourself? How do other people fit into your life?

People: Smug people. Narcissists. Playboys. Playgirls. Hedonists. Sensualists.

Tens

Key Words and Phrases: The finish. The end of a cycle. Completed circumstances. Summation. Completion. Perfection. Permanence. Regeneration. Transformation. Rebirth. A group of people. A family. A community. One too many. Time for a new beginning. The end of one cycle and the start of another. The first shall be last, and the last shall be first. Now you've gone too far.

Corresponding Major Arcana Card: The Wheel of Fortune.

Situation and Advice: The number ten is associated with the Major Arcana card the Wheel of Fortune and with the planet Pluto, which rules Scorpio and the Eighth house. Pluto is the planet of death, birth, and transformation, the cyclic process of growth and decay followed by new growth. Like the Wheel of Fortune card of the Major Arcana, Pluto suggests major life changes brought about by the shifts of fate.

Ten of Wands
The Weight of Ambition

Upright: The burdens of success.

Key Words and Phrases: Carrying a heavy load. Work-related stress. Weighty responsibilities. Determination. Taking on too much. Inability to delegate. Overload. Taking full responsibility. Buried in work. Pressure. Overextension. Loneliness at the top. Hard work. A demanding project.

Heavy responsibilities. Improved status as a result of hard work. Excessive overtime. An onerous burden. Striving for success. Overwork. Worry. Overexertion. Overtaxing oneself. Oppression. Failure to achieve an ambition. Obsessive behavior. The lure of power. All work, no play. Biting off more than you can chew. Romantic maturation. Back strain. Musculoskeletal problems. Slipped discs. Heart problems. If I want it done right, I'll do it myself. He ain't heavy, he's my brother. More than one person can handle alone. You made your bed. Now lie in it. His eyes are bigger than his stomach. The buck stops here.

Situation and Advice: You are struggling now to shoulder your load and meet your many commitments and responsibilities. You may have taken on too many responsibilities and are carrying a heavy load. You are in the final stretch and are wondering if you have enough energy to make it past the goal line.

Despite the oppressiveness of your burden, you do have enough energy to complete the task. Your ambition to succeed and receive acclaim drives you onward. You must, however, realize that you cannot do everything. Learn to delegate responsibility and do not take on more than you can handle. Otherwise, some of your plans will not proceed to completion.

You need to develop a better appreciation of your limits. You may be swamped with work and be feeling the pressure of the load you bear. An excessive focus on career ambitions may be interfering with other aspects of your life. The world will go on turning without you. Overwork can lead to health problems, especially with your back, spine, heart, and musculoskeletal system.

People: An extremely ambitious person. A laborer. Someone who is burdened or overworked. A labor union.

Ten of Wands Reversed: The burden is lifted.

Key Words and Phrases: (+) Relief from stress and pressure. Shifting the load. Delegating wisely.

(–) Misuse of talents. Overweening ambition. Overload. Delays. Failure. Taking on others' responsibilities. Work goes unrewarded. Stuck holding the loot. Mistrust. Unfair burdens. Envy. Deception. Cheating. Running out of steam. Self-imposed obligations. Being led astray. Passing the buck. Wanting excessive control of other people's lives. Stepping on other people's toes. Victimization. Back, heart, and musculoskeletal problems. Much ado about nothing.

Situation and Advice: In its positive aspect, the Ten of Wands reversed signifies the lifting of a heavy load. You are feeling less stress and pressure. You have been able to delegate responsibility wisely to get the job done. Your health is improving now that you have managed your responsibilities more efficiently. You are finally able to put some fun back in your life.

In its negative aspect, the Ten of Wands reversed carries a warning that you will receive little in return for your hard work. Someone may have manipulated you into carrying an unfair share of a burden. The responsibilities you shoulder have felt like a burden for quite some time. Perhaps you don't trust others to do the job right and are afraid to delegate responsibility. You may be suffering the consequences of overweening ambition. Health problems could be the result of physical or emotional overstrain.

People: Someone who causes problems or burdens others.

Ten of Pentacles
Material Abundance

Upright: Family support.

Key Words and Phrases: Strong family ties. Tradition. Comfort. Money. Wealth. Financial security. Success. Security. Stability. A safety net. Generativity. Responsibility. Financial assistance. Sound advice. Accumulation of wealth. Family matters. Ancestral ties. Lineage. Prosperity. A salary increase.

Financial stability. A comfortable home. Happiness. Property. Major purchases or business deals. Good investments. Concern about a parent. Family wealth. Inheritance. Legacies. Pensions. Passing the baton. Inherited abilities. Trusts. Recognition. Reputation. Starting your own family. Major life transitions. Commitment to a traditional way of life. A family occasion like a wedding or birth. Marriage for business or money reasons. An arranged marriage. Corporations. Big businesses. Government work.

Situation and Advice: The Ten of Pentacles depicts several generations of a family enjoying the security of their home. This is a positive card suggesting financial security, inheritance, profitable investments, the passing on of family traditions, major life transitions, the successful sale or transfer of property, the health of family members, and the establishment of firm foundations for family life. Work goes well and a raise in pay is possible. A parental figure, close friend, or family member may assist you. Money from a legacy or pension is possible. You may be in the process of getting married or starting your own family. Marriage may be somehow connected to family requirements or money and business concerns. You wish to bequeath what you value and have learned and earned to future generations. Work involving large corporations or the government is possible.

People: Family members. A dynasty. Wealthy individuals.

◑

Ten of Pentacles Reversed: Family problems.

Key Words and Phrases: Financial loss. Quarrels. Disapproval of family members. Money difficulties. Unstable family finances. Lack of motivation. Worry about an elder. Illness of a parent. The burdens of wealth. Problems with an inheritance. Family fights about money. Domestic problems.

A possible lawsuit. A death in the family. Problems with large corporations or the government. Unsound financial speculation. Restructuring finances.

Situation and Advice: You may feel there is a threat to your security. This is not a time to take a financial risk. You may have an opportunity to increase your income at the expense of job satisfaction or burnout. Money may be tight for a while, and you will probably need to restructure your finances. Perhaps you will need to sell some stocks, a house, or property to make ends meet. You may be concerned about the health or well-being of a parent or older family member. Perhaps a parent is ill and needs medical attention.

You are likely to feel burdened by responsibilities and commitments to those who are close to you. Problems with pensions or legacies could arise. There could be a family fight about an inheritance. You may resent the demands your family is making on your marriage plans or choice of partner. You may feel you were pressured into marriage for the wrong reasons. Unsound financial speculation will lead to losses. There could be problems in dealings with large corporations or with government agencies.

People: Those beset with family problems. Financially burdened individuals.

Ten of Swords

An Irrevocable Ending

Upright: Stabbed in the back. The end of a cycle.

Key Words and Phrases: Ruin. Failure. Defeat. A decisive rupture. A forced change. An emotional cut-off. A decision that alters your life. The death of a matter. Surcease of sorrow. Death of an illusion. A permanent stalemate. Separation. Pain.

Time to let go. Theft. Negative thinking. Distress. Unhappiness. Depression. Loss. Devastation. Bankruptcy. A mugging. Disruption. Hitting bottom. The pits. Disaster. Serious illness. Confronting mortality. A dangerous situation. Collapse. Divorce. Desolation. Hardship. Hazard. A crushing blow. Hitting bottom. Possible travel (maybe over water). Cutting or penetration for medical reasons. Injections. Medical investigations. The only way is up. Unless the grain of wheat falls into the ground and dies, it cannot grow.

Situation and Advice: You have hit bottom. Your plans are not working out. You have reached the outer limits. A situation or relationship is coming to its irrevocable end, and you may be feeling on the threshold of depression because of your loss. You have done all you can and it is time make a definite break or suffer the consequences. This ending is accompanied by a deep sense of loss and sadness. You may be feeling emotionally cut off. Change has been forced upon you and you have little say in the matter. A loss may be related to a legal or career matter, a serious illness, or a separation from an important person in your life. Are you feeling so depressed that you need professional assistance?

Something that has ended may still concern you. You have lost the battle. There is nothing you can do to salvage what is passing out of existence. Just remember that dawn inevitably follows the dark of night. You must let go of a dying circumstance or false beliefs to make way for the future. Like the Tower Trump, the Ten of Swords can indicate sudden clarity of perception and the dispelling of false beliefs. Sometimes travel (especially over water) may be involved in the separation suggested by the Ten of Swords.

People: Those who hit bottom. Those who have suffered a severe loss. Seriously ill persons. Endangered persons.

◐

Ten of Swords Reversed: The worst is over.

Key Words and Phrases: (+) A change for the better. Improvement. Problems abate. The end of a cycle and a new beginning. Emerging from the valley of darkness. Surviving a disastrous situation. The power of prayer. Accepting help from others. Turning to a higher power for assistance. Near death experiences. Overturning a serious threat to life and limb. Light at the end of the tunnel. News about death and dying. An obituary. Return from the dead. The worst is over. Every cloud has a silver lining.

(–) Drastic change. Chronic drawn-out problems. Life-threatening illness. Recurrence of past difficulties. Disruption. Death. The worst is yet to come.

Situation and Advice: You may receive news of a death or a serious illness. Prayer or turning to a higher power can relieve some of the pain you feel. You are emerging from a period of emotional turmoil, hurt, and sadness. The worst is over and your problems are beginning to resolve. Out of your recent pain something of value will emerge. Improvement lies ahead. You or someone close to you will be able to overcome a hazardous situation.

People: Survivors. The long-suffering. Those threatened with death. Those who have had near-death experiences.

Ten of Cups
Joy

Upright: Harmony in personal relationships.

Key Words and Phrases: Lasting happiness in relationships. Tranquillity. Unity. Trust. Rapport. Shared well-being. Giving and receiving love. Good parent-child relationships. Fulfillment. Bliss. Emotional completion. Security. Prosperity. Protection. Contentment. Love. Matrimony. Genuine friendship. Partnership. Compatibility. A joyful family life. Marital bliss. Getting together with friends and family. Serenity. Undying love. Spiritual happiness. Realization of hopes. A happy occasion. A celebration to give thanks.

Situation and Advice: The Ten of Cups is an extremely positive card for matters of love, emotions, values, shared happiness, spiritual growth, and harmonious relationships. It carries a promise of affection, contentment, well-being, and happy family relationships. You may soon attend a happy gathering of friends or family. If you asked about getting married, prospects look good. There may also be a pleasant opportunity for travel.

People: A happy family. A group of friends. Loved ones.

◐

Ten of Cups Reversed: Disrupted joy.

Key Words and Phrases: Disharmony. Marital conflict. Incompatibility. Loss. Sadness. Discontent. Family disagreements. Depression. Pessimism. Arguments. Aggravation. Hurt feelings. A clash of interests. Personality conflicts. Being let down. Loss of friendship. Disrupted family life. Adolescent crisis rocks the family. Impermanence. Adolescent rebellion. An unsettled family routine. Demands made by your children. Delinquent behavior. A celebration canceled. The empty nest.

Situation and Advice: Something happens to disrupt a happy situation, such as a quarrel or clash of interests due to personality conflicts among family or close friends. Teenage children may display adolescent rebelliousness. Someone may make trouble that disrupts the lives of close friends and family. The Ten of Cups reversed may mean a child leaving home, forcing the parents to deal with feelings about an empty nest.

People: A troublemaker. One who does not share in a relationship. A party pooper. A child leaving home. A runaway child. A rebellious teenager. A lonely parent.

෨

Chapter Six

The Court,
Royal, or
Person Cards

The Court, Royal, or Person Cards can represent:
- The people in your life.
- Aspects of your character and personality.
- Your sense of identity and knowledge of yourself.
- The roles you play.
- Events or situations coming into existence.
- Times or seasons of the year.
- Qualities you should cultivate to handle your situation.
- When reversed, they represent shadow aspects of the personality or people who are working against you.

Court or royal cards have two fundamental interpretations. On the one hand, they represent various aspects of yourself that are important in your current situation. On the other hand, Court cards represent other people. They suggest that you are asking about your dealings with others in your life. When many Court cards appear in a reading, there are involvements with many people regarding your question.

Several methods exist to assign the various court cards to particular individuals in the querent's life. One method is to assign astrological signs to each of the four suits, and another method is to assign various cards to individuals according to their age and physical characteristics (see page 24). The physical attributes described in the table should be used only as an approximate guide. In this scheme, Pages represent children, adolescents, and very young adults; Knights represent adults from their early 20s to about 40 years of age, or older adults who are very youthful for their age; Queens and Kings represent mature adults from age 40 on, or younger adults who are very mature for their age.

When a specific sex is attributed to a Court card—a female Queen or a male King, for example—there are a few possible interpretations. One may be that the figure on the card indicates a person of the same sex, such as a Queen representing a strong woman who is influencing the querent. Another may be that the card indicates an aspect of the querent's personality, even if the querent is of the opposite sex. For example, Knights often literally refer to men, but can refer to the role women play that resembles the nature of the Knight (in Jungian terms, a woman's animus, or masculine aspect of her personality). The same holds true for Queens, as men also have Queen-like attributes (in Jungian terms, a man's anima, or feminine aspect of his personality).

~

Pages
Princesses, Knaves, Daughters

Key Words & Phrases: Change. Messages. Messengers. Communication. Important news. Phone Calls. Letters. Information. Friends. Children. Adolescents. Immaturity. Very young men and women (up to their early 20s). Youthful apprentices. Youthful innocence. Flexibility. Movement. An emerging aspect of your personality. Something in the process of formation. New beginnings of situations or enterprises that require attentive nurturing to mature and develop.

Situation and Advice: Pages often refer to the receipt of some form of communication. They suggest a need for more information to make a mature decision and warn against going off half-cocked. Pages frequently appear when you ask a question about a child, and a Page in a reading suggests you may be thinking about a child.

Page of Wands
Esprit de Corps

Upright: Daring action. Vitality. Good news.

Key Words & Phrases: An important and exciting message. Courage. Daring. Optimism. Leadership. Initiative. Extroversion. Being in the limelight. Full steam ahead. Energy. Enthusiasm. Competition. Self-promotion. Vigor. Athletic prowess. Resourcefulness. Creative potential. Inspiration. Faithfulness. Encouragement. Excitement. Quick response. Passion. Sexual arousal. A dynamic event. New ideas. Time to start a creative venture. A message about employment. A message from a friend or relative. An important letter or phone call. An opportunity for new growth. Career change. A new job. Creative writing. The stirrings of creativity. A messenger bearing exhilarating news. Physical exercise. A good sex life. Start spreading the news. This could be the start of something big. Come on, baby, light my fire.

Situation and Advice: Invigorating good news or new opportunities are on the way. Competition is in the air. If you've been waiting for a call to come in for a job interview, it will occur soon. You have much energy, optimism, and enthusiasm at your disposal. You may begin a course of learning. A job or career change is possible. If your question was about romance, expect an ardent and passionate relationship. A love letter may arrive soon. Exhilarating sexual experiences are in the offing. Now is a time to start an exciting new venture. New friendships or romance are possible. You would benefit from some athletic activity at this time.

People: A messenger with exciting news. The bearer of good news. One who promotes optimism and encouragement. Cheerleaders. A courageous, energetic young person. An enterprising youth. An intelligent and restless child. An adolescent. The bearer of good tidings. An ardent young lover. A creative writer. An inspirational or creative person. One who responds quickly and passionately. A stimulating sex partner. Friendly, energetic people. Teachers. Salespersons. Actors. Politicians. Preachers. Inspirational speakers. Coaches. Athletes. Performers.

◐

Page of Wands Reversed: Frazzled. Bad news.

Key Words & Phrases: Upsetting news. Rash communication. A letter of rejection. A curt reply. A quick dismissal. Nay saying. An impulsive decision. A "Dear John" letter. A broken heart. Unwelcome information. Job loss. Feeling exasperated by someone's abrupt treatment of you. Negative attention seeking. Exaggerated self-importance. Acting out. Lack of energy. Discouragement. Obstacles. Indecision. Scattered thinking. Sexual frustration. Unrequited love. Unreliability. Braggadocio. Rumors. Over-dramatization. Arrogance. A troubled sex life. Illness. The 'nays' have it. You're getting on my nerves. Breaking up is hard to do.

Situation and Advice: The reversed Page of Wands symbolizes upsetting news or negative communications. Someone may be making unkind comments about you. A rash or precipitate decision may be causing you consternation. You or someone around you may be acting like a scatterbrained or impetuous child. You may be feeling frazzled or annoyed by someone's curt dismissal of a proposal you would like to discuss more thoroughly. You probably feel you are not being taken seriously.

A downturn in job or career matters is possible, and your own indecision or lack of energy may be the cause. Certain obstacles may be draining your energies. Be cautious with whom you share confidences now because someone may violate your trust and sense of privacy. An undependable, shallow, immature braggart may cause you some difficulty. If your question was about romance, expect to receive unhappy news. Sexual hangups may be interfering with your relationship. If you are an author, your manuscript may be rejected for publication.

People: A prima donna. Someone who breaks your heart. One who craves attention. One who speaks badly of you. An impetuous or insensitive person. Someone who makes precipitate decisions. Someone who tries to dominate you. A showoff. One who cuts corners and can't be trusted. The bearer of bad news. A shallow, undependable, and intrusive person. A busybody. An unreliable, immature braggart. One who can't keep confidences. Someone who is conflicted about sexuality. A scatterbrain.

Page of Pentacles
Studiousness

Upright: A small financial gain. Education.

Key Words & Phrases: A written message. Good news about money and finances. Willingness to learn. Educational opportunities. Attending school. Pursuing an educational degree. An event related to school and education. Slow and steady progress. Patience. Persistence. Thrift. Duty. Realism. Frugality. Kindness. Determination. Respect for material things. Love of nature. Educational opportunities. Eagerness for learning. The beginnings of a solid foundation. Patient development. Open-mindedness. Realistic goals. Well-researched information. Formal study. Learning material values. Skill at detailed work. Technical know-how. Starting a new business enterprise. Methodology. Opportunity to increase income. Beneficial change. Apprenticeship. Scholarship. Detailed paperwork. A message containing useful and practical information. Homework. Documents. Books. Journals. Contracts. Negotiations. News about children.

Situation and Advice: You may soon be presented with an opportunity to make money or engage in a new business venture. Be sure to do your homework so you can be in a position of advantage. Your scholarship will be recognized. Your thoroughness, practicality, and hard work will pay off. From small beginnings, progress will be slow but sure. You may receive a letter or a note that will affect the course of events. If you are about to sign a contract, read all the fine print. Be careful and diligent with any written communications. You could become involved in some kind of research involving close attention to detail and lots of paperwork. Education can benefit you at this time. Pentacles indicate a need to care for physical and material needs.

People: A quiet, reflective and conscientious youth. An open-minded person. Students. Scholars. Those who value the good things in life. One who is willing to learn. A bookworm. An introvert. A reliable friend. Someone you can count on. A hard worker. A practical, dutiful, and sensible person. Someone who is diligent and kind. A lover of nature. A serious student. A researcher. A plodder. A youth who takes learning and material achievements seriously. A secretary. A scribe. A diligent and dutiful youth. Someone involved in commerce. A wheeler-dealer.

◑

Page of Pentacles Reversed: Rebel without a cause.

Key Words & Phrases: An unexpected expense. Bad news. Red tape. A disturbing letter. Delays in negotiations. Mediocrity. Carelessness. Ingratitude. An adverse fiscal report. Money problems. Difficulties with a contract. Closed mindedness. Being illogical. Monotony. Boredom. Ignorance. Rebelliousness. Lack of common sense. Repeating past mistakes. Shoddy research. Superficial knowledge. Materialism. Wastefulness. Extravagance. Moodiness. Laziness. Self-pity. Resentment. Lack of appreciation. Wastefulness. Prodigality. Pettiness. Obstructionism. Selfishness. Jealousy. Ignoring useful information. Self-criticism. Preoccupation with details or technicalities. Ponderous bureaucracy. Excessive conformity. Bad news about a child. Learning disabilities. School problems. Lack of education. A poor choice about an educational matter. A miscarriage. An illness. Can't see the forest for the trees. Take your nose out of the book.

Situation and Advice: You may experience difficulties as a result of not reading the fine print carefully enough. There may be problems with red tape or delays in contract negotiations. Unfavorable financial news is a possibility. Now is a time to use your native intelligence and common sense to avoid repeating past mistakes. Be sure to investigate matters thoroughly rather than relying on superficial knowledge. You might receive an upsetting letter or phone call. Doing too much of your own thing may cause problems. You may fail to see the big picture because of plodding attention to details. A minor health problem is possible.

People: A problem child. A youth with learning disabilities. An unrealistic person. An ingrate. A resentful, jealous, obstructive person. A narrow-minded, selfish technocrat. A petty bureaucrat. Moody young people. Those who have only superficial knowledge. Someone overly fond of luxury. Someone who does not appreciate you. Obsessive-compulsive personalities. Prodigal youths. An ill child. Those who reject or rebel against good advice.

Page of Swords
Quick Thinking

Upright: Decisiveness. Unexpected or upsetting news.

Key Words & Phrases: Strong will. Keen intellect. Penetrating insight. Exciting changes. Forceful or blunt communication. Curiosity. Mental stimulation. Travel. Significant information. Logic. Fairness. Resoluteness. Discretion. Circumspection. Constructive criticism. Spying. Diplomacy.

Good business sense. Dexterity. Agility. Adaptability. Ability to deal with delicate matters. Defensiveness. Delayed plans. A phone call. A message. An important document. A contract or agreement. A legal summons. Professional advice. The beginnings of abstract thought. News about conflict, illness, or strife. Upsetting news. A message heralding change. Say it like it is. Call a spade a spade. He who hesitates is lost.

Situation and Advice: In its positive aspect, you may find yourself in a situation where discretion, quick analysis, and decisiveness are of the essence. Your dispassionate rationality may save the day. You may need to call on a professional advisor for important information to assist you in making a decision. Weigh matters carefully before signing any contract or agreement. Know what you are committing yourself to and what the future ramifications of your current decisions are. The danger is that you may have too many irons in the fire and may leave important initiatives unfinished.

In its negative aspect, you may find yourself in a situation where gossip or rumors play a significant role. Someone may be spreading malicious stories about you, or you may find yourself the object of a blunt verbal assault. The behavior of a young person may upset you. Upsetting news may be on the way. Your plans may be delayed. You may not fully understand the implications of a contract you are about to sign. A young person may cause you aggravation and strife. Someone whom you thought was a friend may not turn out to be so.

People: A spy. A precocious youth. A clever child. Someone who is bright and energetic. A negotiator. A mediator. One who is able to resolve disputes rationally and dispassionately. A defensive person. One who is mentally quick and subtle. One who is furtive, calculating, and unconcerned about the feelings of others. A diplomatic youth. A professional advisor. Those who are both mentally and physically dexterous. Communicators. Scientists. Mathematicians. Linguists. Aviators. Travelers.

●

Page of Swords Reversed: Malice. Hypocrisy. Upsetting news.

Key Words & Phrases: Gossip. Verbal attack. Suspicion. Cunning. Spying. Intrusiveness. Blackmail. Problems. Poor health. A minor illness. Deceit. Misunderstandings. Half-heartedness. Sarcasm. Cynicism. A sharp tongue. A grievance. A legal summons. Backbiting. Cruelty. Belligerence. Nastiness. A forked tongue. Unexpected behavior. Unpredictability. Bad news. Unanticipated events which force a shift of plans. Voyeurism.

Situation and Advice: Someone may be using underhanded methods to gain or spread information. A malicious person may be spying on or working against you. Unexpected problems may surface. You may receive a promise that will be broken later. Read all the fine print before signing any agreements. Misunderstandings are likely. Consider President George Bush's statement made in the face of a staggering budget deficit: "Read my lips; no new taxes." Did he really mean no new taxes?

People: A two-faced gossip. A shady character. Someone who is unconcerned with the feelings of others. One who is cold and calculating. A hypocrite. A blackmailer. A malicious person who spreads rumors. A ruthless or untrustworthy person. A juvenile delinquent. An aggressive child. A clever youth. Someone who feels sick. A youth who acts unpredictably. A spy. Someone who is underhanded or undercover. A furtive, cunning person.

Page of Cups
Birth of New Emotions

Upright: The beginning of friendship. An invitation.

Key Words & Phrases: Increased emotional sensitivity. A social invitation. Love. Warmth. Attraction. Comfort. Kindness. The beginning of creativity. A discussion about feelings. Tender emotions. A new phase in a relationship. Creative imagination. Quiet study. Intuition. Imagination. Inspiration. Introversion. Psychic ability. Friendliness. Thoughtfulness. Inspiration from a friend. News about a happy emotional event like a birth or a wedding. A love letter.

New feelings. A new stage of emotional development. The emergence of hidden talents. Artistic ability. A fresh plan. Esthetic sensibility. A good idea. An important message. News about a birth or marriage. Starting a new project. Contact with a friend. Fondness for working in solitude. Teaching. Training. Education. A child. Children. A homosexual person.

Situation and Advice: You may soon hear about the birth of a child, wedding plans, engagement, or other happy emotional news. You are entering a period of new feelings and attitudes, a time of emotional rebirth. You may be renewing an emotional tie or starting a new relationship. You are entering a new phase of emotional growth that requires learning to trust all over again. A thoughtful, sensitive young person may surprise you with good news. You are entering a period of new emotional development, sensitivity, and maturity. If you are starting a new job, it may involve careful attention to emotional issues. A child or children may figure importantly in your current or future life. The Page of Cups may also represent a homosexual person who will influence the situation.

People: An affectionate child. A gentle, artistic youth. A homosexual person. Someone who helps or comforts you. An artist. A poet. A teacher. An educator. A friendly, helpful person. A sensitive, thoughtful, introverted, cooperative, quiet, dreamy, imaginative, psychic, emotional, or dependent youth. One who meditates. A mascot. A gentle, loving, non-aggressive, passive youth. A student. A trainer. One who studies and learns in solitude. Someone interested in learning about emotional issues. A young friend.

◑

Page of Cups Reversed: Frivolousness. A spoiled child.

Key Words & Phrases: Emotional immaturity. Insecurity. Unhappiness. Living in a world of fantasy. Daydreaming. Escapism. Isolation. Shallowness. Whimsicality. Laziness. Dropping out. Irresponsibility. Promiscuity. Lack of common sense. Muddled thinking. Deception revealed. Flirtatiousness.

Failure to plan for the future. Discomfort. Lethargy. An unhappy child. Throwing the baby out with the bath water. A fading relationship. Diminished social interactions. Drug or alcohol problems.

Situation and Advice: You may be concerned about a child's emotional well-being. Perhaps you are witnessing the consequences of spoiling your child or being a spoiled child yourself. Your capriciousness, lack of discipline, laziness, or lack of dedication may be causing difficulties. For some reason you are not living up to your potential or making use of your talents. Your cavalier attitude may be a problem. You may be wasting time and energy on pipe dreams and living in a world of unreality. Sometimes this card warns of escapism through drugs or alcohol. A relationship may be ending or fading away, or there may be a definite decrease in your social activities. You may be ignoring important flashes of intuition.

People: A spoiled child. A drug addict or alcoholic. Someone who lives in a fantasy world. A dreamer. A visionary. A scatterbrain. A muddled thinker. A frivolous, immature youth. A fair weather friend. An unhappy child. A poor student. A dropout. Someone who does not plan for tomorrow. An emotionally disturbed youth. A child of divorce. Those who spread malicious gossip to avenge their hurt feelings. Lazy, selfish people.

~

Knights
Princes, Sons

General Key Words & Phrases: A matter of consequence about to happen. New people and experiences entering your life. The coming or going of matters. Restlessness. Energy. Strength. Constructive force. Courage. Changeability. Movement. Drive. Action. Haste. Readiness for battle. Energetic young people. Mature adolescents. Young men from late teens through mid-thirties. Active male figures. Champions. Seekers. A knight in shining armor. The quest for knowledge. Situations involving schools, colleges, or universities.

Knight of Wands
Escape from Difficulty

Upright: Change is in the air. Creative energy.

Key Words & Phrases: An important event related to an enterprise. New people. New ideas and experiences. Impetuousness. Not wanting to settle down. An important visitor. A business trip. Perpetual motion. Change of environment. Departure from custom. Quick decisions. Swift action. Haste. Adventure. Challenge. Ambition. Charisma. Energy. Love of fun. Sense of humor. Enthusiasm. Optimism. Excitement. Generosity. Love of sports. Athletic activities.

Confidence. Vision. Perspective. An abrupt departure. Relocation. Flight. Movement. Getting away. Travel over water. A journey. A new job. A vacation. Sexual adventures.

Situation and Advice: Change is in the air. A matter of considerable importance is emerging in your life. You may be about to move or embark on a creative project or a long journey, possibly related to business. Your motive may be to get away from an oppressive person or circumstance. You are entering or leaving a significant situation. An important person from afar may play a role in your life now. Perhaps you are changing jobs or residences. Your confidence and enthusiasm may help you achieve an important goal. Someone may present you with helpful business ideas. If you are about to go on vacation, you will have a pleasant holiday. Romantic relationships blossom with the promise of an exciting sex life. You are full of energy and enthusiasm.

People: Travelers. Negotiators. Debaters. Movers. Competitors. Individualists. Active, ardent, energetic people. Those who enjoy being alive. An impetuous young man who acts quickly and decisively. One who does not want to settle down. Someone involved in new projects. Someone with a good sense of humor. A person of haste. Fun-loving people who have trouble committing themselves as they are given to many interests and distractions. Sportsmen. Those who love a challenge. An exhilarating lover. The hare (of the tortoise and the hare).

◑

Knight of Wands Reversed: Impatience.

Key Words & Phrases: Egotism. Indecision. Instability. Opportunism. Lack of follow-through. Stress. Rapid change. Disruption. Procrastination. Foolish haste. Unreliability. Bossiness. Argumentativeness. Violence. Dissipation.

Aimlessness. Recklessness. Jogging in place. Disputes. Lack of energy. Despondency. Frustration. Jealousy. Promiscuity. Fickleness. One-night stands. Fluctuating employment. A journey delayed. Problems with a move or relocation. Slam, bam, thank you, ma'am. Love 'em and leave 'em.

Situation and Advice: Your haste and lack of follow-through may be causing problems. There may be instability regarding your employment or other projects. You may be feeling stressed out by the rapid changes in your life. Irresponsible, pushy, domineering, argumentative, or rash behavior will only alienate those around you and make matters worse. If you asked about a relationship, your prospective partner may have problems with commitment and be interested only in sexual novelty.

People: A liar. An opportunist. One who blows with the wind. A charming but untrustworthy person. An argumentative young person. A lover of conflict. A bigot. A promiscuous person. One who promises much but does not deliver. Unreliable, irresponsible persons. Vagabonds. Gigolos.

Knight of Pentacles
Slow, Steady Progress

Upright: Tangible progress.

Key Words & Phrases: An important event related to
material concerns. New people. New experiences. Common
sense. Improved finances. Business travel. A sensible course
of action. Diligence. Dependability. Patience. Perseverance.
Conservative measures. Unexpected sources of money or
income. Industriousness. Practicality. Conventionality. Wise

discrimination. Thoroughness. Reliability. Security. Practical know-how. Methodical work. Attention to detail. Caution. Calmness. Kindness. Faithfulness. Seriousness. Loyalty. Thoughtfulness. Consideration. Trustworthiness. Service. Work orientation. Simplicity of character. Love of animals and nature. A hard worker. Careful planning pays off. Enjoyment of simple pleasures. Propagation. My word is as good as gold. Slow but sure. Time heals all wounds. You can't be too careful. Good fences make good neighbors.

Situation and Advice: Chances are you consulted the cards about issues related to employment, property matters, or financial security. You may be on the verge of a new or unexpected source of prosperity. Money may come in from many sources. A long-standing venture will reach a positive outcome. Slow and steady progress assures success. Your diligent, hard work pays off. A loyal friend may come to your aid, or you may render service to others. You may travel in connection with business. Property and real estate matters go well. If your question was about starting a family, the Knight of Pentacles shows the desire and ability to propagate. If it represents an aspect of your personality, you may be more interested in tangible results than in the feelings of others. If you asked about romance, you can expect a steady, secure relationship with a faithful lover.

People: Sensible, conscientious, dependable people. Accountants. Money managers. Tradespersons. Craftspersons. Mechanics. Those who work in industry. Machinists. Engineers. Mathematicians. Business travelers. Land owners, managers, or developers. An easygoing, diligent person. Those who are good with their hands. Reliable, patient, conventional, trustworthy, hard-working people. A serious, methodical person. Someone who is work-oriented and unaware of the feelings of others. A loyal friend. Someone who perseveres to reach a goal. A lover of nature and animals. A veterinarian. Someone fond of children. Someone lacking imagination. Farmers. Lovers of the outdoors. Kind and faithful lovers. The tortoise (of the tortoise and the hare).

◐

Knight of Pentacles Reversed: Financial instability.

Key Words & Phrases: Greed. Money problems. Delays in business. Dishonest monetary dealings. Being underpaid. An impasse. Dullness. Plodding. Lack of inspiration. Indolence. Idleness. Stodginess. Tedium. Carelessness. Meanness. Irresponsibility. Wastefulness. Avarice. Lack of planning. Staleness. Lack of progress. Haste. Stagnation. Obstacles. Impatience. Scattered energies. Depression. Dissatisfaction. Apathy. Weakness. Complacency. Timidity. Excessive conservatism. Inertia. Refusal to take sensible risks. Unethical financial dealings. Get a life.

Situation and Advice: You are feeling uninspired and have reached some sort of impasse. Perhaps you are being too conservative or sticking to outworn methods that are no longer effective. If your question was about finances, money matters are currently encumbered. Perhaps you are being underpaid or are asking too little compensation for all the work you are doing. You are likely to be finding romance dull and lifeless. Your apathy and depression are preventing you from enjoying life.

People: Plodders. Dull, dim-witted people. Wastrels. Bums. Those engaged in dishonest financial transactions. Those who live off the hard work of others or refuse to work at all. An irresponsible person who may involve you in bad debts. Someone who is too hasty and makes mistakes. A greedy, mean, rapacious person. A diffident, uninspired, complacent person.

Knight of Swords
Rapid Comings and Goings

Upright: Forthrightness. Sudden changes.

Key Words & Phrases: An unexpected situation. An important event related to a matter of intellect or conflict. New people. New experiences. Swift or impulsive action. Quick solutions. Mental stimulation. Leadership. Ambition. Confidence. Fearlessness. Assertiveness. Aggressiveness.

Decisive action. Persuasiveness. New ideas. Force of intellect. Mental challenges. Professional advice. Analytical problem-solving ability. Restlessness. Diversity. Versatility. Mercurial energy. Communication. Strength. Use of force. Gallantry. Virility. Single-mindedness. Resoluteness. Protection during difficult times.

Situation and Advice: You may enter a conflictual situation with frenzy and excitement, only to have it pass quickly and chaotically out of your life. Expect to be active and on the go. Swords often herald a period of struggle or competition in which you need to take quick and firm action. A strong, assertive, and gallant youth may come to your defense. If you put your mind to it, you are capable of steadfast commitment toward a goal. Now is a time to follow your head rather than your heart. Be strong and decisive, and approach situations with a steel-trap mind. Sound professional advice can spell the difference between success and failure. Swords have difficulty with emotions and do not bode well for romantic relationships. The Knight of Swords also warns against impulsive or rash behavior.

People: A champion. A leader. A strong, assertive, and decisive person. One who gets what he or she wants. A professional advisor. A clever young man. Lawyers. Those involved in law enforcement. Engineers. Communicators. Those involved in intellectual occupations. Economists. Those with technological expertise. An overbearing, aggressive, domineering, and impatient person. A strong, dependable, helpful, and gallant youth. An intellectual. Someone who involves you in a conflict. Those who are bright and successful in business but also somewhat ruthless or selfish in pursuing their goals. A self-absorbed and insensitive young person. Clever, sprightly persons. Someone who is more at home with thoughts than feelings.

○

Knight of Swords Reversed: Trouble. A quick exit.

Key Words & Phrases: Upset. Harsh words. Cruel behavior. Conceit. Braggadocio. Injustice. Bad judgment. Impulsivity. Excessive haste. Rash actions. A sudden disappearance. A precipitous departure. Prejudice. Quarrels. Selfishness. Impatience. Bad advice. Rashness. Pushiness. Bossiness. Bigotry. Meanness. Confrontation. Disagreement. Too rapid a pace. Scattered thinking. Chaotic behavior. Lack of focus. Unsolicited and unhelpful counsel. Extravagance. Sarcasm. Slyness. Deceit. Belligerence. Excessive force. Bullying. Violence. Subterfuge. Time to lay low. When the going gets tough, I get going. Trying to catch flies with vinegar rather than honey.

Situation and Advice: This is not the time to initiate a new project. Someone may be actively opposing or upsetting your plans. Sarcastic words only serve to alienate those around you. Without warning a person or situation may suddenly depart from your life. A significant man in your life may make an unanticipated exit. Your own thinking may be scattered and lacking focus. You need to cultivate patience or you may end up in a quarrel. Avoid harsh words and impulsive decisions. Someone may be trying to bully you for selfish reasons, or your own dictatorial behavior may be causing problems.

People: A bossy person. A bigot. A dictator. One who thinks only of oneself with no regard for others. A man who makes a quick exit. A troublemaker. An aggressive young man. An unbalanced, immature person. An enemy. A bully. A gossip. Someone who opposes and upsets your plans. A know-it-all. A stubborn, belligerent, disrespectful, and cocky young man. A sly, stealthy person. A scatterbrain. A violent person.

Knight of Cups
New Relationships

Upright: Romance. Artistic talent.

Key Words & Phrases: An important event related to relationships and emotional concerns. New experiences. A social invitation. A holiday with friends. A proposal. An offer. A new opportunity. A new love. Seduction. Imagination. Sensitivity. Art. Music. Dance. Dreams. Intuition. Kindness. Empathy.

Sympathy. Following your dream. Rose-colored glasses. Caring for those less fortunate. Moodiness. Narcissism. A tempting offer. Utopian idealism. A marriage proposal. To dream the impossible dream. Follow your bliss.

Situation and Advice: You may meet someone new with whom you fall in love or who introduces you to a new emotional experience. Someone may present you with an offer that is hard to resist. You may find yourself taking a holiday with friends. An invitation or an opportunity for a new relationship may be in the near future. Be sure of how you feel to avoid being easily led by others. Your greatest assets at this time are your gentleness, sensitivity, and idealism.

People: Romantic young men. Idealists. Dreamers. Champions of the underdog. Lovers. Refined, artistic, intuitive people. Dancers. Musicians. Artists. Psychics. Psychologists. Therapists. Counselors. Salespersons. A passive person who is easily influenced by others. Emotionally oriented people. A romantic person who brings love into your life. A paramour. A seducer. A tempter. Your ideal man or woman. An amiable, intelligent young man full of new ideas and proposals. Romeo and Juliet.

Knight of Cups Reversed: The Tricky Dick Card.

Key Words & Phrases: Untrustworthiness. Illusion. Escapism. Lies. Half-truths. Trickery. Irresponsibility. Embellished stories. Fantasy. Deception. Manipulation. Seduction. Fraud. Weakness. Embezzlement. Immaturity. Insincerity. Flattery. Obsequiousness. Vagueness. Fickleness. Fear of commitment. Inconsistency. Passivity. Spinelessness. Excessive narcissism. Passive-aggressive traits. Instability. Not telling the whole truth. Lack of realism. Things are not what they seem.

Situation and Advice: You may receive an offer that seems too good to be true. Someone is probably lying to you. Check the details carefully and read all the fine print or you could regret your decision. Avoid being too passive and easily influenced by others. You are in danger of being misled. Get sound advice from an impartial third party. A loved one may disagree with you. Beware of being hoodwinked and bamboozled.

People: Weaklings. Sycophants (brown-nosers). A lover who cheats on you. A swindler. Someone who misleads you by being deliberately vague or not telling the whole truth. A habitual liar. Someone who is immature and lazy. A hopeless romantic. A narcissistic, passive-aggressive individual. One who lacks self-confidence and takes no responsibility for his or her actions. Someone with a fragile sense of identity and poor personal boundaries. An obsequious (fawning) person.

∼

Queens
Mothers

Key Words & Phrases: Queens stand both for women who are actual people in your life and for different aspects of your personality. They are mother figures and often symbolize mature women with some kind of authority or personal power. Queens can also represent men who share the character traits demonstrated by the queens, e.g., creativity, love of nature, caring, fondness for children, et cetera. They are less likely than Pages and Knights to represent situations. Queens can also represent a new level of understanding or awareness. Several Queens in a reading may signify meetings or gatherings of many women.

Queen of Wands
Career Woman

Upright: Balanced family and career interests.

Key Words & Phrases: Queen of hearth and home. *Joie de vivre* (love of life). Majesty. Rulership. Ambition. Center of attention. Social position. Popularity. Fondness for sex. Self-assertion. Demonstrativeness. Competence. Leadership ability. Good business sense. Versatility. Tirelessness. Passion.

Warmth. Vivacity. Courage. Enterprise. Confidence. Foresight. An attractive, magnetic, mature woman. Success of an enterprise. Love of home. Independence of thought. Generosity. Love of nature. The power of positive thinking.

Situation and Advice: An attractive, sensible woman may have good advice to offer. The energy, independence of thought, kindness, and generosity of the Queen of Wands promises a successful outcome to any venture she initiates. She is a career-minded woman with a head for business who can also be the life of the party. This extroverted Queen enjoys healthy and spirited competition. Her competent, assertive air wins others over to her cause.

People: Enterprising women. Career-minded women. A business associate. A socially well-positioned single woman. A female boss or supervisor. A sensible, mature, helpful woman. A woman in command. A protectress who fiercely defends her interests and those of her friends. A vibrant, energetic, fun-loving, and assertive woman. An entrepreneur. A woman involved in many projects. A devoted wife and mother. A married woman of high energy and enthusiasm who successfully runs her home and also pursues outside interests. A helpful friend who is well liked. An outspoken, witty, but sometimes caustic and aggressive woman who champions her supporters. A kind, loyal, generous, confident, competitive woman who enjoys enterprise and the limelight and also values her home and family life. A country woman.

◑

Queen of Wands Reversed: The shadow side of the feminine.

Key Words & Phrases: Egotism. Narrow-mindedness. Unbridled ambition. Jealousy. Demandingness. Ruthless competition. Deception. Envy. Moodiness. Manipulation.

Seduction. Lies. Strictness. Domination. Disorganization. Infidelity. Untrustworthiness. Bitterness. Self-centeredness. Emotional blackmail. Interference. Paranoia. Irritability. Hatred of male authority. Neuroticism. Feminism gone awry. Penis envy. The end justifies the means.

Situation and Advice: A neurotic and rigidly inflexible woman may interfere with your plans by insisting on getting her own way. This ruthlessly ambitious woman will use any means at her disposal to get what she wants. You or someone close to you may be resorting to emotional blackmail to block another's efforts at independence. Beware of sticking your nose where it doesn't belong. Don't try to impose your values on everyone around you.

People: An unyielding, temperamental woman who demands her own way and can't get beyond her neurotic hangups. Those who are exceedingly businesslike. A woman who is domineering, bitter, strict, and possibly unfaithful. Someone who interferes in others' affairs. A busybody. A poor listener. Those who are always right even when they're wrong. Prudish, moralistic persons who try to impose their values on others.

Queen of Pentacles
Practical Manager

Upright: A sensible approach.

Key Words & Phrases: Organization. Fertility. Prosperity. Sensuality. Love of nature. Hospitality. Shrewdness. Abundance. Ownership. Fondness of luxury. Responsibility. Resourcefulness. Good business sense. Steady employment. The good things in life. Security. Creativity. Wealth. Common sense. Confidence. Nurturance. Emotional maturity. Solid learning. Firm foundations. A green thumb. A beautiful home or environment. Taking care of one's physical and emotional needs. Good money management. The garden of earthly delights.

Situation and Advice: This card signals success in business and financial matters. A sensible, practical approach brings steady progress. The Queen of Pentacles can indicate fertility or a pregnancy. It is a card of material abundance and sensual delights. You may have dealings with a shrewd businesswoman, or you may apply practical, conservative measures to your own affairs.

People: A businesswoman. A good organizer. A voluptuous woman. A shrewd, talented, creative woman of wealth. A patron of the arts. Someone fond of the good things in life. A practical woman with business acumen. A sensible money manager. A maternal, nurturing, down-to-earth person. Someone concerned with the welfare of others. A capable woman who is both a mother and businesswoman. A steadfast, sensuous woman who enjoys luxury and has a good sense of material values. One who works hard for material success. A helpful friend. A team player. A benefactress. A philanthropist. A provider. A woman who likes to display her wealth.

◑

Queen of Pentacles Reversed: Greed.

Key Words & Phrases: Brooding. Irresponsibility. Lack of common sense. Stagnation. Vacillation. Distrust. Suspicion. Selfishness. Narrow-mindedness. A sense of entitlement. Conspicuous consumption. Gluttony. Money problems. Pretentiousness. Self-aggrandizement. Putting on airs. Rapacity. Fiscal recklessness. Laziness. Dependency. Fear of

failure. Insecurity. Instability. Fears. Self-doubt. Lack of motivation. Sexual frustration. Wastefulness. Poor money management. Boastful showiness. Overindulgence.

Situation and Advice: A pretentious, unhappy woman may
be causing problems. You or someone around you may be
overly concerned with outward appearances instead of with
what is truly valuable. Greed or fiscal irresponsibility may be
causing difficulties. Perhaps you do not have enough money
to achieve your goal. Your own fears and self-doubts can lead
to a sense of insecurity that hinders your progress. To modify
John F. Kennedy's famous quote, you may be asking not what
you can do for your country, rather you may be focusing on
what your country can do for you.

People: A stingy or petty woman. An insecure, unstable
woman. A fearful person. A glutton. Someone who takes but
gives little in return. A moody, depressed woman. Someone
who is lazy, suspicious, distrustful, lacks motivation, feels
insecure, and neglects her responsibilities. A wastrel. An
extravagant person. Someone with no common sense. A
grasping, rapacious person. Someone with a great sense of
entitlement. Name droppers. Status seekers. Gold diggers. An
ostentatious woman who flaunts her wealth with little concern for the suffering of others.

Queen of Swords
Intelligent and Solitary

Queen of Swords

Upright: A woman alone. Head over heart.

Key Words & Phrases: Strong will. Sharp wit. Sarcasm. Autonomy. Ambition. Keen intellect. Analytical ability. Aloofness. Thought dominates feelings. Perceptiveness. Keen insight. Fair judgment. Right decisions. Communication. Teaching. Professional advice. Independence. A steel-trap mind. Determination. Career-mindedness. Good counsel. Diplomacy. Craft. Helpful assistance. Standing up for yourself. Widowhood. Being alone. I wasn't born yesterday.

Situation and Advice: This is a card of "going it alone." Autonomy, aloofness, and independence are key themes. Now is the time to stand up for yourself and be clear about your wants and needs. You have learned to be independent during periods of loneliness. Your keen intellect and sense of fairness have put you in good stead. You are far more interested in career and ambitions than in emotional matters. Your keen sense of discrimination helps you to separate the wheat from the chaff. You may have dealings with a woman who has known sorrow. If you asked about romance, the prospects are bleak at this time. This card warns that your emphasis on cool, rational thought has strangled your emotional expression.

People: A distant, uninvolved parent. A woman who has known sorrow and who now remains aloof. A cool, calm, and collected individual. One who has suffered loss or hardship. An intelligent, witty, analytical woman. A professional woman who can fight on your behalf. A female advisor (doctor, lawyer, et cetera). A female college professor. A woman involved in a technical career. An educator. A journalist. A judge. A divorced, widowed, or separated woman. A woman without children. A woman who has suffered yet remains strong and courageous. An aloof, intellectual woman who manipulates situations to her advantage. A strong-willed, ambitious, but cold woman. An idealistic, progressive, humanitarian woman. One who highly values prestige and success. A career-minded woman who has little interest in developing her love life.

◐

Queen of Swords Reversed: A real bitch.

Key Words & Phrases: Misuse of speech or intellect. Disregard of law. Misinformation. Sarcasm. Browbeating. Intolerance. Bigotry. Complaining. Betrayal. Retaliation. Manipulation. Resentment. Emotional blackmail. Unreliability. Rigidity. Unscrupulousness. Pettiness. Lack of perspective. Excessive intellectuality. Narrow-mindedness. Gossip. Malicious lies. Bias. Prejudice. Deceit. Cunning. Rumors. Bad news. Vindictiveness. Bitterness. Loss. Coldness. Untruthfulness. Grief. Misery. Whining. Loneliness. It's my way or the highway. Misery loves company. Mirror, mirror on the wall, who's the fairest one of all?

> Heaven has no rage like love to hatred turned, nor hell a fury like a woman scorned.
>
> —William Congreve, *The Mourning Bride* (1697)

Situation and Advice: A domineering, vindictive woman may be secretly trying to discredit you and thus prevent you from obtaining a position you desire. You must not allow hard times to leave you feeling embittered and devoid of tender emotions. Someone with little regard for your rights or feelings may try to force you to do things his or her way. Perhaps you are feeling the wrath of a woman you slighted or treated unfairly.

People: An angry woman who feels she was treated unfairly. A spiteful gossip. A sly, vindictive, underhanded, manipulative woman who (often secretly) opposes you. Someone who is hostile and embittered as a result of hardship or emotional losses. A biased woman, prone to spreading rumors and breaking confidences. One who puts people down and can't be trusted. Someone who twists the facts to her advantage. One who feels above the law. A clever, verbally skillful, secret enemy.

Queen of Cups
A Caring Woman

Upright: Deep feeling. Nurturing.

Key Words & Phrases: Queen of emotions. Sensitivity. Otherworldliness. Intuition. Perception. A choice based on sincere feelings. Imagination. Remembrances. Visions. Dreams. Kindness. Psychic ability. Empathy. The sixth sense. Sympathy. Affection. Reserve. Introspection. Artistic creativity. Gentleness. Emotions. Mystery. Occult interests. Prophecy. Divination. Mysticism. Psychology. Counseling. Atmosphere.

Love of music and art. Generous. Fondness for home and family. A loving friend. The stirrings of the heart.

Situation and Advice: The Queen of Cups suggests an opportunity to turn inward to examine your feelings about a matter. Your hunches and intuitions are reliable guides. Pay special attention to dreams and psychic perceptions. A loving friend may come to your assistance, or you may have the opportunity to show someone how much you care. Your mother or a mother substitute may play a significant role in near future events.

People: One's mother. One who feels deeply. One who understands his or her own feelings. An artistic, emotional, imaginative, visionary, empathetic, caring woman. A devoted wife and mother. A nurse. A helper. A good listener. A social worker. A helpful, understanding, caring woman. A lover of animals. A woman capable of mysticism or prophesy. A woman deeply involved in her inner world and in the realm of fantasy. A woman of intuition and keen perception. An intensely emotional, passionate and loyal woman. Cups always represent people who may be too easily influenced by others.

◗

Queen of Cups Reversed: A fickle woman.

Key Words & Phrases: Fickleness. Vanity. Gullibility. Poor judgment. Exaggeration. Embellishment. Oversensitivity. Self-indulgence. Laziness. Superficiality. Silliness. Self-deception. Confusion. Indecision. Daydreaming. Moodiness. Negative thinking. Morbid preoccupations. Emotional disturbance. False hopes. Illogic. Clouded judgment. Uncontrolled emotions. Flirtatiousness. Infidelity. Little regard for reality. Lack of sympathy. Gossip. Unreliability. Irresponsibility. Dependency. Perversity. Hysteria. Changing with the wind. Escapism. Unreality. Alcohol or drug abuse. Enabling. Co-dependence. Needless self-sacrifice. Mental illness. Living in a fantasy world. Fatal attraction.

Situation and Advice: Chances are your emotions are clouding your judgment. You may be unaware of some important information or someone may be deceiving you. Choose your advisors carefully. If you asked about romance, you are likely to experience disappointment through the infidelity of your lover. You may be involved in a co-dependent relationship. Are you foolishly and needlessly sacrificing your life for someone who does not appreciate you? Are you enabling another's addictive behavior? In a very negative spread the Queen of Cups reversed could represent a fatal attraction.

People: Women who love too much. A charming busybody. Enablers of addiction. Those who sacrifice themselves unnecessarily for others. A fair-weather friend. An unfaithful lover. A hysterical, overly emotional woman whose attitudes change with the wind. A masochist. A borderline personality. An unreliable woman who can't be trusted with a secret or a sensitive matter. An unsympathetic person. A lazy, self-indulgent woman. A woman dominated by her emotions and unswayed by rational thought. One who abuses drugs or alcohol.

∼

Kings
Fathers

Key Words & Phrases: Kings stand for actual people in your life or for different aspects of your personality. Kings are father figures and they usually symbolize mature men of stature, leadership, and authority. Kings are less likely than Pages and Knights to represent situations. When they represent aspects of our personalities, Kings reflect our force of will, initiative, principled action, and ability to get things done. Kings can also represent publicity, public recognition, honors, awards, and celebrations. Several Kings in a reading sometimes indicate gatherings of many men.

King of Wands
Leadership

Upright: Enterprise.

Key Words & Phrases: Being in charge. Wit. Charm. Strength. Inspiration. Motivation. Maturity. Fatherliness. Intelligence. Ambition. Decisiveness. Independence. Courage. Liveliness. Enthusiasm. Love of challenge. Fondness for excitement. Passion. Loyalty. Activity. A commanding presence.

Charisma. Optimism. Generosity. Encouragement. Creativity. Professionalism. Healthy competition. Impulsiveness. Unexpected income. Mediation. Arbitration. Negotiation.

Situation and Advice: You may receive sound advice from a strong, mature, and generous man. In relationships you are able to appreciate your partner's point of view. You may have a chance to mix with interesting people. You are able to negotiate well and convey your point of view. If given routine work to do, however, you are likely to become irritated by details. If you asked about romance, get ready for a sexual adventure.

People: A decisive leader. The person in charge of an enterprise. A devoted father and husband. A generous, mature man who is loyal and committed to a monogamous relationship and family life. A skilled communicator. A secure but somewhat impulsive businessman who is married with a family. An honest, trustworthy, professional man. Someone who can help you financially. An entrepreneur. An adventurous man who takes charge and initiates many projects. An optimistic, fun-loving, passionate, generous person who dislikes details and is prone to hasty action. A virile, adventurous lover. A good negotiator. Someone who inspires others to creative achievement. Mediators. Arbitrators. Inspiring speakers and evangelists. Journalists. Teachers. Preachers. Gamblers. Salespeople. Those involved in promotions or marketing.

◑

King of Wands Reversed: Intolerance.

Key Words & Phrases: Bossiness. Self-righteousness. Arrogance. Lies. Deviousness. Dogmatism. Strictness. Prejudice. Bigotry. Inflexibility. Opposition. Antagonism. Disagreement. Quick temper. Controversy. Aggression. Unyielding. Ruthlessness. Despotism. Insensitivity. Tyranny.

Hypocrisy. Egotism. Self-seeking. Suspicion. Being overpowered. Misogyny. Resentment of female authority. Womb envy. Do what I say, not what I do. It's my way or the highway.

Situation and Advice: An arrogant person in authority may take an intolerant or unyielding stance. You may need to stand your ground rather than do something you know is wrong. You should also consider whether you are being autocratic and insensitive to the feelings of others. This is also a time to be on the lookout for con artists and their get-rich-quick schemes. If it looks too good to be true, it probably is.

People: A liar or devious person. A con artist. An overbearing, dogmatic person. An opinionated, stubborn, and controlling man. A biased man who opposes your plans or tries to engage you in a controversy. One who lacks concern for the feelings of others. One whose main focus is self-promotion. Mercenaries. Unscrupulous televangelists. Some used car salesmen.

King of Pentacles
Worldly Success

King of Pentacles

Upright: Security minded. Sound financial advice.

Key Words & Phrases: Steady progress. Ambition. Shrewdness. Practicality. Business ability. Wealth. Patience. Power. Stability. Reliability. Commitment. Satisfaction. Organizational skills. Acclaim. Status. Discipline. Control. Thoroughness. Contentment. Gentleness. Kindliness.

Calmness. Love of nature. Financial ability. Leadership in industry. Mathematical acumen. Common sense. Generosity. Perseverance. Staying power. Hard work. Earned success. Skillful management. Good use of the land. Increased income. Professional success. Sound investments. Real estate transactions. Ownership. Achievement through persistent effort. Climbing the corporate ladder. Money in the bank. Protection. Money talks.

Situation and Advice: The King of Pentacles suggests involvement in business matters and in organizing the financial aspects of your life. Present and future security is a priority now. You may be in line for a promotion or a salary increase. You can succeed at practical ventures. Real estate and property matters go well. Your patience, honesty, kindness, and loyalty are rewarded. You can receive sound financial advice. A practical, conscientious approach brings success.

People: A conscientious worker. A financial advisor. A leader of industry. Financiers. Engineers. Mathematicians. Property owners. Real estate developers. Businessmen. Those who work with the land. A devoted father who understands his children. A methodical, responsible, steady, reliable, taciturn, conservative man. A good manager. A financially secure man who is married with a family. Bankers. Investors. Stock brokers. Merchants. A good money manager. Someone who is good with mathematics. An ambitious man who will work long and hard to reach his goals. A patriarch. A patron of the arts. A generous man of wealth. Someone preoccupied with financial matters. A provider. A protector. An honest and loyal friend.

◑

King of Pentacles Reversed: Lack of business sense. Vulgarity.

Key Words & Phrases: Materialism. Dullness. Preoccupation with money. Meanness. Bigotry. Superficiality. Insensitivity. Greed. Fraud. Dishonesty. Influence peddling. Disloyalty. Clumsiness. Heavy-handedness. Crudeness. Rudeness. Pornography. Rigidity. Stubbornness. Autocracy. Poor management. Excessive worry about finances. Placing career and money above all else. Dilettantism. Workaholism. Keeping up with the Joneses. Paranoia. Disorganization. Money can't buy you love. The end justifies the means. Everything has its price.

Situation and Advice: You may need to deal with a man who is mean, crude, grasping, bigoted, dishonest, vulgar, or miserly. In your own life you should be careful not to measure success solely in terms of money. The King of Pentacles reversed also warns against dishonest actions motivated by greed and materialism. Be careful not to make crude or vulgar comments that offend others in your life.

People: A bully. A dullard. A dictator. A wastrel. One who mismanages money. Someone who will do anything for money. An uninteresting, materialistic, opinionated, bigoted, superficial person. A male chauvinist pig. A sexist bigot. An impoverished man. A stingy, plodding, suspicious man. A self-indulgent person. Someone prone to angry outbursts. A man who is overly worried about financial matters.

King of Swords
Authority and Command

Upright: Cool rationality. Sound advice.

Key Words & Phrases: Truth. Control. Balanced judgment. A fair decision. An analytical mind. Professionalism. Intelligence. Innovation. Ambition. Self-assertion. Aggression. Authority. Drive. Keen discrimination. Repartee. Objectivity. Rationality. Equality. Justice. Arbitration. Law and order.

Expertise. Charm. Cooperativeness. Conviction. Prudence. Good counsel. Logic. Clear thought. Keen intellect. Power of analysis. Diplomacy. Lofty ideals. Strength of character. Commitment. Specialization. More head than heart. Being out of touch with one's feelings.

Situation and Advice: A decision you have been awaiting will be fair and impartial. An intelligent professional may provide you with sound business or legal advice. You may be acting in an overly cool and intellectual manner to the exclusion of feelings and softer ways of relating to others. You are capable of much originality now. You desire to break the mold and free yourself from the restrictions of conventionality. You need to consider whether you are out of touch with your feelings and perhaps afraid of entering into an intimate relationship with another. Others may feel you are disregarding their opinions.

People: One who is his own person and resents any limitations imposed by others. A commanding, aggressive person. An unemotional, aloof, intelligent, independent, analytical man of authority who makes balanced judgments and gives excellent advice. One who is out of touch with his or her feelings. One who fears intimate contact with another. Someone with an official title. Military people. Politicians. A leader. An authority. A lawyer. A doctor. A judge. An arbitrator. A specialist. A government official. A professional. A man who will fight for your interests. An authority figure with moral standing but little interest in feelings or individual problems. An intelligent man who enjoys learning and the study of abstract truth. A man who looks before he leaps. Someone with expertise in the social sciences or the field of communication. One who can view a situation impartially and unemotionally. A private person who keeps his own counsel. One's father. An aggressive boyfriend.

◑

King of Swords Reversed: Premeditated malice.

Key Words & Phrases: Exploitation. An unfair decision. Prejudice. Grandiosity. Sarcasm. Selfishness. Ruthlessness. Deviousness. Scheming. Poor judgment. Suspicion. Accusation. Injustice. A domineering attitude. Unfairness. Bias. Vengeance. Overcaution. Cruelty. Hardness. Severity. Cynicism. Opinionatedness. Manipulation. Tyranny. Lust for power. Legal problems. Intimidation. Sadism. Revenge. Violence. Aggressiveness.

Situation and Advice: You may be suffering an injustice. Someone may be deceiving or intimidating you through ruthless schemes. You may be exploiting others in your life. Your sarcastic comments may have wounded someone close to you. You may have been hurt by someone else's words. You may be the victim of an unfair verdict in a legal proceeding.

People: Sadists. A ruthless, suspicious, sarcastic, vindictive, cruel man. A cruel bully. Someone corrupted by power. Someone who is overly cautious. A cold-hearted man who is callous, treacherous, violent, or unjust. A cunning, aggressive bigot.

King of Cups
Wise Counsel

Upright: Compassion.

Key Words & Phrases: Assistance. Feelings. Imagination. Respect. Trust. Consideration. Understanding. Elegance. Responsibility. Reliability. Secrecy. Generosity. Wisdom. Culture. Kindness. Sophistication. Wealth of knowledge. Professionalism. Dignity. Reserve. Protection. Concern.

Nurturance. Caring. Healing. Empathy. Good advice. Negotiating skills. A good listener. A good friend.

Situation and Advice: A man of culture and intelligence will listen to you and offer sound advice. You may be called upon to lend a compassionate ear to a friend or a family member. You are involved in a situation in which caring and empathic assistance are of utmost importance. A mature, emotionally stable man will offer you sympathetic understanding. Your father or a father surrogate may figure prominently in upcoming events.

People: One's father. An educated, cultured and literate man. A mature, emotionally stable person. A mature man who is easy to talk to. A professional. A trusted advisor. A bachelor. Those willing to accept extra responsibility. Men associated with the Law or the Church. A man of dignity who is quiet, kind, well-respected, trustworthy, empathic, and who gives good advice. A man of the cloth. A teacher. Someone interested in the arts and sciences. A man in the helping professions. A man of ideas. A kind doctor. A judge or lawyer. A businessman. A counselor. A good friend. A negotiator. An artist. Someone who understands unconscious motivations. A man in touch with his emotional life.

◖

King of Cups Reversed: Sleaziness.

Key Words & Phrases: Bad advice. Scheming. Insecurity. Immaturity. Neurotic behavior. A false front. Worthless suggestions. Double dealing. Con games. Loss. Power plays. Deception. Dishonesty. Insincerity. Self-deception. Fraud. Entangling alliances. Manipulation. Self-indulgence. Treachery. Violence. Untrustworthiness. Laziness. Weakness. Selfishness. A ruthless thirst for position or power. A sting operation. Escapism. Sexual exploitation. Drug or alcohol abuse. Dependency. Addictive behavior. Unbridled narcissism. Too good to be true.

Situation and Advice: The advice of a suave professional may prove untrustworthy. Someone may be using you by playing on your emotions for his or her own selfish gain. There is a danger of your becoming the victim of a con artist or an underhanded scheme. Beware of a charming man who tries to con you into a dubious project; you are bound to suffer in the end. Remember that if an offer sounds too good to be true, it probably is.

People: A narcissistic personality. A manipulator. A con artist. One who looks out only for himself. A man without scruples. A lazy, self-indulgent man. Those who spoil their loved ones. Those who toy with others' emotions for selfish gain. An antisocial personality. A parasite. A treacherous man who misleads and denigrates you. A swindler. Dishonest people. A womanizer. Those who prey on the emotional pain of others. An alcoholic or drug addict. A gigolo.

❧

Appendix A

Astrology and the Tarot

Although the Tarot and astrology share many correspondences, these two occult disciplines are independent fields of study. Many students come to the Tarot from astrology, and vice versa. It is important to remember that there is no exact one-to-one correlation between astrological and Tarot symbolism. In fact, astrological associations between the Tarot Trumps and astrological attributions differ from one author to another.

The astrological associations provided in this book reflect those commonly in use among modern Tarot experts. Bear in mind that the Tarot cards have meaning in their own right independent of astrology. Arthur Edward Waite could not have said it better when he wrote in *The Pictorial Key to the Tarot*:

> The true Tarot is symbolism; it speaks no other language and offers no other signs. Given the inward meaning of its emblems, they do become a kind of alphabet which is capable of indefinite combinations and makes true sense in all.

Waite also emphasized that the Tarot "is not, by attribution or otherwise, a derivative of any one school of literature of occultism; it is not of Alchemy or Cabalism or Astrology or

297

Ceremonial Magic." Rather, said Waite, the Tarot "is a presentation of universal ideas by means of universal types."

Psychoanalyst Carl Gustav Jung would later call these universal ideas "archetypes of the unconscious mind." The power of the Tarot derives from its capacity to allow us to tap into the archetypal images, feelings, and human interactions symbolized by the cards. There is nothing magical or mystical about the Tarot. The cards are merely tools that allow us to experience facets of our human inheritance as sentient, spiritual beings.

The reader should regard links between astrology and the Tarot as suggesting further nuances of Tarot symbolism. The Tarot cards speak for themselves independent of astrology. Each student of the Tarot must discover the meanings of the cards anew. If making astrological connections helps you to understand the cards, read on. If not, simply ignore this appendix.

The tables here list some of the popular methods of attributing astrological symbolism to the cards in the Tarot. There are various methods of attributing signs and planets to the pip cards. Most involve the succession of signs in an element (Fire, Earth, Air, Water) according to their modality (Cardinal, Fixed, or Mutable). Browsing the tables will allow you to see the patterns involved in making such assignments.

Seasons and Compass Directions

Some authors derive compass directions and seasons from astrological symbolism. The usual directions assigned to the suits are as follows:

Suit	Direction	Element/Season
Cups	North	Water (The sign Cancer begins the Summer)
Pentacles	South	Earth (The sign Capricorn begins the Winter)
Wands	East	Fire (The sign Aries begins the Spring)
Swords	West	Air (The sign Libra begins the Fall)

In Witchcraft, compass directions are assigned differently to the elements: Earth is North, Fire is South, Air is East, and Water is West. Because I come to Tarot from astrology, I stick to the astrological assignments.

A Useful Exercise in Astrology and the Tarot

Readers who are versed in astrology will find the following exercise an excellent way to become familiar with the Major Arcana cards. Obtain a copy of your birth chart. Referring to Table 1, write the name of the corresponding Major Arcana card next to each planet. Then write the name of the corresponding Major Arcana card next to each house cusp.

Separate all the Major Arcana cards from your deck and place each card on your natal horoscope in the positions determined by the above procedure. Study the meanings of the Major Arcana as they relate to the meanings of the houses the cards occupy in your birth chart.

Table I: Astrological Associations of the Major Arcana
(This version is popular in English speaking countries.)

Number	Card	Astrological Association
0	The Fool	Uranus
1	The Magician	Mercury
2	The High Priestess	Moon
3	The Empress	Venus
4	The Emperor	Aries
5	The Hierophant	Taurus
6	The Lovers	Gemini
7	The Chariot	Cancer
8	Strength	Leo
9	The Hermit	Virgo
10	Wheel of Fortune	Jupiter
11	Justice	Libra
12	Hanged Man	Neptune
13	Death	Scorpio
14	Temperance	Sagittarius
15	The Devil	Capricorn
16	The Tower	Mars
17	The Star	Aquarius
18	The Moon	Pisces

Continued on next page

Number	Card	Astrological Association
19	The Sun	Sun
20	Judgement	Pluto
21	The World	Saturn

Table II: Popular Astrological Associations of Pip Cards

The Hermetic Order of the Golden Dawn was a short-lived but very influential society of occultism. It originated in England during the late 1800s and attracted such prominent figures as the poet William Butler Yeats, the magician Aleister Crowley, and the inventor of the most popular Tarot deck, Arthur Edward Waite. The rituals and teachings of the Golden Dawn continue to influence practitioners of occultism and high magic today (for more on the Golden Dawn, see The Golden Dawn by Regardie [Llewellyn, 1989]). A.T. Mann is a prominent Tarot scholar who is well versed in astrology and the occult sciences.

Wands:	Golden Dawn	A. T. Mann
Ace	Root of Fire	Power of Fire
2	Mars/Aries	Mars/Aries
3	Sun/Aries	Sun/Aries
4	Venus/Aries	Jupiter/Aries
5	Saturn/Leo	Sun/Leo
6	Jupiter/Leo	Jupiter/Leo
7	Mars/Leo	Mars/Leo
8	Mercury/Sagittarius	Jupiter/Sagittarius
9	Moon/Sagittarius	Mars/Sagittarius
10	Saturn/Sagittarius	Sun/Sagittarius

Pentacles:	Golden Dawn	A. T. Mann
Ace	Root of Earth	Power of Earth
2	Jupiter/Capricorn	Saturn/Capricorn
3	Mars/Capricorn	Venus/Capricorn
4	Sun/Capricorn	Mercury/Capricorn
5	Mercury/Taurus	Venus/Taurus
6	Moon/Taurus	Mercury/Taurus
7	Saturn/Taurus	Saturn/Taurus

Pentacles:	Golden Dawn	A. T. Mann
8	Sun/Virgo	Mercury/Virgo
9	Venus/Virgo	Saturn/Virgo
10	Mercury/Virgo	Venus/Virgo

Swords:	Golden Dawn	A. T. Mann
Ace	Root of Air	Power of Air
2	Moon/Libra	Venus/Libra
3	Saturn/Libra	Uranus/Libra
4	Jupiter/Libra	Mercury/Libra
5	Venus/Aquarius	Uranus/Aquarius
6	Mercury/Aquarius	Mercury/Aquarius
7	Moon/Aquarius	Venus/Aquarius
8	Jupiter/Gemini	Mercury/Gemini
9	Mars/Gemini	Venus/Gemini
10	Sun/Gemini	Uranus/Gemini

Cups:	Golden Dawn	A. T. Mann
Ace	Root of Water	Power of Water
2	Venus/Cancer	Moon/Cancer
3	Mercury/Cancer	Pluto/Cancer
4	Moon/Cancer	Neptune/Cancer
5	Mars/Scorpio	Pluto/Scorpio
6	Sun/Scorpio	Neptune/Scorpio
7	Venus/Scorpio	Moon/Scorpio
8	Saturn/Pisces	Neptune/Pisces
9	Jupiter/Pisces	Moon/Pisces
10	Mars/Pisces	Pluto/Pisces

~

Decans are a method for dividing each sign of the zodiac into three equal ten-degree segments. Each decan has a planetary or sign association. In astrology, we always begin counting at zero degrees of the sign Aries, which has three decans (0–10 degrees, 10–20 degrees, and 20–30 degrees of Aries). Tarot experts have used at least three different methods to associate decans with astrological rulerships. The oldest method is to assign planets to each decan in Chaldean order, that is, in reverse order of the planets' speed of motion. The Chaldeans only knew the seven visible planets which were, in order from slowest to fastest, Saturn, Jupiter, Mars, Sun, Venus, Mercury, and the Moon. Because Aries is ruled by Mars, he gets the first decan. The second decan goes to the Sun, and the third goes to Venus, because the Sun and Venus are the next in Chaldean order.

The Hindus used a different system for decans. They attributed a sign rather than a planet to each decan. The first decan of Aries belongs to Aries. The second and third decans of Aries belong to the two other Fire signs (Leo and Sagittarius) in the order of the zodiac. The same logic applies to other signs. There are four elements: earth, air, fire, and water. Each element has three signs, which form the basis for decan assignments:

Element	Signs
Earth	Taurus, Virgo, Capricorn
Air	Gemini, Libra, Aquarius
Fire	Aries, Leo, Sagittarius
Water	Cancer, Scorpio, Pisces

Some Tarot authors call the Ace of each suit the "root" of the element, and begin assigning decans in Hindu order starting with the second decan.

Table III: Other Astrological Associations of Pip Cards

	Hindu Decans	Chaldean Decans	Alternative Hindu Decans
Wands:			
Ace	Root of Fire	Fire	Aries/Aries
2	Aries/Aries	Mars	Aries/Leo
3	Aries/Leo	Sun	Aries/Sagittarius
4	Aries/Sagittarius	Venus	Leo/Leo
5	Leo/Leo	Saturn	Leo/Sagittarius
6	Leo/Sagittarius	Jupiter	Leo/Aries
7	Leo/Aries	Mars	Sagittarius/Sagittarius
8	Sagittarius/Sagittarius	Mercury	Sagittarius/Aries
9	Sagittarius/Aries	Moon	Sagittarius/Leo
10	Sagittarius/Leo	Saturn	Summation of Fire

	Hindu Decans	Chaldean Decans	Alternative Hindu Decans
Pentacles:			
Ace	Root of Earth	Earth	Capricorn/Capricorn
2	Capricorn/Capricorn	Jupiter	Capricorn/Taurus
3	Capricorn/Taurus	Mars	Capricorn/Virgo
4	Capricorn/Virgo	Sun	Taurus/Taurus
5	Taurus/Taurus	Mercury	Taurus/Virgo
6	Taurus/Virgo	Moon	Taurus/Capricorn
7	Taurus/Capricorn	Saturn	Virgo/Virgo
8	Virgo/Virgo	Sun	Virgo/Capricorn
9	Virgo/Capricorn	Venus	Virgo/Taurus
10	Virgo/Taurus	Mercury	Summation of Earth
Swords:			
Ace	Root of Air	Air	Libra/Libra
2	Libra/Libra	Moon	Libra/Aquarius
3	Libra/Aquarius	Saturn	Libra/Gemini
4	Libra/Gemini	Jupiter	Aquarius/Aquarius
5	Aquarius/Aquarius	Venus	Aquarius/Gemini
6	Aquarius/Gemini	Mercury	Aquarius/Libra
7	Aquarius/Libra	Moon	Gemini/Gemini
8	Gemini/Gemini	Jupiter	Gemini/Libra
9	Gemini/Libra	Mars	Gemini/Aquarius
10	Gemini/Aquarius	Sun	Summation of Air
Cups:			
Ace	Root of Water	Water	Cancer/Cancer
2	Cancer/Cancer	Venus	Cancer/Scorpio
3	Cancer/Scorpio	Mercury	Cancer/Pisces
4	Cancer/Pisces	Moon	Scorpio/Scorpio
5	Scorpio/Scorpio	Mars	Scorpio/Pisces
6	Scorpio/Pisces	Sun	Scorpio/Cancer
7	Scorpio/Cancer	Venus	Pisces/Pisces
8	Pisces/Pisces	Saturn	Pisces/Cancer

Continued on next page

	Hindu Decans	Chaldean Decans	Alternative Hindu Decans
9	Pisces/Cancer	Jupiter	Pisces/Scorpio
10	Pisces/Scorpio	Mars	Summation of Water

Table IV: Alternative Astrological Associations of Trumps

(This version is popular in South America.)

Number	Card	Astrological Association
0	The Fool	Neptune (rather than Uranus)
1	The Magician	Taurus (rather than Mercury)
2	The High Priestess	Cancer (rather than the Moon)
3	The Empress	Venus
4	The Emperor	Jupiter (rather than Aries)
5	The Hierophant	Leo (rather than Taurus)
6	The Lovers	Gemini
7	The Chariot	Capricorn (rather than Cancer)
8	Strength	Mars (rather than Leo)
9	The Hermit	Saturn (rather than Virgo)
10	Wheel of Fortune	Sagittarius (rather than Jupiter)
11	Justice	Libra
12	Hanged Man	Pisces (rather than Neptune)
13	Death	Pluto (rather than Scorpio)
14	Temperance	Aquarius (rather than Sagittarius)
15	The Devil	Scorpio (rather than Capricorn)
16	The Tower	Uranus (rather than Mars)
17	The Star	Virgo (rather than Aquarius)
18	The Moon	The Moon (rather than Pisces)
19	The Sun	The Sun
20	Judgement	Mercury (rather than Pluto)
21	The World	Aries (rather than Saturn)

Appendix B

Numerology and the Tarot

In the older Tarot decks, the twenty-two Major Arcana were the only cards with allegorical drawings. The sixteen Court cards depicted the Page, Knight, Queen and King of each suit, and the forty Pip cards merely showed the number and suit of each card.

The word "pip" refers to the markings that show the numerical order of the card. Because the original Tarot decks had only numerical markings on the Pip cards, the divinatory meanings of the Pips relied on the numerological symbolism of each card combined with the meaning attributed to its suit. The student of the Tarot needs to know something about numerology to appreciate the symbolism of the pip cards.

The symbolic significance of numbers has a long history in Western philosophy. Pythagoras, who gave us his famous theorem of geometry in the sixth century B.C., believed numbers to be the essence of being. He discovered that the musical scale can be expressed in mathematical ratios, and he described the "music of the spheres" based on the idea that harmonic ratios between the heavenly bodies produce music as the planets travel through space. Pythagorean numerology led to the invention of the astrological theory of aspects (sextiles, squares, trines, oppositions) during the Hellenistic period and thus to the rise of modern Western astrology. Pythagoras' theory of numbers became the basis for many Western divinatory systems, including the modern Tarot.

According to Barbara Walker, the number of Tarot cards in a standard deck—namely seventy-eight—probably derives from numerological divination. There are twenty-one different combinations of throws of two dice as there are twenty-one numbered major trump cards. The Fool card is numbered zero and may have been added later to the original twenty-one trumps. There are fifty-six possible combinations of the throws of three dice as there are fifty-six minor arcana cards. Furthermore, the sum of the numbers one through twelve (for the twelve signs of the zodiac) is 78, that is, $1 + 2 + 3 + 4 + 5 + 6 + 7 + 8 + 9 + 10 + 11 + 12 = 78$. Such numerological correspondences did not escape the notice of the early occultists who influenced the creation and development of the traditional Tarot deck.

This chapter will describe the symbolic significance of each digit from 0 through 9 as they are used in the Tarot. In addition, I will discuss the ideas of the "life path" or "birth force" number and the usefulness of calculating the "personal year" number.

The key numbers used in numerology are the ten digits (0, 1, 2, 3, 4, 5, 6, 7, 8, 9) and the master numbers (11 and 22). These concepts are helpful in Tarot delineation and in other forms of divination. Becoming familiar with your life path and personal year numbers will give you further insight into the meanings of the Pip cards of the Tarot.

Your Life Path, Birth Force, or Destiny Number

The Life Path number is a number derived from your exact day, month, and year of birth. To find your life path number, add the numbers of your day, month, and year of birth. Take this sum and add the digits together until you get either a master number (11 or 22) or a single digit (0 through 9). That is your life path or birth force number. It has to do with your fundamental make-up and the major lessons you must learn in this lifetime.

Here's an example of a young man born May 8, 1981. First, we add together the day, month and year:

Day	8
Month May=	5
Current Year	1981
Sum	1994

Now add the digits in this sum: $1 + 9 + 9 + 4 = 23$

Because 23 is not a single digit or master number, we add its digits together: $2 + 3 = 5$.

The life path or destiny number of this young man is 5. He will need to learn the constructive use of freedom during his lifetime.

Now calculate your own life path number following the same procedure.

The Personal Year Number

Calculating the personal year number is similar to calculating the life path number. The only difference is that you use your birthdate in the current year instead of the actual year of birth. The personal year number tells you the numerological significance of the current year in your life.

Here's an example. Suppose you were born May 31, 1951, and the current year is 1995. To find your current personal year number, add together the numbers in your current year's birth date: May 31, 1995. Here goes:

Day	31
Month May=	5
Current Year	1995
Sum	2031

Now add together all the digits in 2031: $2 + 0 + 3 + 1 = 6$.

This person's personal year number for 1995 is 6. You will learn that a 6 year is characterized by a focus on home, family, close relationships, and marriage. Knowing your personal year number helps put the current year in perspective. In a Tarot spread, a predominance of sixes will have a similar significance.

Numerological Significance of the Digits and Master Numbers

If you understand the numerological significance of the numbers on the Pip cards, you will be able to work more productively with the Tarot. This section will review the traditional meanings of the ten digits and of the two master numbers 11 and 22. Find your life path number and current personal year number in the list below. Meditate on the significance of these two numbers as they relate to your life history. Calculate the personal year numbers for other significant years in your life. How do those numbers relate to what occurred during those years?

Zero: Zero is the number of nothingness and potentiality. Ancient numerologists regarded the circle (O) as the perfect form. Zero is a symbol of the Cosmic Egg, the archetypal feminine creatrix of life, and of immortality. Zero precedes all numbers and symbolizes the continuous cycle of life: birth, death, and rebirth. You are exactly zero years old when you first emerge from the womb. A circle has no beginning and no end. Zero symbolizes boundlessness, pure potentiality, and limitless freedom. A circle with a dot at the center is a symbol for the sun, which to astrologers represents the central core of the personality. Jung regarded circular figures as mandalas expressive of the archetype of the Self. The Fool Trump is the only Tarot card to bear the number zero. Zero cannot appear as a life path or personal year number.

One: I am. One is a number of the start of a cycle, of singularity, initiation, fresh action, originality, progress, ambition, courage, exciting change, new beginnings, planting seeds, the start of an enterprise, having babies, new ventures, inner strength, conviction, decisiveness, confidence, leadership, aggressive energy, independence, and individuality. In geometry, one corresponds to a single point—the first inkling that something exists. The Aces of the Minor Arcana each bear the number one and symbolize the seeds or starting points of each of the four suits. The four Aces are the initiating forces of their corresponding elements (fire, earth, air, water). The Major Arcana cards corresponding to one are The Magician (I), The Wheel of

Fortune (X), and The Sun (XIX). Astrologically the number one is associated with the sun.

Two: We are. Two is a number of balance, choice, harmony, moderation, pairs of opposites, duality, polarity, partnership, friendship, relationships, group activities, cultivation, reflection, development, affection, affirmation, patience, quiet waiting, tending the garden, confirming a new direction, cooperation, diplomacy, tact, persuasion, sympathy, devotion, and working with others. In geometry two points determine a line. The cards numbered two give direction to the seeds planted by the Aces. The Major Arcana cards corresponding to the number two are the High Priestess (II), Justice (XI), and Judgement (XX). Astrologically the number two is usually associated with the moon.

Three: We create. Out of the partnership of the number two come offspring, births, children, new plans, and creative ventures. Three is a number of joy, procreation, completion, parenthood, completion, unfolding, recreation, romance, travel, pleasure, happiness, enthusiasm, planning, preparation, optimism, imagination, fun, entertainment, art, talent, creativity, the written or spoken word, benefits and fruits of partnerships, adaptability, and self-expression. Sometimes three signifies death that makes way for new life. In geometry three points determine a plane. Threes extend the direction set by the twos and give a broader perspective. The Major Arcana cards corresponding to three are the Empress (III), the Hanged Man (XII), and the World (XXI). Astrologically the number three is often associated with Jupiter.

Four: Four is the number of foundations, of the structure of reality. The four dimensions of the physical world are length, width, breadth, and time. A table has four legs. A compass has four directions. Four is a number of manifestation and of laying foundations in the material world. Four translates the plans of the threes into reality. Four relates to business, security, construction, property and real estate matters, organization, routine, perseverance, discipline, efficiency, memory, will, effort, energy, challenge, hard work, order, logic, measurement, reason, stability, method, restrictions, limitations, accuracy, systematization, classification, productivity, management, dependability, pragmatism, service, and firm foundations. Four is a number of actualization and solidity as well as of persistence and stubbornness. Four refers to temporal power, parents, and authority figures. In astrology the fourth harmonic deals with the consequences of our actions and their impact on the material world. The Major Arcana cards corresponding to four are the Emperor (IV) and Death (XIII). Astrologically the number four is commonly associated with Uranus.

Five: Five challenges and disrupts the well-established solidity of the four. Five is a number of crisis and of adjustment due to feedback. Five signifies adaptation, disruption, adventure, challenge, competition, travel, freedom, activity, expanded horizons, new opportunities, resourcefulness, self-promotion, marketing oneself, romance, excitement, risk-taking, breaking out of a rut, deciding on a new direction, variety, progressiveness, versatility, professional advancement, new friendships, socializing, juggling many abilities, and change. Significant shifts or adjustments in family, home, or career are often heralded by the number five. Creative solutions can emerge out of periods of instability and wondering where you are going with your life. In astrology the fifth harmonic relates to the search for order and form to bring order out of chaos. The Major Arcana cards corresponding to five are the Hierophant (V) and Temperance (XIV). Astrologically the number five is usually associated with Mercury.

Six: Six is the number of harmony restored after the disruption of the number five. Six is the calm after the storm of the fives. It is a number of peace, calm, contentment, self-acceptance, cooperation, satisfaction, harmony of opposites, regularity, equilibrium, and striving for perfection. Six relates to home, family, duty, close relationships, friendship, love, patience, justice, reconciliation, marriage, domestic responsibilities, remodeling, family obligations, assistance, caring for and attending to the needs of others, and responsibility. In astrology the sixth harmonic deals with the expression of joy, affection, and vitality. The Major Arcana cards corresponding to six are the Lovers (VI) and the Devil (XV). Astrologically the number six is frequently associated with Venus.

Seven: Seven is a spiritual number. Seven refers to respite, introspection, contemplation, evaluation, soul development, biding time, pondering choices, sorting out options, intellectual pursuits, study, meditation, analysis, research, objectivity, unique approaches, specialization, unusual solutions, thoughtfulness, understanding, planning, patient waiting, solitude, wisdom, occult studies, spiritual awareness, truth, intuition, philosophy, and technical or scientific matters. Like the fives, sevens tend to disrupt the harmony of the sixes and bring greater variety, activity, expansion, experimentation, and imagination into the life. The Major Arcana cards corresponding to seven are the Chariot (VII) and the Tower (XVI). Astrologically the number seven is often associated with Neptune.

Eight: Like the fours, eight is a number of order, achievement, recognition, power, regeneration, money, progress, worldly success, advancement, organization, structured patterns, financial stability, opportunity, status, money, work, executive ability, sound judgment, capability, authority, material satisfaction, business acumen, setting priorities, and accomplishment in the material world. In geometry eight points can determine a solid cube. The Major Arcana cards corresponding to eight are Strength (VIII) and the Star (XVII). Astrologically the number eight is usually associated with Saturn.

Nine: As the final single digit number, nine represents the end of a cycle or phase of life and the preparation for entering a new phase of existence. Nine signifies the final integration of the previous eight stages of the cycle. Nine refers to completion, perfection, purification, giving, detachment, attainment, transition, conclusion, termination, ending, compassion, loss of an aspect of one's life to make way for a new cycle, clearing the decks, finishing matters, forgiveness, charity, teaching, counseling, selfless giving, brotherhood, humanitarian ideals, release, and letting go. In astrology the ninth harmonic relates to wisdom, ideals, and spiritual knowledge. The Major Arcana cards corresponding to nine are the Hermit (IX) and the Moon (XVIII).

Astrologically the number nine is frequently associated with Mars.

Ten: Ten is a transition point from one cycle to another. Ten is a number of completion and final ending. As one more than nine, ten often signifies "one too many." In numerology 10 reduces to $1 + 0 = 1$, the start of a new cycle, the time for another spin of the wheel of fortune. The Major Arcana card corresponding to ten is the Wheel of Fortune.

Eleven: Eleven is a master number symbolizing insight, spiritual understanding, inspiration, awareness, revelation, illumination, intuition, creativity, idealism, teaching, wisdom, compassion, and enlightenment. In numerology 11 reduces to $1 + 1 = 2$, and master number 11 is a higher octave of 2. The Major Arcana card corresponding to eleven is Justice; however, Strength is card eleven in some decks. Astrologically the number eleven is often associated with Pluto.

Twenty-two: Twenty-two is also a master number representing self-discipline and broad-based mastery with spiritual awareness. There are twenty-two Major Arcana cards in the Tarot. Twenty-two is the number of the master builder who achieves material success on a large scale to benefit humanity. In numerology 22 reduces to $2 + 2 = 4$, and master number 22 is a higher octave of 4. The Major Arcana card corresponding to twenty-two is the Fool (also zero); the cycle ends where it starts.

The following list summarizes some commonly used astrological associations between numerology and astrology:

1	Sun	6	Venus
2	Moon	7	Neptune
3	Jupiter	8	Saturn
4	Uranus	9	Mars
5	Mercury	11	Pluto

Bibliography

Abraham, Sylvia. *How to Read the Tarot*. St. Paul, MN: Llewellyn, 1994.

Almond, Jocelyn, and Keith Seddon. *Tarot for Relationships*. Northamptonshire, England: Aquarian Press, 1990.

Aprenda a Tirar el Tarot Astrologico. *Predicciones* (Revista de Astrologia, Ciencias Ocultas y Disciplinas Alternativas), Año 2, Numero 10, Julio 1992, pp. 72-76.

Benares, Camden. *Common Sense Tarot*. Van Nuys, CA: Newcastle, 1992.

Bishop, Barbara J. *Numerology: Universal Vibrations of Numbers*. St. Paul, MN: Llewellyn, 1992.

Butler, Bill. *The Definitive Tarot*. London, England: Rider & Company, 1975.

Campbell, Joseph. *Myths to Live By*. New York: Viking, 1972.

Capra, Fritjof. *The Tao of Physics*. Boston: Shambhala, 1991.

Case, Paul Foster. *The Tarot: A Key to the Wisdom of the Ages*. Richmond, VA: Macoy Publishing, 1947.

Clarson, Laura. *Tarot Unveiled: The Method to its Magic*. Stamford, CT: U.S. Games Systems, 1988.

Connolly, Eileen. *Tarot: A New Handbook for the Apprentice*. North Hollywood, CA: Newcastle, 1979.

DiPietro, Sylvia. *Live Your Life by the Numbers*. New York: Signet, 1991.

Eliade, Mircea. *Rites and Symbols of Initiation*. New York: Harper & Row, 1958.

Ericsson, Stephanie. *Simply Divine*. Utne Reader. March/April 1992, pp. 111-114.

Fairchild, Gail. *Choice Centered Tarot*. Smithville, IN: Ramp Creek Publishing, 1981.

Fenton, Sasha. *Supertarot*. Northamptonshire, England: Aquarian Press, 1991.

Garen, Nancy. *Tarot Made Easy*. New York: Simon & Schuster, 1989.

Gerulskis-Estes, Susan. *The Book of Tarot*. Dobbs Ferry, NY: Morgan & Morgan, 1981.

Greer, Mary. *Tarot Constellations*. Van Nuys, California: Newcastle, 1987.

————. *Tarot for Your Self.* Van Nuys, California: Newcastle, 1984.

Gray, Eden. *A Complete Guide to the Tarot.* New York: Bantam, 1970.

Guiley, Rosemary Ellen. *The Mystical Tarot.* New York: Signet, 1991.

Jung, Carl Gustav. *Collected Works of C.G. Jung.* Bollingen Series XX, Vols. 1-18. Princeton: Princeton University Press, 1959.

Kaser, R.T. *Tarot in Ten Minutes.* New York: Avon, 1992.

Lawrence, D. Baloti. *Tarot: Twenty-two Steps to a Higher Path.* Stamford, CT: Longmeadow Press, 1992.

Lind, Frank. *How to Understand the Tarot.* Northamptonshire, England: Aquarian Press, 1969.

Mann, A. T. *The Elements of the Tarot.* London, England: Element Books, 1993.

Masino, Marcia. *Easy Tarot Guide.* San Diego, CA: ACS Publications, 1987.

McLaine, Patricia. *The Wheel of Destiny.* St. Paul, MN: Llewellyn, 1991.

Mueller, Robert; Echols, Singne E. and Sandra A. Thomson. *The Lover's Tarot.* New York: Avon, 1993.

Nichols, Sally. *Jung and Tarot: An Archetypal Journey.* York Beach, ME: Samuel Weiser, 1980.

Peach, Emily. *The Tarot Workbook.* New York: Sterling, 1990.

Pollack, R. *Tarot Readings and Meditations.* Northamptonshire, England: Aquarian Press, 1990.

Pond, David and Lucy. *The Metaphysical Handbook.* Port Ludlow, WA: Reflecting Pond Publications, 1984.

Renee, Janina. *Tarot Spells.* St. Paul, MN: Llewellyn, 1990.

Sargent, Carl. *Personality, Divination and the Tarot.* Rochester, VT: Destiny Books, 1988.

Semetsky, Inna R. *Introduction of Tarot Readings into Clinical Psychotherapy—Naturalistic Inquiry.* Unpublished Master's Thesis, Pacific Oaks College, Pasadena, CA, October 1994.

Sharman-Burke, Juliet. *The Complete Book of Tarot.* New York: St. Martin's Press, 1985.

————. *The Mythic Tarot Workbook.* New York: Simon & Schuster, 1988.

Shavick, Nancy. *The Tarot.* Quogue, NY: Prima Materia Books, 1985.

Waite, Arthur Edward. *The Pictorial Key to the Tarot.* Secaucus, NJ: Citadel Press, 1959.

Wilmer, Harry A. *Practical Jung.* Wilmette, IL: Chiron Publications, 1987.

Index

☽ REACH FOR THE MOON

Llewellyn publishes hundreds of books on your favorite subjects! To get these exciting books, including the ones on the following pages, check your local bookstore or order them directly from Llewellyn.

Order by Phone
- Call toll-free within the U.S. and Canada, 1-800-NEW WRLD
- In Minnesota, call (651) 291-1970
- We accept VISA, MasterCard, and American Express

Order by Mail
- Send the full price of your order (MN residents add 7% sales tax) in U.S. funds, plus postage & handling to:
  Llewellyn Worldwide
  P.O. Box 64383, Dept. 1-56718-400-6
  St. Paul, MN 55164–0383, U.S.A.

Postage & Handling
- **Standard** (U.S., Mexico, & Canada)

If your order is:

  $20.00 or under, add $5.00

  $20.01–$100.00, add $6.00

  Over $100, shipping is free

(Continental U.S. orders ship UPS. AK, HI, PR, & P.O. Boxes ship USPS 1st class. Mex. & Can. ship PMB.)

- **Second Day Air** (Continental U.S. only): $10.00 for one book + $1.00 per each additional book
- **Express** (AK, HI, & PR only) [Not available for P.O. Box delivery. For street address delivery only.]: $15.00 for one book + $1.00 per each additional book
- **International Surface Mail:** Add $1.00 per item
- **International Airmail:** Books—Add the retail price of each item; Non-book items—Add $5.00 per item

Please allow 4–6 weeks for delivery on all orders.
Postage and handling rates subject to change.

Discounts
We offer a 20% discount to group leaders or agents. You must order a minimum of 5 copies of the same book to get our special quantity price.

Free Catalog
Get a free copy of our color catalog, *New Worlds of Mind and Spirit*. Subscribe for just $10.00 in the United States and Canada ($30.00 overseas, airmail). Visit our web site at www.llewellyn.com!

Visit our website at www.llewellyn.com for more information.

Robin Wood Tarot

CREATED AND ILLUSTRATED BY
ROBIN WOOD

INSTRUCTIONS BY ROBIN
WOOD AND MICHAEL SHORT

Tap into the wisdom of your subconscious with one of the most beautiful Tarot decks on the market today! Reminiscent of the Rider-Waite deck, the Robin Wood Tarot is flavored with nature imagery and luminous energies that will enchant you and the querant. Even the novice reader will find these cards easy and enjoyable to interpret.

Radiant and rich, these cards were illustrated with a unique technique that brings out the resplendent color of the prismacolor pencils. The shining strength of this Tarot deck lies in its depiction of the Minor Arcana. Unlike other Minor Arcana decks, this one springs to pulsating life. The cards are printed in quality card stock and boxed complete with instruction booklet, which provides the upright and reversed meanings of each card, as well as three basic card layouts. Beautiful and brilliant, the Robin Wood Tarot is a must-have deck!

0-87542-894-0
boxed set: 78-cards with booklet $19.95

Shapeshifter Tarot

D. J. Conway
AND
Sirona Knight
ILLUSTRATED BY Lisa Hunt

Like the ancient Celts, you can now practice the shamanic art of shapeshifting and access the knowledge of the eagle, the oak tree or the ocean: wisdom that is inherently yours and resides within your very being. The *Shapeshifter Tarot* kit is your bridge between humans, animals and nature. The cards in this deck act as merging tools, allowing you to tap into the many different animal energies, together with the elemental qualities of air, fire, water and earth.

The accompanying book gives detailed explanations on how to use the cards, along with their full esoteric meanings, and mythological and magical roots. Exercises in shapeshifting, moving through gateways, doubling out, meditation and guided imagery give you the opportunity to enhance your levels of perception and awareness, allowing you to hone and accentuate your magical understanding and skill.

1-56718-384-0
Boxed kit: 81 full-color cards, instruction book   **$29.95**

Legend
The Arthurian Tarot

Anna-Marie Ferguson

Gallery artist and writer Anna-Marie Ferguson has paired the ancient divinatory system of the tarot with the Arthurian myth to create *Legend: The Arthurian Tarot.* The exquisitely beautiful watercolor paintings of this tarot deck illustrate characters, places and tales from the legends that blend traditional tarot symbolism with the Pagan and Christian symbolism that are equally significant elements of this myth.

Each card represents the Arthurian counterpart to tarot's traditional figures, such as Merlin as the Magician, Morgan le Fay as the Moon, Mordred as the King of Swords and Arthur as the Emperor. Accompanying the deck is a decorative layout sheet in the format of the Celtic Cross to inspire and guide your readings, as well as the book Keeper of Words, which lists the divinatory meanings of the cards, the cards' symbolism and the telling of the legend associated with each card.

1–56718–267–4
Boxed set:
Book: 6" x 9", 272 pp., illus., softcover
Deck: 78 full-color cards
Layout sheet: 21" x 24", four-color $34.95